VENDETTA

Also by James Neff

The Wrong Man

Unfinished Murder

Mobbed Up

City Beat

VENDETTA

BOBBY KENNEDY VERSUS JIMMY HOFFA

JAMES NEFF

For Sara,
All the best!
James Neff

LITTLE, BROWN AND COMPANY
New York • Boston • London

For Maureen, Jameson, and Chris
And especially Dorothy

———————————————

Little, Brown and Company
Hachette Book Group
1290 Avenue of the Americas, New York, NY 10104
littlebrown.com

First Edition: July 2015

Little, Brown and Company is a division of Hachette Book Group, Inc. The Little, Brown name and logo are trademarks of Hachette Book Group, Inc.

The publisher is not responsible for websites (or their content) that are not owned by the publisher.

The Hachette Speakers Bureau provides a wide range of authors for speaking events. To find out more, go to hachettespeakersbureau.com or call (866) 376-6591.

ISBN 978-0-316-73834-7
Library of Congress Control Number: 2015939408

10 9 8 7 6 5 4 3 2 1

RRD-C

Printed in the United States of America

CONTENTS

VENDETTA

PROLOGUE: DARK FORCES

THE WEATHER IN THE NATION'S capital was so uncharacteristically sunny and warm on Friday, November 22, 1963, that attorney general Robert F. Kennedy interrupted a big Justice Department meeting about fighting organized crime to take lunch outdoors at Hickory Hill, his rolling Civil War–era estate about three miles outside Washington, DC. Among those joining him for tuna sandwiches and tomato soup at tables by the swimming pool were the US attorney in Manhattan, Robert Morgenthau, and RFK's wife, Ethel Kennedy.

At quarter to two, just as Kennedy prepared to head back to the Justice Department, a workman who had been painting a new wing at the Kennedy home sprinted toward them. He wore a painter's cap and held a transistor radio in one hand and shouted words nobody at first could quite make out. Just then a telephone extension at the pool rang with a call from FBI director J. Edgar Hoover.

Bobby Kennedy knew something was wrong, because Hoover never called him at home. "I have news for you," the FBI director said. "The president's been shot."

After he hung up, RFK clapped his hand over his mouth, and Morgenthau saw a look of "shock and horror" on his friend's face. Ethel rushed to his side, and for a few seconds he was speechless. Then he choked out the words, "Jack's been shot. It may be fatal."

The phones at Hickory Hill rang all that afternoon as family and friends called or arrived unbidden to try to provide some comfort. At half past two, Hoover phoned again, and in an affectless tone this time informed RFK, "The president's dead."

By then, Jim McShane, head of the US Marshals Service, had his men posted on the perimeter of the Kennedys' six-acre estate. RFK, McShane, and others were worried that the attack on the president might be part of a broader assault on the nation's leaders, and he wanted to protect Kennedy's family.

When Justice Department spokesman Ed Guthman showed up, he and RFK paced back and forth across the lawn as Bobby's anguished words spilled out. The two men had met seven years earlier in Seattle, after Guthman published a string of exposés in the *Seattle Times* about Teamsters union corruption. RFK had just gotten started as chief counsel for what became known as the Senate Rackets Committee hearings, a massive, groundbreaking investigation that exposed dirty alliances between labor racketeers and business leaders and transfixed millions of television viewers as hoodlums, fixers, and crime bosses took the fifth while being hectored by the boyish, occasionally fumbling Bobby Kennedy. His target in chief turned out to be defiant, charismatic Teamsters president Jimmy Hoffa.

"There's so much bitterness," RFK told Guthman that Friday afternoon. "I thought they'd get one of us....I thought it would be me."

Under the bright skies at the Miami International Airport only a few days earlier, President Kennedy did not encounter bitterness but rather an adoring crowd of about five thousand people in this southern city. Many had pushed up against a temporary chain-link fence along the tarmac, and after his brief remarks, they clapped and cheered, their voices swelling "into a wild howl."[1] It was five in the afternoon, seventy-four degrees, and a warm wind blew JFK's reddish-brown hair over his forehead. Kennedy, in a dark blue suit and green tie, laughed at the glorious crowd and, with the barest hint of a limp, stepped toward the throng clamoring along the fence.

"Please, Mr. President," a burly Secret Service agent said. "Follow the route we've—"

"Give me a minute, boys," Kennedy said. "I've got to talk to these people."

At the fence, women were crying and tried to reach over to kiss him. "God bless you, my boy!" one woman shouted. Men reached for his lapels, as if to slow him down for an instant to make a connection. A small boy held up his Yogi Bear doll, hoping to hand it to him.

One of the Secret Service agents implored, "Please, please! Mr. President!" and eventually they steered him to his convertible limousine.

Arrangements already had been made for Teamsters president Jimmy Hoffa to visit Miami when his nemesis in the White House finished his early campaign swing in south Florida. Hoffa despised the Kennedys and used the might of the nation's biggest, most powerful union to try to thwart their crusade to jail him. Months earlier, the Justice Department brought criminal charges against him in both Chicago and Nashville.

Hoffa was wrapping up business at a midday meal at a Miami restaurant on Friday, November 22, when radio reports swept through the city that President Kennedy had been shot. The awful news from Dallas was relayed by public-address systems in department stores, by dispatchers to the city's scores of cab drivers, and by tearful busboys crowded around transistor radios back in the kitchen.

Hoffa rose to his feet, stepped up on his chair, and began to cheer. "I hope the worms eat out his eyes," he would later say.

Soon Hoffa called one of his lawyers, Frank Ragano of Tampa, Florida, whose second-most-famous client was the Mafia's Florida boss, Santo Trafficante Jr. "Have you heard the good news?" Hoffa asked the young lawyer. "They killed the son of a bitch. This means Bobby is out as attorney general. Lyndon will get rid of him."[2] Asked by reporters that weekend about his reaction to the assassination, Hoffa replied at one point with a brutal, offensive truth: "Bobby Kennedy is just another lawyer now."

In time, searing grief would paralyze Robert Kennedy. But by Friday afternoon, he suspected that dark forces were behind his brother's murder — that the "they" who would "get one of us" could be the mob or Hoffa, targets of his own ruthless pursuit. Before he left for the airport to meet Air Force One, carrying the body of his slain brother, RFK called trusted associates in the Kennedy network, some of whom referred to themselves as the Band of Brothers, loyalists working in agencies across all areas of government, men with maverick streaks that enabled them to operate outside bureaucratic lines.

He talked to Walter Sheridan, the soft-spoken, intense head of the Get Hoffa squad, a team of prosecutors and accountants working full-time to bring legal action against the aggressive Teamsters president. Sheridan, an ex-FBI agent dedicated to RFK, dogged Hoffa for years. He had developed informants inside the Teamsters headquarters and seemed to know the labor leader's every move. A year earlier, Sheridan had heard from a turncoat Teamsters official close to Hoffa who, if he was to be believed, said that Hoffa discussed killing RFK with explosives or a long-range rifle as he drove in his convertible. Was it such a stretch that Hoffa might have turned his anger from one Kennedy brother to the other?

When RFK asked whether he thought Hoffa might be a suspect, Sheridan replied with a not unsurprising yes. Bobby asked his friend to fly to Dallas and monitor the official investigation. Make back-channel inquiries and look for anything that has to do with Hoffa.

Sheridan quickly booked a government-rate flight, made his way to Dallas, and began sleuthing.

CHAPTER 1

The Blinding

SHORTLY BEFORE MIDNIGHT ON APRIL 5, 1956, *New York Daily Mirror* labor columnist Victor Riesel, his twenty-three-year-old secretary, and two frightened union members settled into the broadcast booth of a radio station in midtown Manhattan. Riesel, a short, peppery, dark-haired man with a pencil-thin mustache, was on a mission. For years he had used his Inside Labor column to attack racketeering figures who had wormed their way into union leadership. Now, at age forty-one, he hosted a popular talk-radio show, and his syndicated column ran in nearly two hundred newspapers. Riesel was at the height of his influence.

One week earlier, federal prosecutors in New York City had launched a grand jury investigation into suspected mob infiltration of the International Brotherhood of Teamsters and other local unions. Riesel made no secret that he was going to appear before the grand jury and share all he knew about the "manicured mobsters" and "muscle men" who belonged to the "crime syndicate."

The two union members accompanying Riesel to the WMCA

studio had been beaten up for complaining about a father-son team of hoodlums who ran their local union. Riesel let the two dissidents spill their grievances on air and praised their courage. "It's a tough mob, and it's tied in with the toughest mobs in New York and Chicago," he told his audience.[1]

When the radio show ended, at 2:00 a.m., Riesel and his secretary, Betty Nevins, accompanied the two men to the street, where they nervously checked under their car's hood to see if a bomb had been hidden there while they were on the air. After seeing them drive off safely, Riesel and Nevins rode in her car to Lindy's, the all-night Broadway restaurant made famous by writer Damon Runyon as a hangout for theater swells, gangsters, and cops. Following them to Lindy's but hiding in the shadows, staying well back, was a young man carrying a small glass jar of concentrated sulfuric acid.

Riesel got his start in the world of labor as a young boy attending union meetings with his father, Nathan, who founded an embroiderers' local of the International Ladies' Garment Workers Union. In the 1920s, his father fought to try to keep the union's leadership free of Communists and racketeers. For his troubles, Nathan was beaten up by union goons — once, in 1942, so viciously that despite a series of operations he ended up disabled for life.

Victor Riesel had worked in a series of dreary jobs — hatmaker, embroiderer, mill worker — while taking industrial-relations classes at night at Manhattan's City College. Like many, Riesel felt that being a union officer was a moral calling; it wasn't simply a way to make a living or pursue power. He believed unions were supposed to be watchdogs that protected workers against rapacious businessmen and shady politicians — the means to guarantee everyday citizens decent wages, safety at work, and personal pride. With a college degree, fierce ambition, and a slangy prose style, he started out at the tiny but influential *New Leader,* the liberal anticommunist weekly. In 1942, he landed as labor editor at the *New York Post,* where he wrote Inside Labor several days a week. Eight years later, he and his column moved to the Hearst tabloid the *New York Daily Mirror.*

Riesel gained influence in the 1940s as an anticommunist crusader during the Red scare, using his column as a seal of approval for public figures and labor leaders who wanted to whitewash their liberal or leftist pasts. He let labor leaders — Ronald Reagan, president of the Screen Actors Guild, for example — write guest columns in which they apologized for their youthful but "mistaken" ideology. (Among the conservative-leaning leadership of the Screen Actors Guild, Riesel's imprimatur boosted Reagan's career.)

By the spring of 1956, even though his column appeared in 193 newspapers, Riesel did not wield the influence of such columnists as Walter Lippmann or Joseph Alsop. But within the labor movement, Riesel's views carried heft — and could even put a spark into a New York City federal grand jury.

"My father taught me a hatred of goons," he would later say. "The first chance I got, I went after them.…The mob placed a 'terror tax' on society, raising the price on everything from clothing to artichokes — anything that could be delivered."[2] In city after city, Riesel had seen investigations into labor racketeering come and go, launched in the wake of a public outrage then slowly stymied by frightened witnesses, public apathy, and the shifting political fortunes of striving prosecutors. But he was excited about this latest investigation in his backyard.

The United States attorney for the southern district of New York, Paul Williams, had empaneled a grand jury and targeted seven newly chartered Teamsters locals that were run by men sharing a distinguished pedigree: all were associates of prosperous underworld kingpin John "Johnny Dio" Dioguardi. And all had lengthy rap sheets—bookmaking, robbery, drug dealing, murder, assault, rape. These seven locals were a subspecies of labor unions known as paper locals, essentially shell unions that existed on paper—with a bona fide charter from the international union—but didn't have members, only officers with votes to cast. Perhaps foolishly, Riesel revealed that he was going to be the grand jury's star witness. The investigation, he wrote in his column, could end up bringing down "the Mr. Bigs of the American crime syndicate."

What Riesel and others didn't yet know was that it was Jimmy Hoffa, an ambitious but as yet little-known Teamsters vice president from Detroit, who had quietly connived to get the international union to provide the charters to his good friend Dio.

For Hoffa to become president of the Teamsters, as he hoped, he would need the support of the influential New York joint council. Hoffa had a plan to put one of his loyalists, John O'Rourke, in control of the association of fifty-six New York–area Teamsters locals, with a total of 125,000 members. Each of these fifty-six locals could cast up to seven votes, one from each officer, and the forty-nine votes of the seven newly chartered Dio locals would be enough to swing the top job to Hoffa's man.

As for Dio (said to be the inspiration for the mobbed-up labor boss Johnny Friendly in the blockbuster 1954 film *On the Waterfront*), he and his crew would make a fortune from the charters. As newly minted labor officials, they could threaten to unionize a company unless they were given bribes. Or if an honest union was trying to unionize a particular company, the head of the company might pay off Dio to sign its employees to a sweetheart deal—lower wages and fewer benefits. Either way, workers were exploited. Among Dio's crime associates were James "Jimmy Doyle" Plumeri, Anthony "Tony Ducks" Corallo, and Thomas "Three-Finger Brown" Lucchese, all made members of the Mafia.

It was easy to spot Riesel, five foot four, wearing a fedora, and his young secretary, tall, with shoulder-length blond hair. After dinner, they walked to her car, parked on the corner of 51st and Broadway. There, a thin, dark-haired young man stepped out of the shadows near the Mark Hellinger Theatre and walked up to them. He wore light-colored trousers and a tan jacket and said not a word.

Thinking the man wanted a handout, Riesel slipped his hand into his pocket, feeling for a quarter. At that moment, the man, swinging underhand, emptied the small jar of acid in Riesel's face.

"My gosh! My gosh!" Riesel cried, his hands clawing his skin. Nevins pulled him back into Lindy's to try to get help.

Meanwhile, the assailant walked off, then began running up an alley. Blocks away, he caught the attention of a policeman who told him to stop.

He had just been robbed, the man told the policeman, and he pointed up the street to an imaginary assailant. When the officer took off in that direction, the man who destroyed Riesel's eyes slipped away.

Riesel was driven to nearby Saint Clare's Hospital, where doctors tried to flush out the acid, hoping to save his sight. The pain was unbearable, beyond imagining, Riesel would later say. His eyes and face felt like they were on fire.

Within hours, the *Mirror* had a photographer with Riesel in his hospital room, capturing images of the columnist in bed, his face and right hand heavily wrapped in white gauze. "I feel like a chump because I was caught flat-footed," Riesel lamented. "I should have realized what was taking place."

News of the horrific attack splashed across front pages around the country, provoking outrage. Offers of reward money flooded in from the Newspaper Guild, the *Mirror*, and papers from all over. United States attorney Williams called it "an out-and-out threat and a black effort to intimidate witnesses" from aiding his grand jury investigation. He said Riesel "has been working very closely with this effort and we hold him in the highest regard as a man of honor and principle."[3]

That morning in Chicago, Jimmy Hoffa breezed into a meeting with other Teamsters leaders and made a beeline to national warehouse organizer Sam Baron, a slight, silver-haired man. Hoffa liked to ridicule Baron for being an idealist, a goody two-shoes. Baron held an important post within the Teamsters, was proud of his accomplishments for workers, and as a result was willing to tolerate Hoffa's bullying for the greater good.

Ten years younger, built like a fireplug, with blocky fists and dark, slicked-back hair, Hoffa stubbed a thick finger in Baron's chest. "Hey, Sam, a buddy of yours got it last night."

Baron replied that he didn't know what Hoffa was talking about.

"Your buddy Victor Riesel. Somebody threw acid in his face. The son of a bitch should have had it thrown on the hands he types with, too."[4]

Baron was horrified, but Hoffa just laughed.

A few minutes later, Hoffa took a telephone call from a top Teamsters official in New York City. "Gee, that's a shame about Riesel," Hoffa said over the phone. "I hope they got the bastard that did it."

After he hung up, one of Hoffa's associates asked about his newfound sympathy for Riesel.

"Don't be stupid," Hoffa replied. "You know that phone's tapped."

———

IN EARLY 1956, ROBERT F. Kennedy, the thirty-year-old chief counsel for the US Senate's Permanent Subcommittee on Investigations, was also spending time in New York City looking into the underworld. But unlike the work of Riesel or the grand jurors, his efforts were strictly unofficial and took place late on weekend nights as he zoomed around town with detectives in unmarked squad cars.

It was Johnny Dio and his associates who drew Kennedy to Manhattan. At the time, Kennedy still knew nothing of Jimmy Hoffa; off and on for the past year, Kennedy and members of the investigations subcommittee had been digging into suspected procurement fraud, focusing on the millions of dollars the Pentagon paid to private companies to provide military uniforms. As the subcommittee would later show, government officials took kickbacks from mobbed-up apparel makers in exchange for overpriced contracts. A devout Catholic, Harvard-educated, the son of one of the country's richest (and most detested) men, Bobby Kennedy knew little about labor unions and even less about organized crime. But he became fascinated by its sinister practices and was determined to learn what he could about the secret society. In his earnest, hardworking fashion, he sought out experts to give him an underworld education. Asking around, he was told about two top federal narcotics agents who had created a flowchart of New York mob families that traced who did what in the drug trade. He met with the agents. They in turn introduced him to fellow agents in New York, who let him join them on ride-alongs.

After finishing up his work on Fridays in Washington, he would fly to New York, where the Kennedy family had a luxurious apartment. Late at night, RFK and the squad went from drug buy to drug bust across the five boroughs, kicking in doors, rousting dealers, and developing snitches. It was aggressive crime-busting in the wide-open era before strict search warrants and Miranda warnings. Often joining them on raids were New York City narcotics detectives—tough Irish cops battling bad guys and possessing qualities that RFK admired and that fit his own self-image.[5]

Kennedy came across Johnny Dio's name time and again as the Senate subcommittee dug deeper. A thug and enforcer in the 1930s, Dio helped his crime bosses control a network of dress shops, pattern cutters, shoulder-pad makers, and subcontractors that fed New York's huge garment industry, which, at its peak, supported three hundred thousand jobs. He had perfected the garment-district shakedown. Dio and Mafia member James "Jimmy Doyle" Plumeri, who was also Dio's uncle, set up an association of truck owners and operators who paid them hefty dues. Garment manufacturers had to use these truckers if they didn't want acid thrown on their merchandise or thuggish picketers blocking their storefronts — or if they didn't want Dio, just a bit more forthrightly, instructing his minions to beat up drivers and owners who wouldn't pay up.

It was classic mob strong-arming—violent, effective, and increasingly public. In 1932, Dio was wounded in a shoot-out tied to the rackets, which brought police attention to his trucking monopoly. Twice in the 1930s, with much fanfare in the newspapers, he and his uncle were indicted for coercion and extortion. Both times they were acquitted; witnesses and victims had a habit of abandoning their complaints. Crusading New York special prosecutor Thomas E. Dewey brought the two to trial again in 1937. Evidence showed they were getting $500 from each truck driver in the garment district plus a tariff on every suit and topcoat made in the city, a torrent of illicit cash. "At the trial, frightened witnesses testified how recalcitrant employers and employees were beaten when they refused to pay," the *Mirror*, Riesel's employer, reported. One man testified that he was beaten so badly by Dio thugs he spent two weeks in bed. Another said that gangsters "threatened to cut off his ears" if he didn't comply.[6] Dio and Plumeri could afford the best lawyers, but in the midst of Dewey's popular anticrime juggernaut, they were outmatched. In the middle of the trial, Dio and Plumeri halted the damaging revelations by pleading guilty, in Dio's words, to "racketeering, stealing, extorting, that is all."[7] He served three years thirty miles up the Hudson River in Sing Sing.

After prison, Dio found success with nonunion dress factories out of state, one of which, Rosemary Fashions (named after his daughter), made dresses that sold for $2.98. But he couldn't stay away from the garment district, the mile-square midtown Manhattan neighborhood packed with hundreds of apparel manufacturers. Workers, mainly women, many of them immigrants, put in long hours for low pay—all of them linked by delivery trucks that moved merchandise from shop to subcontractor to wholesaler to delivery dock. Fiercely competitive, subject to seasonal demands, dependent on Teamsters, the garment trade by its nature was vulnerable to labor racketeers.

There were richer and more powerful crime lords in New York than Johnny Dio, but he showed a knack for capturing public attention. Known as Dapper Mr. D, Dio dressed in well-tailored suits, picked up the checks for friends at the best steak houses in New York, schmoozed at the Luxor Baths, the popular Runyonesque steam room, and found his name linked in gossip columns to Baby Lake, a celebrated chorus girl at the Latin Quarter, a fancy Times Square nightclub. At Christmas, friends recalled, Dapper Mr. D would give his wife a shoe box of cash, with a note saying, "Honey, why don't you buy yourself something nice?" They and their two sons and a daughter lived in an estate in Freeport, Long Island, where Dio was said to enjoy cooking fine Italian cuisine at family dinners each Sunday.

In the early 1950s, Dio took a different path to power, becoming a union official himself. He was awarded charters for six locals with the United Automobile Workers of the American Federation of Labor (not to be confused with the union of the same name run by Walter Reuther, associated with the Congress of Industrial Organizations, or CIO). Dio and his locals, membership in which grew to five thousand, attracted the attention of the farsighted Hoffa, who was laying the groundwork to become Teamsters president. If he could get his friend Dio to bring the locals into the Teamsters union, they would be part of the Teamsters' influential Joint Council 16. Hoffa already had strong support from Teamsters leaders in the Midwest and the South. With Dio's connivance, he could extend his influence into new territory, the East Coast.

At first, it did not go as smoothly as Hoffa planned. He repeatedly wheedled Teamsters president Dave Beck to let Dio into the union, but to his credit, Beck initially refused. Meanwhile, the AFL kicked Dio and his unions out of the federation for running a corrupt operation and exploiting dues-paying members.

In 1955, Hoffa assigned Eddie Cheyfitz to clean up Dio's public image in order to ease him into the union. Eddie Cheyfitz was a dandyish, red-haired Washington lawyer-lobbyist who worked for Hoffa and the Teamsters and whose law partner was a rising star on the national legal scene, Edward Bennett Williams.[8] Cheyfitz, on a $60,000 annual retainer with the union, had his work cut out for him.

But by this time, Hoffa undisputedly wielded more power than Beck. Whenever labor reporters pointed this out to him, the rotund, bald-headed labor boss ranted, and his face turned red. At a 1955 press conference after a meeting of the union's executive board, Beck asked Hoffa: "Who's in charge here, Jimmy?" Hoffa smiled and said dutifully, "You are, Dave." Beck beamed at the room full of reporters, as if to say, "See, those stories you're writing aren't true."

In late 1955, Hoffa displayed his clout by persuading the second in command at Teamsters headquarters, Einar Mohn, to approve seven new Teamsters charters that ended up with Dio. Dapper Mr. D and his sharks lost no time in signing sweetheart deals with dozens of small companies that made everything from ladies' clothes to dog food to candy. Business owners funneled their payoffs to Dio by sending consulting fees to Dio's cutout, Equitable Research Associates.[9]

Building on Hoffa's aggressive lobbying, Dio had his paper locals use their votes to cast out the seventy-four-year-old president of Teamsters Joint Council 16, Martin Lacey. Lacey filed a lawsuit in early 1956, charging election fraud, but Beck didn't back him, and Lacey gave up the fight before long. Once Hoffa's man, John O'Rourke, took over as president of the powerful post, Hoffa was one step closer to becoming president of the country's toughest, biggest union. The only drawback: Lacey's lawsuit was what brought Hoffa, Dio, and the phony locals to the attention of the chief federal prosecutor in Manhattan.

In August of 1956, the FBI and US attorney Williams announced that they had cracked the Riesel case. The "mastermind" behind the acid blinding, the FBI said, was labor racketeer Johnny Dio. According to agents, Dio called an April 1—Easter Sunday—meeting at a lower Manhattan candy store run by one of his associates, Gondolfo Miranti. There he announced he needed someone to rough up Riesel for $1,000. Miranti, an ex-con, didn't want to handle the beating himself, so he passed the assignment down the food chain until he had scrounged up twenty-two-year-old Abraham "Abie" Telvi, a less-than-brilliant low-level thug. Telvi was told his victim was a disc jockey named Mr. Marshall whose wife wanted him hurt because he had been unfaithful.

Miranti pointed out "Mr. Marshall" to Telvi one night after Riesel left his late-night radio show. Telvi, a sturdy six-footer, said he could easily handle the five-foot-four man, whom he planned to beat up. The next night, the evening of the assault, Miranti gave Telvi a bottle of sulfuric acid to throw in the victim's face, explaining, "This is easier and you can get away faster."[10]

It wasn't. Telvi got caught in the backsplash, and several acid drops burned the right side of his face. With a paste of baking soda covering his wounds, Telvi hid in a bakery belonging to a friend for a few days. He was shocked at the lurid headlines and told friends he was upset that "higher-ups from uptown" had lied to him about his victim. He had blinded a politically connected newspaper columnist, bringing heat on himself and his family. Telvi decided he needed to get out of New York and had his brother drive him to

Youngstown, Ohio. There he stayed hidden for two months while his burns healed and police investigated the crime four hundred miles away in Manhattan.

Telvi returned to the Lower East Side that summer, angry and unappreciated. With the tabloids treating the Riesel blinding as a crime of the century, Telvi decided he had been underpaid. He demanded $50,000. Through channels, the young hitter was promised that he'd be getting an additional payment in two weeks. Which he did: a fatal gunshot wound to the back of his head. On July 28, his body was discovered dumped into a gutter on a Lower East Side street. Young Abraham Telvi had learned to keep mob secrets the hard way.

Even after the arrests of Dio, Miranti, and other coconspirators, puzzling loose ends remained. Dio's supposed motive behind the acid attack—to intimidate Riesel and keep him from cooperating with the grand jury—did not make sense to journalists and others following the case. Riesel hadn't written specifically about Dio in more than a year. Why would hot-tempered Mr. D wait so long for revenge? And if Dio had been investigated nearly every step of his adult life, what provoked him to act against Riesel this time? Frank Hogan, the New York district attorney, had pursued Dio even during the previous few years, tapping his telephone, convicting him for not paying state income taxes (Dio served only two months), even arresting him over parking violations. Given the scrutiny, why would Dio put himself at risk by going after Riesel?

The likely responsibility for the Riesel attack emerged from examining the timing of events and focusing on the man who had the most to lose without Dio's assistance.

The paper locals grand jury commenced in late March. By Sunday, April 1, only three days after the grand jurors started their questioning, Dio put the Riesel plan in motion. Hoffa, who disliked Riesel, was informed of the crime's success only hours after it happened and appeared thrilled with its horrific results.

The acid attack on Victor Riesel came when much was at stake for Hoffa.[11] Johnny Dio would forever be known as the man who blinded Victor Riesel, and the crime guaranteed that police would try to nail him for the rest of his life. But the labor columnist believed that someone else, a higher-up, had told Dio to terrorize him. Riesel, who had a long recipro-cal relationship with FBI director J. Edgar Hoover, based his belief on information he obtained from Bureau sources. (In a letter, Hoover once thanked Riesel for being a "staunch friend" who helped to blunt "our Red-tinged critics at every move".)[12] "The FBI is convinced Jimmy Hoffa ordered the attack," Riesel would one day explain. The columnist added that he, too, was convinced of Hoffa's guilt.[13]

All roads led back to Hoffa. But in 1956 the man who would become his equal, chief counsel Kennedy, was riding with cops deep into the New York night, getting his bearings in a treacherous business, working his way around the mob's networks and relationships—and he wasn't able to read the map, at least not yet.

CHAPTER 2

Life Is a Jungle

BOBBY KENNEDY WAS LOOKING FOR new targets. The Permanent Subcommittee on Investigations had held twenty-nine days of hearings about fraud in the procurement of military uniforms; on July 10, 1956, RFK and the staff issued a second report about mobbed-up companies that had pushed up the costs of navy caps, army jackets, and the like. But beyond that, he had run out of revelations.

That summer Clark Mollenhoff, Washington bureau chief for the *Des Moines Register* and the Minneapolis *Star Tribune*, promoted a target to Kennedy: Detroit Teamsters boss Jimmy Hoffa. For the past three years, in a sustained crusade of muckraking, Mollenhoff had reported one exposé after the other about Hoffa and the Teamsters.

Kennedy wasn't familiar with Hoffa, so Mollenhoff provided a lengthy explanation and gave him copies of his news articles. Mollenhoff had been after Hoffa since 1953, when the reporter was assigned to look into complaints from a local business about brutal tactics by Teamsters officials in Minneapolis.

Mollenhoff, a lawyer and member of the Newspaper Guild, was sympathetic to unionism. He expected to find that the complaints were little more than grousing by a company trying to save a buck by driving out its union. Instead, what he found shocked him. Hoffa employed hoodlums as union stewards, men who thought nothing of threatening or beating members who wanted a say in how their locals were operated. Furthermore, a car-hauling company was funneling money to Hoffa in exchange for a sweetheart deal that over the years saved it hundreds of thousands of dollars. Mollenhoff outlined one such arrangement in an article that began, "The wife of James R. (Jimmy) Hoffa was on the payroll of the rackets-ridden jukebox local of the Detroit teamsters union at $100 a week, but she never went near the office."

Few reporters investigated the nation's 1.4-million-member International Brotherhood of Teamsters. For one, Teamsters drivers delivered newspapers in most cities — and in general, newspapers owners and editors didn't go out of their way to antagonize their distributors. In addition, newspapers were susceptible to union pressure. Unlike automobiles or timber or other products, newspapers were perishable, especially in cities with competing dailies. Bundles of undelivered newspapers delayed by trumped-up work stoppages ended up in trash bins. "Old news" is a pejorative term for a reason.

Not surprisingly, Mollenhoff's exposés had little impact on Hoffa and almost none in the nation's capital. When Hoffa next ran across Mollenhoff, at the Mayflower Hotel in Washington, Hoffa greeted him with a smirk. Looking up at the six-foot-four, 250-pound reporter, the stumpy labor boss said, "Hiya, poison pen." Then Hoffa tried an approach that had worked successfully with other reporters. "Now, lookit here, Clark. They don't pay newspaper reporters enough for you to be giving me the bad time that you've been giving me." Hoffa looked him in the eye, and then coolly said, "Everybody has his price. What's yours?"[1] An unnerved Mollenhoff decided to treat the offer as a joke. "You don't have enough money, Jimmy," he replied.

Kennedy wasn't sold on Mollenhoff's idea, even after reading the reporter's hard-hitting stories. RFK knew little about how unions worked and less about how business owners and union officials colluded. Kennedy had grown up tended by nannies, schooled in private academies, and exposed to powerful businessmen and politicians through his father's connections.

Joe Kennedy was the son of a Boston saloon keeper who also served as a ward boss in Boston. Joe went to Harvard, then picked banking as a career, a Waspish domain far from his Irish Catholic roots. He became a successful trader on Wall Street in the 1920s, where he was known as an unsentimental, brusque operator who famously said, "Only a fool holds out for the top dollar." That philosophy, and holdings from his bank, Columbia Trust, helped shelter him from the 1929 stock market crash – he came out with tens of millions of dollars of his wealth intact and invested in liquor, movie studios, and commercial real estate.[2]

A tycoon at a relatively young age, Joe Kennedy became bored with business and never talked about it with his children. "Listening to them talk about money," said Charles Spalding, a close friend of the Kennedy brothers, "was like listening to nuns talking about sex."[3] Joe Kennedy's informal curriculum at the family dinner table included politics and world events but not labor racketeering. RFK would later admit that even after Mollenhoff had tutored him about Hoffa, he found it hard to accept that bankers, lawyers, company executives, and union leaders colluded at the expense of rank-and-file workers.

So the naive Kennedy put Mollenhoff off, saying he doubted that his subcommittee was the proper jurisdiction for such a probe. As an arm of the Senate's Committee on Government Operations, the Permanent Subcommittee on Investigations was supposed to study ways to make the federal government more effective by exposing waste, fraud, and inefficiencies. The Senate Labor Committee was the proper place for an investigation into suspected Teamsters corruption, Kennedy told the reporter.

Mollenhoff considered RFK's demurral to be a lame excuse.[4] The Senate Labor Committee had a reputation of being overly friendly with big labor. Senators were wary not only of labor's prowess in telling its rank and file how to vote but also of its ability to raise millions of dollars in campaign contributions. Hoffa liked to remind politicians of this fact. "There are two ways to play politics," Hoffa would say. "You either make speeches or else you spend dough. We spend lots of dough. We got connections in the right places. We expect to keep them."

But Mollenhoff would not give up. He had collected documents from an earlier short-lived US House investigation into the Teamsters, and he pointed out to Kennedy that Hoffa had unexplained wealth. Despite humble roots and a career as a union officer, he owned a fleet of trucks and interests in a farm, a brewery, a race track, and a girls' camp in Wisconsin. Mollenhoff tried to goad Hoffa into making his income and net worth public. "I won't tell the Internal Revenue Service, so I'd be a damned fool to tell you," Hoffa told the newsman.

Mollenhoff eventually found a tactic that seemed to work on Kennedy, who prided himself on his toughness and found it almost impossible to back down when challenged. "I taunted him by questioning his courage to take on such an investigation," Mollenhoff would later explain.[5]

Kennedy still had doubts. At the time, publicity about the paper locals scandal was confined to New York, and Dio hadn't yet been arrested for being the ringleader of the acid attack on Victor Riesel. The Detroit labor leader freely admitted being friends with various underworld figures, including some who had been convicted of using unions to shake down businesses. But the International Brotherhood of Teamsters and its see-no-evil president Dave Beck were not a hot topic in Washington.

RFK told the reporter that his Hoffa proposal seemed promising on paper, but he had one reservation: Who the hell had ever heard of Jimmy Hoffa and Dave Beck?

"If you do your job right," Mollenhoff replied, "everybody will have heard about 'em — and you, too."[6]

That summer, Bobby Kennedy turned to the political fortunes of his brother John F. Kennedy, senator from Massachusetts. Bobby had managed his brother's successful Senate race in 1952, and now, after four years in the Senate, Jack Kennedy was toying with the idea of getting his name on the Democratic ticket as vice president to Adlai Stevenson, the former Illinois governor who ran unsuccessfully against Dwight Eisenhower in 1952. A favorite of liberal Democrats and the big labor unions, Stevenson had secured the Democratic nomination for president in 1956.

This time, Stevenson broke with tradition and announced he was going to let delegates select his running mate at the Democratic National Convention in Chicago in mid-August. Party insiders and the press listed the front-runners as Kennedy, senator Hubert Humphrey of Minnesota, and Estes Kefauver, the first-term senator from Tennessee. Kefauver was little known outside his state until he suddenly made a national name for himself in 1951 as chief inquisitor of televised Senate hearings on organized crime. The Kefauver hearings, which traveled to fourteen cities in 1950 and 1951, riveted the public by providing the first televised look at such real-life mob figures as Joe Adonis and Frank Costello, who, time and again, under questioning by Kefauver and others, refused to answer and "took the fifth," making it a household term.

At the last minute, Jack surprised Bobby by asking him for help getting on the ticket with Stevenson at the Democratic convention. Their father thought he had talked Jack out of trying it before he left the country for a vacation on the French Riviera. He believed the popular Eisenhower would whip Stevenson, and with his son on the ticket, pundits might put some of the blame for a loss on JFK's being Catholic.

Robert Kennedy had a complicated relationship with his father. With his fortune secured but his own political ambitions unrealized, Joseph P. Kennedy devoted himself to promoting the political futures of his competitive clan — "My job is my children," he once said — particularly those of his two oldest sons, Joe Jr. and Jack.

Thin and bookish, Jack was beset by illnesses all his life. He achieved fame during World War II as skipper of *PT-109*, one of the navy's quick, mahogany-hulled patrol torpedo boats. After a Japanese destroyer sunk his vessel in August of 1943, lieutenant junior grade John F. Kennedy heroically brought his surviving crew members to safety on a small Pacific island. Kennedy towed one injured sailor by the strap of the man's life jacket, clenching it in his teeth. A year later, his oldest brother, Joe Jr., a naval aviator based in London, volunteered for a near-suicide mission: piloting a plane full of explosives into the Nazis' hidden V-1 launching pads on the French coast. He had planned to parachute out well before impact. But the plane accidentally exploded before reaching its target. There were no survivors.

The Kennedys retreated into grief, particularly Joe. He had invested much of his ambition into his oldest son, generally agreed to be the most athletic, charming, handsome, and likeliest to succeed of the Kennedy men.

Some of Bobby's closest friends held a less-than-charitable view of the patriarch. Kenneth "Kenny" O'Donnell, who met Bobby at Harvard and became a trusted and lifelong friend, felt that Joe Kennedy brutalized his third son. "His father was a very autocratic, strict, controlling fellow—not a nice guy," O'Donnell, who worked in JFK's Boston office, would later say. "We used to tease Bobby and say, 'Why don't you tell him off once in a while?' Bobby would get this horrified look and say, 'Have you met my father? You tell him off. I like it the way it is. He doesn't pay attention to me, and I like it that way.'"[7]

Bobby looked up to his older brother Jack, whose wit, social graces, and academic accomplishments were far beyond his. Eight years apart in age, they were not close growing up. As his older brothers had, Bobby was determined to test himself in the greatest challenge of his generation, fighting in World War II. His plan was to become a navy pilot, following Joe Jr.'s path. But halfway through officer candidate school he failed the aptitude test for flight training. It was May of 1945, and it looked as though he was going to miss the war before he got out of OCS. Fortunately, his father had connections.

Eight years earlier, President Roosevelt had appointed Joseph Kennedy ambassador to Great Britain, America's most prestigious diplomatic post, at the Court of St. James's. Calling on friends such as secretary of the navy James Forrestal, Kennedy had gotten the service to name a new 2,200-ton destroyer after his fallen son. So RFK enlisted as a seaman and shipped out in early 1946 to serve aboard the ship named after his brother, assuming duties he knew to be far inferior to the heroics performed by his higher-ranking brothers. The turn of events had to be a disappointment to someone driven to please his father and determined to display toughness and selflessness, the virtues that would define Kennedy men in the years to come.

By April of 1946, Jack had decided to run for Congress in Massachusetts's eleventh district, home to the navy shipyard in Charlestown. Coincidentally, the *Joseph P. Kennedy Jr.* had docked there on April 11, and Bobby arranged leave for April 22, when Jack was set to announce his candidacy for the US House. It's unclear whether Bobby was too busy helping his brother or too unhappy with the turn of his life to care, but he didn't return to duty on the destroyer at 0800 hours on April 23, as required. Instead he went AWOL, not returning to his post until after two in the morning on April 25, absent without leave for nearly two days. Kennedy went before a captain's mast, the navy version of misdemeanor court, and was fined and hit with a ten-day restriction aboard the ship. Despite going AWOL, he was honorably discharged on May 27. It appears he never told anyone about his misconduct.[8]

At the 1956 national nominating convention, the two Kennedy brothers and O'Donnell were novices at securing votes from the delegates and ran around the convention floor "like a couple of nuts," O'Donnell would later recall. "We didn't know two people in the place." Inexperienced in national political maneuvering, the three young men were unsure which state leaders held power over which delegates, and Bobby offended some of them with brusque demands for support. After the first round of balloting ended, no Democratic candidate for vice president held a majority, but JFK, to the surprise of many, was in second place. In the second round of balloting, JFK was briefly in the lead but still fifteen votes short of a majority. Then delegates for a few of the lesser candidates threw in with Kefauver, putting him over the top. The Kennedys hated to lose; Jack, unsmiling, gave a gracious concession.

Bobby stayed angry about the loss, unable to hide his disappointment. Later, he encountered Mollenhoff, who was wrapping up his reporting, on the convention floor. Mollenhoff brought up Hoffa and the Teamsters again and needled RFK.

"Well, goddamn it, do you believe me now?" Mollenhoff wanted to know. "Kefauver did his investigations five years ago, and it got him enough clout to beat your brother's butt."

This time RFK was more open to Mollenhoff's arguments for going after Hoffa. "Well, why don't you come down and let's talk about it?" Kennedy told him.[9]

Then about a week after the Democratic convention, news broke that made Bobby's decision whether to pursue Hoffa vastly easier. In New York, FBI agents arrested Johnny Dio on charges of ordering the acid attack on Riesel. The news was huge, making front-page headlines across the country. RACKET CZAR ACCUSED AS RIESEL CASE MASTERMIND, said the *Washington Post*'s front page. The story also mentioned Dio's paper locals strategy in New York "on behalf of James R. Hoffa, a Teamster Union vice president."

RFK finally decided: he would ask senator John L. McClellan, chairman of the investigations subcommittee, to look into labor racketeering and, in particular, Jimmy Hoffa.

By early September Kennedy got approval from McClellan to take a quick sniff around suspected labor racketeering nationally. He wanted to see if the topic was important enough for the subcommittee and, from RFK's point of view, compelling enough to capture the attention of voters and the press.[10] In his memoir about his work on the subcommittee, Bobby would later characterize this early effort as "a nationwide survey of the labor scene," making no mention of Hoffa. But the Teamsters boss was clearly in Kennedy's sights from the beginning. RFK and McClellan arranged a meeting for September 11 with FBI director Hoover to discuss "ways to curb Teamster...Jimmy Hoffa."[11] Senate records show that, as a first step in scrutinizing Hoffa, a subcommittee investigator that September retrieved two years' worth of Hoffa's personal income tax returns from the files of a federal tax-court case against him. The records showed that despite appearances—Hoffa's off-the-rack business suits, the modest bungalow in Detroit—he and his wife, Josephine, were well-to-do. They enjoyed a net income of $35,000 in 1954 and $37,000* the year before; his union salary was augmented by a partnership in an oil exploration company and other business interests.[12]

Two weeks later, under the signature of Senator McClellan, Kennedy asked the Internal Revenue Service for access to Hoffa's "income tax returns, penal files, and related documents" going back to 1948.[13]

The IRS regarded personal tax returns as confidential records to be used by its auditors to see if people and businesses were cheating on their taxes. Outside agencies could use them to investigate suspected tax-related crimes, but even then, investigators could inspect tax returns only at IRS headquarters. They could take notes but were not allowed to have photostats made. McClellan's request for the Hoffa returns was so unusual that IRS commissioner Russell Harrington himself wrote to the senator, warning him that a committee

---

* This amounts to about $324,000 in 2015 dollars.

investigator would only be permitted to inspect the Hoffa returns in room 5571 of the Treasury Department "upon presentation of proper credentials."

At this early stage in a preliminary investigation, the Senate subcommittee and its chief counsel had amassed little evidence that Hoffa was a tax cheat; Bobby, however, had suspicions based on Hoffa's many outside business interests and his practice of dealing mostly in cash. His sweeping up of tax returns would become an ingrained practice of the McClellan committee. (The IRS would only curtail this tactic many years later.) Kennedy's top financial investigator, Carmine Bellino, a former supervisor of the FBI's accounting division, knew the value of tax returns for providing leads and would rely heavily on them.

Late that fall, as Kennedy got deeper into backgrounding Hoffa and labor, he took a trip to Seattle to meet with a colleague of Mollenhoff's, reporter Ed Guthman of the *Seattle Times*, a Pulitzer Prize winner who had been investigating Teamsters president Dave Beck off and on for eight years. Guthman had broken the story about the Teamsters doling out an expensive perquisite to Beck. It paid $163,000 for Beck's spacious home on the shores of Lake Washington, just north of the Seattle city limits, and then allowed him and his family to live there rent free. There was more. Sources inside the Teamsters told Guthman that Beck was a thief, diverting union funds to pay for personal expenses. But Guthman couldn't pin down the story. Beck was the most powerful man in the state of Washington, with friends in law enforcement, and union insiders were afraid of him. Guthman needed help.

In meeting with Kennedy, he had to decide whether he'd

resort to an investigative reporting gambit: trade his tips and research to a congressional investigator who had subpoena power and might get closer to the truth in exchange for the investigator's promise to leak anything newsworthy back to him exclusively. Guthman was wary of Robert Kennedy; in the northwest corner of the country, the reporter knew him only as the little brother of a handsome Massachusetts senator with a reputation as a millionaire playboy.

"Can you trust him?" Guthman asked Mollenhoff. He replied yes.

To keep his mission quiet, Kennedy checked into Seattle's venerable Olympic Hotel using a fake last name, Rogers. He met Guthman for dinner and listened as the newsman told him about unhappy Teamsters drivers who felt stung by sweetheart contracts and were threatened at union meetings when they dared to complain. When RFK asked for their names, Guthman held back, wondering if this neophyte investigator was serious. Did he even know how to protect sources?

By the next morning, Guthman decided to reveal their names, persuaded by RFK's earnestness and concern. When Kennedy met with Guthman's sources, he was struck that one of their chief complaints about Beck wasn't a pocketbook issue but the labor leader's pompous refusal to let members have a say about how their locals were run. Indeed, Beck bragged that he ran his union the way executives ran General Motors — time-honored, top-down management.

Beck wasn't always such a stuffed shirt. Like Hoffa, he grew up poor and loved to remind people of that fact. His father barely made a living as a carpet installer. To help the family finances, young Beck peddled newspapers, sold fish he caught in Puget Sound, and killed wharf rats that he delivered to public health officials. (They paid him a five-dollar bounty for each one that tested positive for bubonic plague.) Beck climbed from Teamsters organizer to local president to head of the giant Western Conference of Teamsters with his advocacy of "business unionism." He convinced business owners that they would profit from the stability created by paying somewhat higher wages to workers. Chambers of commerce loved him. A florid, fleshy man with a bald head, Beck used his power to insinuate himself into Seattle's political and cultural establishment. He bought downtown real estate, gas stations, and other small companies. By the 1950s, Beck, a Republican, had become more powerful in Washington State than the governor. President Eisenhower welcomed him at visits to the White House, referring to him as the Republicans' labor statesman. Behind his back, Beck was known as His Majesty the Wheel.

In Seattle, Kennedy was steered to a man who urged him to explore Beck's dealings with Nathan Shefferman, a Chicago "labor consultant." In fact, Shefferman was a fixer, a middleman between companies and union leaders willing to sell out. Typically, he took large fees from companies in exchange for persuading "friendly" union officials, for a price, to agree to a substandard contract. Sears, Roebuck and Company, it would later come out, used Shefferman to arrange sweetheart contracts that affected thousands of Teamsters drivers and warehouse workers throughout the country. The connivance saved the giant retailer millions of dollars.

Several days before Christmas, Kennedy and Carmine Bellino landed in Chicago during a snowstorm and met with Shefferman at his office in the Loop. He chatted amiably, insisting he had nothing to hide. When they served him with a documents subpoena, he let them borrow his books and financial documents for a day or two. Toting the bundles of ledgers and documents, RFK and Bellino pushed through the snow and past shoppers on Michigan Avenue to return to their rooms at the Palmer House hotel, wondering what they'd find.

Bellino was a genius of forensic accounting. In the previous few years, he had worked on three congressional investigating committees that needed help tackling tricky white-collar criminal matters, including the hearings about uniform procurement. He could take stacks of receipts, canceled checks, phone records, bank statements, contracts, and (when he could get them) federal tax returns and quickly spot transactions out of order or numbers that didn't match up. For example, a canceled check creased down the middle drew Bellino's suspicions. It likely meant someone had folded it in half and slipped it in his pocket or a wallet. That didn't mean it was a payoff; but depending on the payee, such checks were flagged for closer scrutiny.

Bellino spread out the ledgers and papers and got to work, looking for missing entries, large checks made out to "Cash," and other red flags. Within an hour, he had seen enough to conclude that Beck was diverting union funds to Shefferman for "consulting" — which actually meant serving as a personal shopper for Beck, spending tens of thousands of Teamsters dollars on personal goods for Beck and his family: golf clubs, outboard motors, a freezer, chairs, love seats, twenty-one pairs of nylon stockings. "We had come to the startling but inescapable conclusion," Kennedy later wrote, "that Dave Beck, the president of America's largest, most powerful labor union, was a crook."

Kennedy had to decide what to do next. Bellino had seen two other congressional investigations into union rackets get started then falter as political pressure closed them down. "Unless you're prepared to go all the way," Bellino warned Bobby, "don't start it." RFK replied, "We're going all the way."

Over the Christmas holiday, Bobby and his family joined

the rest of the Kennedy clan at the family's Hyannis Port complex on Cape Cod. There he announced excitedly what he wanted to do next with the McClellan committee — investigate the criminal infiltration of labor unions. He planned to expose the way they exploited the workers they were supposed to protect.

Joe Kennedy couldn't believe what he was hearing. It was, he announced, "politically dangerous," a foolish idea that would only hurt Jack's presidential chances in 1960. It would destroy the support he would need from labor unions.

If Jack had strong feelings at the time, he kept them to himself. But Joe "was really mad," RFK's sister Jean recalled. "He was really, deeply emotionally opposed."[14] Bobby and his father fought over his plans throughout the holiday, turning their disagreement into a bitter fight that was, Jean recounted, "the worst ever." Jack's friend LeMoyne "Lem" Billings, who was at Hyannis Port that Christmas, witnessed part of the clash. "The old man saw this as dangerous, not the sort of thing, or the sort of people to mess around with," Billings recalled.[15]

But after years of following his father's wishes, Bobby refused to bend this time. Finally he'd found a project that matched his needs: one that took on bad guys, required courage, aided victims, and, despite his father's judgment, might pay off politically for the Kennedys. It was too good an opportunity to pass up.[16]

Back in Washington a few days after Christmas, Bobby outlined his findings for Senator McClellan. He found the Arkansas lawyer, a stern Baptist from an antilabor state, an easy sell on launching a full-blown committee investigation into the Teamsters and labor racketeering. But their plans ran afoul of members of the Senate's Committee on Labor and Public Welfare, who believed that hearings about unions should be within its jurisdiction. In a compromise, a "select," or special, committee was created with four senators from the Committee on Labor and Public Welfare and four from the Committee on Government Operations, with Democrats and Republicans in equal number. McClellan was chair, and RFK was chief counsel.

By the end of January in 1957, the bipartisan Select Committee on Improper Activities in the Labor or Management Field was in business. Democrats on the committee included McClellan; Sam Ervin of North Carolina; Patrick McNamara, a Michigan trade unionist; and John F. Kennedy of Massachusetts. The Republicans were conservative Barry Goldwater of Arizona; Karl Mundt of South Dakota; Irving Ives, a New York liberal; and Bobby's former boss, the booze-addled demagogic commie hunter from Wisconsin, Joe McCarthy.

Four years earlier, from January to July of 1953, Robert Kennedy served as assistant counsel for McCarthy's Permanent Subcommittee on Investigations, a rocky experience that affected how he planned to run this new special Senate committee. At the time, RFK was twenty-seven years old, married, and jobless and well aware that he had subordinated his career to the demands of Jack and his father, not without consequence. On his short shore leave from the navy in 1946, he helped Jack kick off his first congressional campaign, returned two days late, and was slapped with AWOL charges. In 1952, he reluctantly gave up his first job as a lawyer, working in the Internal Security Section of the Justice Department, to move to Massachusetts and run Jack's floundering Senate campaign. Representative Kennedy eked out a narrow victory over incumbent senator Henry Cabot Lodge Jr. "If Bobby hadn't come up to take over that campaign and if he hadn't been Jack Kennedy's right-hand man from that point on, without question, Jack Kennedy would have lost," close friend and campaign aide Kenny O'Donnell would later say.[17] Even so, he felt he hadn't accomplished much and was getting nowhere. He was a "really very cross, unhappy, angry young man," family friend Lem Billings was to say—a man with a chip on his shoulder and an unpleasant eagerness to tell people off.[18]

Like Joe McCarthy, Bobby believed that infiltration by Communists into the US government was a genuine threat. In the third year of the Korean War stalemate against Communist China, such beliefs were common, particularly among many Catholics, who felt the godless belief system of Communism was the work of the devil himself. "I liked him," Bobby said after first meeting the vulgar, hard-drinking, hammy, antiestablishment Irishman. McCarthy dated RFK's sister Eunice a few times, then sister Pat, and stayed overnight at the Kennedy complex in Hyannis Port. He joined in their touch football and softball games. Among the clannish Kennedys, McCarthy grew closest to Joe Kennedy, who in turn generously supported America's most famous Irish Catholic politician with campaign cash. He returned the favor by not campaigning in Massachusetts for his Republican colleague Senator Lodge, which helped Kennedy become the rare Democrat to defeat an incumbent while the Eisenhower landslide enabled Republicans to take the White House and both houses of Congress.

After the 1952 campaign, Bobby was amenable when his father asked McCarthy to give him a position as chief counsel on the Senate Permanent Subcommittee on Investigations, for which McCarthy, a member of the majority party, was the new chairman. O'Donnell was aghast that Bobby would join McCarthy. Time and again, he argued with RFK against it, noting that the senator's slipshod hunt for supposed government-employed subversives was an international disgrace. "McCarthy could prove your mother was a Communist by his way of reasoning," O'Donnell told him. The new Massachusetts senator didn't want his brother to take the job, either, but not because of Senator Joe's anti-Red beliefs. JFK himself was a strong anticommunist; in the 1940s at House Labor Committee hearings, he got favorable coverage in the Boston press for his heavy-handed interrogation of suspected Communists in the union movement. But gifted politician that he was becoming, Jack Kennedy felt that the growing public distaste for McCarthy's methods would besmirch Bobby's reputation should his younger brother ever run for elective office. In time, Jack's prediction proved true.

Even with his father's connections, Bobby quickly learned that he faced competition for chief counsel. McCarthy was being importuned by Dick Berlin, chairman of the Hearst media empire, and George Sokolsky, influential conservative Hearst columnist, to hire the well-connected, aggressive Roy Cohn, a brilliant but unscrupulous boy-lawyer on the make from New York who had helped prosecute the Justice Department's case against accused Soviet spies Julius and Ethel Rosenberg. McCarthy, feeling squeezed between his powerful patrons, hired them both, but the more experienced albeit younger Cohn took the chief counsel prize.

The two young men clashed in their first encounter, Cohn would recall.

"[RFK] walked in, sat down, and he looked me over very carefully, as though he was, you know, sizing up a piece of merchandise or something. And he said, 'You know,' he said, 'you puzzle me very much.' So I said, 'Well, I'm sorry I puzzle you. Why do I puzzle you?' And he says, 'Well, Morton Downey' — referring to Morton Downey, the singer and the

Coca-Cola executive who was a longtime close friend of the Kennedy family—'Morton thinks you're a great guy, and so do some people. But a lot of other people think you're no good. I just don't know which side to go with'.... So I said to him, 'Well, I don't know that I've really offered myself up for inspection or judgment on your part, and I wouldn't really worry too much about the whole thing. Maybe let's go on the assumption that the people thinking I'm a bad guy are right, and since we apparently are not going to have particularly much to do with each other, I don't think it should be a problem that's really going to have to trouble you all that much.' "[19]

While Cohn and McCarthy hectored suspected pinkos in the State Department, assistant counsel Kennedy and a young investigator named LaVern Duffy dug through maritime statistics and trade reports to document the trade carried on by US allies with Communist China. Kennedy complained that Cohn was not doing any legwork, interviewing witnesses, or confirming facts about suspected subversives; rather, he was making slashing personal attacks on government workers without hesitation. If Cohn and McCarthy had the goods, fine, then fire away, RFK believed. Instead, Cohn and his committee sidekick, G. David Schine, undertook "no real spadework that might have destroyed some of their pet theories."[20] When he resigned after six months, Bobby later said, "I told [McCarthy] I thought he was out of his mind and was going to destroy himself."[21] Although he worked for the polarizing senator for only six months, RFK was forever linked to him because he refused to disavow McCarthy's conduct, even after the Senate voted overwhelmingly in 1954 to censure him. Kennedy considered loyalty a defining virtue.

In terrible health when the McClellan hearings started, McCarthy would die of acute liver inflammation only four months later. On May 7, at the Appleton, Wisconsin, funeral mass in the St. Mary Parish Catholic church, Bobby sat far from sight in the choir loft, his head bowed in prayer. He was the only Kennedy family member to attend the service for the family's destructive, damaged old friend. Outside the church, Bobby asked reporters to please not mention that he had come to pay his respects, and most complied. "I thought there was important work to do," he would later say of his decision to work for the man whose name defined the Red scare era. "I was wrong."

In the first week of what became known as the McClellan hearings, chief counsel Kennedy had only six investigators. It wasn't enough. Soon he and McClellan went on a hiring spree and within six months had thirty-five investigators, twenty stenographers and clerks, and forty-five accountants on loan from the General Accounting Office. Deploying more than one hundred workers, they had assembled the largest investigative team to operate out of Congress.

Days after the committee was formed, RFK heard from Eddie Cheyfitz, the public relations man and lawyer who was on a $60,000-a-year retainer from the Teamsters. You've got to see Hoffa, Cheyfitz insisted to RFK. Sure, Jimmy was wild and reckless trying to organize in Detroit in the 1930s, but so was everybody else. Hoffa wants to clean up the corruption and cares about the working man, unlike Beck. He wants to meet you and will answer any questions you have, Cheyfitz insisted. You'll like him.

Other than the part about answering questions, none of what Cheyfitz said turned out to be true. Cheyfitz had an unusual history for a Washington insider. A former member of the Communist Party and a labor organizer, Cheyfitz abandoned the party in 1939 because of the Nazi-Soviet nonaggression pact. He had been a mine workers' union official, wrote a book on collective bargaining, worked as lobbyist for the powerful US Chamber of Commerce and for the Motion Picture Association of America, then handled the Teamsters' public relations and lobbying on a generous retainer from Dave Beck.

Hoffa had known Cheyfitz for a few years and didn't trust him. When Cheyfitz showed up in Detroit, Hoffa would chew him out, suspecting that Beck had sent Cheyfitz there to spy on him, to find out if Hoffa was making moves to oust him as Teamsters president. Cheyfitz convinced Hoffa he wasn't a spy. When he offered to help Jimmy scrub his own roughneck image, Hoffa took him up on it. By 1956, Cheyfitz had Hoffa speaking at the Harvard Business School about transportation economics. "In the past two years there's been an organized move to change his personality," Bernard Marcus, a Philadelphia Teamsters official, privately told committee investigators. Hoffa was "very inarticulate, stumbled all over himself. [Now] Hoffa has glibness. He didn't have it before. There is an organized move to promote Hoffa nationally. He's done everything except kiss babies."[22]

Hoffa also benefited from an enormous fund-raising dinner in his honor in Detroit in April of 1956. The city council declared April 20 James R. Hoffa Day in honor of "his dynamic leadership, courageous labors, and valuable sense of civic duty." The dinner was attended by the who's who of Michigan's establishment: labor leaders, heads of hospitals and trucking firms, the Catholic bishop of Chicago, a prominent rabbi from Philadelphia, the former Wage Stabilization Board chairman, and, of course, Dave Beck. Ford, General Motors, Sears, Montgomery Ward, and other Detroit- and Chicago-based corporations bought blocks of the $100-a-plate tickets. With much fanfare at the dinner, it was announced that Hoffa was donating all the proceeds, some $250,000, to build the James R. Hoffa Children's Home of Jerusalem, which broke ground four months later in Israel. The dinner went a long way toward scrubbing Hoffa's unsavory image in Michigan and portraying him as a broad-minded leader with interests in international affairs.

By then, Cheyfitz had switched his primary allegiance from Beck to Hoffa, knowing that Beck was weak, under investigation by the IRS, and no match for Hoffa's growing support across the 1.4-million-member union. Even so, Hoffa at first still didn't completely trust Cheyfitz. In front of others, Hoffa made a show of saying, "You're my lawyer now," while handing Cheyfitz a dollar, officially making the exchange a contract; thenceforth, Hoffa believed, everything Cheyfitz learned from him was protected by lawyer-client privilege. As a result, in early 1957, Hoffa could confidently give damaging information about Beck to Cheyfitz, who suggested to Kennedy that his investigators dig even deeper into Shefferman's activities. At the same time, Cheyfitz gave Kennedy a polished spiel that downplayed Hoffa's thuggish friends and brutish tactics.

When Cheyfitz told Hoffa he ought to meet with Bobby Kennedy, he replied, "For what? I got nothing to talk to him about."[23] Despite the lawyer-client relationship, Hoffa didn't confide to Cheyfitz the method by which he planned to smack down Kennedy's investigating committee: find someone to infiltrate it as a spy.

Informants, espionage, and surveillance had long been tools of the trade on both sides of the labor-management equation. In Detroit, the well-known and most extreme example was found at Ford Motor Company, where founder Henry Ford built the company's notorious "service bureau," a network of some eight thousand union infiltrators, spies, strikebreakers, and agents provocateurs who incited others to violence so they would be arrested, discrediting the union. Hoffa had his own network of friendly cops, newspaper reporters, judges, lawyers, and lawmakers. One of them, Miami lawyer Hyman Fischbach, told Hoffa he knew a lawyer and former Secret Service agent named John Cye Cheasty who had applied to be an investigator on the McClellan committee.

Hoffa trusted Fischbach, who was reported to be close to gambling kingpin Meyer Lansky, and told him to bring Cheasty to Detroit for a meeting. It would be, Hoffa pledged, worth his while.

Cheasty, a tall, pudgy, forty-nine-year-old Brooklyn man on a partial disability retirement pension, was between jobs as a private investigator and needed the money. He asked Fischbach his client's name, and instead of answering, the lawyer pulled out an address book and pointed to a name, Jimmy Hoffa.

Cheasty whistled. "Well, Mr. Big himself."[24]

"Nothing but the best," Fischbach replied.

Cheasty took the trip to Detroit, wondering just what assignment the Teamsters boss might have in mind. Late that night Hoffa told him: take that job with the committee, spy on Kennedy and the investigators, then report back. Hoffa said he wanted names of witnesses the committee was going to call, the kinds of questions that would be asked, any helpful documents. He promised Cheasty $2,000 a month for nine months.*

If he had qualms about the Hoffa assignment, the former PI kept them to himself. If he got a job with the committee,

---

* Nearly $17,000 a month in 2015 dollars.

he told Hoffa, he'd go along with Hoffa's plan. Delighted, Hoffa gave him $1,000 in cash to start and told the former federal agent that he was now part of "triple coverage." Hoffa said he already had a "spy" in the office of Senator McCarthy and "a girl on the Hill."[25]

The next day, after returning to New York, Cheasty called Kennedy, identified himself, and said, "I have information that will make your hair stand on end." He met with Kennedy in his Senate office the following day and outlined Hoffa's scheme. What upset Cheasty perhaps the most, he said, was that his friend Fischbach thought he'd be even remotely interested in Hoffa's offer. From what he'd seen, Hoffa was a threat to the country and should be stopped.[26]

Kennedy could barely believe this stunning development. He took Cheasty to McClellan and had him repeat his story. The senator then called FBI director J. Edgar Hoover, who came over within minutes and took Cheasty with him back to FBI headquarters for interviews. The government didn't have enough to bring charges against Hoffa yet, but now that Cheasty had agreed to be a double agent, Hoover told RFK to put him on the committee payroll.

Eventually, Eddie Cheyfitz convinced Hoffa that there was little to lose by talking to Kennedy. Cheyfitz had seen Hoffa deploy rough but effective charm when he wanted to. Quick on his feet, drop-forged in all-night negotiations, Hoffa was gifted at defending himself and making a case, and Cheyfitz truly thought Hoffa had a chance to disarm the chief counsel a bit. Perhaps the committee might be satisfied with taking down Beck, in itself a mighty accomplishment, and leave Hoffa alone. Hoffa agreed, and a date was set for a quiet dinner at Cheyfitz's home in suburban Chevy Chase on February 19.

Bobby wanted something more tangible than small talk at the arranged dinner and asked Mollenhoff to suggest some questions he could ask Hoffa. The reporter sent RFK a three-page memo entitled "Individuals Who Hoffa Should Be Questioned About," which gave details on eighteen men with the Teamsters who had rap sheets. Bobby, or, more likely, Bellino, underlined each name and instructed a staffer to "make lead cards" to ensure that the men would be investigated by the Rackets Committee.[27]

That evening, Hoffa and Kennedy arrived separately in a snowstorm at Cheyfitz's white brick home. Bobby was a few minutes late, delayed by a call from the FBI, telling him how things had gone an hour earlier. To prove his bona fides to the Teamsters boss, Cheasty had met Hoffa near his hotel and, with Kennedy's blessing, passed him the names of four witnesses at the upcoming hearings.

When he met Hoffa, RFK was struck by how short he appeared; Mollenhoff's accounts of Hoffa's power and reach must have made him seem larger. Hoffa stood a bit over five foot five, weighed a solid 180 pounds, and wore his dark hair slicked straight back and his suit pants cuffed over white socks. Hoffa said that RFK gave him a wimpy handshake. He recalled: "I can tell how he shakes hands what kind of fellow I got. I thought, 'Here's a fella thinks he's doing me a favor by talking to me.'"

Cheyfitz offered drinks, but Hoffa made a point of saying he didn't drink, and RFK chimed in that he didn't drink (in fact, he was a light drinker). Hoffa seemed friendly and polite but he circled back, again and again, to talking about toughness. He had been in many picket-line brawls with cops and rented company goons, and he had won those battles. Hoffa wore those picket-line scars as though they were a Purple Heart. It was no secret that he had a long arrest record for assaults and violence, but he had beaten the rap in nearly all of them. "I do to others what they do to me, only worse," Hoffa told Kennedy—if employers crossed him, he would destroy them.

Such boasts were second nature for Hoffa, the posturing of the picket line and the bargaining table. He routinely used intimidation and strategic doses of violence to achieve his ends. Even two decades after labor's "bloody thirties," Hoffa would still get on the telephone and order the beatings of nonunion workers a thousand miles away or instruct a crew of organizers to intimidate nonunion drivers with gunfire, taking care to aim over their heads.[28]

"I guess I should be wearing my bulletproof vest," Kennedy said, trying to make a joke.

Hoffa's upbringing couldn't have been more different from Kennedy's. His family had little money, and after age seven he had no father to push him along. James Riddle Hoffa was born on Valentine's Day, 1913, in Brazil, a small coal-mining town in central-west Indiana, the third of four children born in as many years to John Cleveland Hoffa and Viola Riddle Hoffa. He was named after his uncle James who owned a bar where the right password got you past several locked doors and into an illegal gambling parlor.[29] Jimmy's father, who finished the ninth grade, ran a steam-powered drilling machine for a coal prospector. The work took him across the southern end of the state, and John Hoffa was often away from home for several days at a time or longer as he searched for promising new mineral seams. By that time, Indiana's coal boom was playing out, and Viola Hoffa had to take in laundry from Brazil's better-off citizens to earn extra money. On October

19, 1920, Jimmy Hoffa's father died at age thirty-eight, having lingered for months after an apparent massive stroke. In time, Teamsters literature would give John Hoffa's cause of death as coal-dust poisoning. At age seven, Jimmy was left with memories of a weekend father who took his children fishing and to whatever circus or medicine show came through town. In an age before Social Security death benefits and public assistance, Viola had little choice but to take in more laundry and enlist her kids to join the fight to subsist. Hoffa and his brother, Bill, eighteen months older, trapped birds, snared rabbits, and caught fish for the supper table. Generously interpreting what had strayed into the public domain, they harvested apples, pears, strawberries, hickory nuts, and walnuts — anything within arm's reach or a few steps inside a fence. The family's livelihood, the "Hoffa home laundry," depended on Viola's large black cast-iron stove, cords of firewood to heat the water tubs, and half a dozen clunky flatirons. Jenetta, his older sister, ironed; Jimmy and Bill cut and stacked wood, hauled out ashes, and delivered clean laundry and collected payments; Nancy, the youngest, folded. Working full-time while keeping four children under control, Viola Hoffa relied on a leather strap to discipline the boys and spoonfuls of castor oil for the girls.

In 1924, she sought better fortunes and moved her family to Detroit, which was growing by one thousand residents a week, thanks to the burgeoning auto industry. Eventually she landed a steady, low-paying job at Fisher Body's Fleetwood plant, where she and other women, many of them immigrants from central Europe, finished and polished chrome radiator caps. Jimmy cleaned basements, ran errands, and sacked potatoes at a grocery store. He and Bill made two dollars a day handing out advertising leaflets at shift changes outside

Ford's massive River Rouge plant. The handbills touted patent medicines—"phony junk about how to cure the clap and syphilis," according to Bill Hoffa.[30]

Their working-class Detroit neighborhood was mostly populated by people of Hungarian, Polish, and Slavic descent. The Hoffa children were viewed as "hillbillies," outsiders to be taunted and attacked, Hoffa's brother would later say. "Most of the kids in school were Hunkies, and if they got you down, they'd stomp you and knife you. They never got Jimmy or me down. Jim always could take care of himself, and if he couldn't, I would help. With the guys we had to fight, you always had to make your first sucker punch count. Many's the time Jim and I held them off, standing back-to-back."[31]

Jimmy dropped out of school after ninth grade. "It didn't seem right to have to spend so much time at inconsequential pursuits"—schooling—"before being able to get down to man's business," Hoffa later said.[32] He landed a job stocking goods at a department store, Frank & Seder, ten hours a day, six days a week, for twenty cents an hour. He turned his $12 weekly paycheck over to Viola, who doled out spending money. After the 1929 stock market crash, with department store spending in a slump, Hoffa found work at Kroger Grocery and Baking Company, which had offices and warehouses several blocks from his family home and employed some of his neighbors. He snagged a loading dock position, saying he was eighteen and impressing a supervisor with his stocky, muscular build and eagerness to work. He made thirty-two cents an hour unpacking produce from trucks. Despite the high pay, it was frustrating, almost desperate work. He started his shift at four thirty in the afternoon but sat idle and unpaid part of the time because the workers were compensated only for time spent unloading. He put in sixty hours to get paid for forty-eight. In the teeth of the Great Depression, at least he had a job.

The Kroger night-shift foreman, Al Hastings, whose nickname was the Little Bastard, was "the kind of guy who causes unions," Hoffa was to say. Hastings fired anyone who irritated him, and there was a limitless supply of unemployed men willing to take the place of those who were fired. With no job security, Hoffa felt powerless and humiliated, day after day. "This guy was real sadist," Hoffa would later say. "He thoroughly enjoyed screaming out commands and then cursing a man and threatening to fire him if he didn't move quick enough. He was a little tin Jesus in the warehouse, and the only time he smiled was when he fired somebody."[33]

The Kroger warehouse workers began to talk about forming an independent union. Of the 175 men covering all the shifts, five of them stepped up to serve as coordinators — one of them eighteen-year-old Jimmy Hoffa. There were two others in their late teens, Frank Collins and Bobby Holmes, who would remain lifelong friends of Hoffa's. Together they covertly hatched plans for a walkout when the time was right.

In May of 1931, Hastings ignited the spark. He made a big show out of firing two men for stepping out to a midnight food cart, as was the routine for many workers. Hoffa and the other four decided it was time to take action. The moment came on a warm night three days later, when a truck of highly perishable Florida strawberries pulled into the dock. When they had the berries halfway unloaded, Hoffa put down his crate, and the others walked away from the packing lines and gathered on the loading dock. Hastings knew what was afoot and screamed at them to return to work. The gang of five demanded to speak to the boss, a night supervisor named Blough. Hastings refused, and threatened mass firings, but the chant went up: "We want Blough! We want Blough!" Supervisor Blough showed up and quickly promised to discuss working conditions if the workers finished unloading the berries.

Over the next few days, Hoffa, thirty-six-year-old Sam Calhoun, and the other three reached an agreement with Kroger management guaranteeing a half-day minimum pay, lunch breaks, washrooms, permission to smoke, and other issues that made the job slightly more bearable. The Kroger workers later affiliated with the Teamsters, and Jimmy, who proved his skill at organizing, took a job as a business agent for Teamsters Joint Council 43 and Local 299. He didn't have a salary but instead was paid for each worker he signed up.

Unionizing a company could be dangerous work. It wasn't until the mid-1930s, with labor-friendly New Deal legislation, that private-sector workers were guaranteed the basic right to organize, bargain collectively for pay and working conditions, and take collective action. Even so, strikes were often bloody, violent conflicts, with authorities typically enforcing order by arresting strikers. "It was the open shop capital of the world," Hoffa once said of Detroit in the 1930s. "Every time you went near a place to organize you'd get picked up and sent to jail. The police beat you on the head with nightsticks. It was a mess. We fought on the streets. The employers hired every hoodlum strikebreaker in town. We used to laugh to see the police and the ex-cons lined up against us."[34]

Looking for new members, Hoffa and other Teamsters organizers set their sights on the rapidly expanding car-hauling industry—the tractor-trailer rigs that, by 1935, were hauling two million new cars a year to dealers. Most car haulers were small, with fewer than a dozen or two drivers, and highly competitive. Rather than sign up workers, Teamsters organizers for Local 299 used a brutally effective tactic. They would tell a company to enroll its drivers in the Teamsters or else their trucks would be bombed. When owners refused, trucks were blown up. "In the mid-1930s," according to historian Thaddeus Russell, "the local gained a reputation as the most violent, lawless union in an unusually violent, lawless city."[35] Employers could be just as savage. Someone shot Bill Hoffa in the stomach while he walked a picket line outside a Detroit grocery store, mistaking him for his rabble-rousing younger brother. The wound was serious, but he recovered. No one was arrested.

Hoffa often said, "Life is a jungle," and he believed he had survived because he was the fittest, mentally and physically. He had come of age in the mass unionism of the 1930s, when the Teamsters broke with the idea of narrow craft unions — carpenters, film editors — and swept up warehouse workers, jukebox mechanics, long-haul truckers, and assorted "riff-raff," to use the disapproving term of Teamsters president Dan Tobin. The charismatic Teamsters leader named Farrell Dobbs, a Trotskyite who'd had tremendous success organizing Minneapolis truck drivers under a citywide contract, influenced Hoffa deeply. Dobbs had boosted membership and fed union treasuries by insisting on uniform, citywide contracts that stabilized the city's unstructured trucking system, which consisted of hundreds of companies. With the higher wages came lower turnover and more experienced workers, and the companies made more money. Young Hoffa had spent hours listening to Dobbs — "a far-seeing man" — talk about the inevitable flaws of capitalism, its role in the Depression, and the economic future of American society. Hoffa rejected socialism but "plainly regarded capitalism as a racket that the strong manipulated to their advantage — a system where everyone was on the take, morality was bullshit, and no holds were barred."[36]

By the time of the McClellan hearings, Hoffa and Beck stood at the opposite end of labor's political spectrum from Walter Reuther, president of the United Automobile Workers, another Detroit labor power and the face of the American labor movement. Reuther held on to his ideals from the

1930s; he was still committed to union democracy, the cause of social justice, and liberalism at home and abroad. Hoffa dismissed such strivings with a favorite put-down — "naive." "I don't want to change the world," Hoffa said. He just wanted power and money — and planned to destroy anyone who got in his way.

———

IF BOBBY KENNEDY HAD KNOWN SOMETHING of Hoffa's background, their first meeting might have gone more smoothly. With Cheyfitz trying to break the ice, Hoffa and Kennedy warily sat down for their roast beef dinner. Bobby questioned Hoffa about his upbringing, what kind of schooling he had had, how much a union official made in salary, how he spent his workday. Hoffa, who was particularly attuned to class slights, felt insulted. "It was as though he was asking, with my limited education, what right did I have to run a union like this," Hoffa said.[37]

After dinner, the men moved to the living room, where Hoffa sat on a couch and Bobby stood with his back to a fire in the fireplace. Cheyfitz prodded them to get into more controversial matters.

Kennedy asked Hoffa about the paper locals in New York City tied to Johnny Dio, who was then under indictment for the blinding of Victor Riesel. Hoffa's answer surprised Bobby. "In discussing the paper locals of New York, he said that he took full responsibility for them.... He said Dio had nothing to do with the operation," RFK put in a memo two days later.[38]

Kennedy asked Hoffa about a Minneapolis Teamsters official convicted of federal and state labor racketeering charges (one of the eighteen men listed in Mollenhoff's memo). Why did you keep him in his job?

A different Teamsters leader brought that man to Minneapolis, Hoffa said, and he knew "right from the beginning that it was a very bad mistake." As the night moved on, Hoffa answered each of Kennedy's questions, appearing "disarmingly frank," RFK wrote in his memo.[39] Perhaps Cheyfitz had the right idea with this peace mission after all.

Around 9:30 that evening, Ethel Kennedy called Cheyfitz's home and asked for her husband. Hoffa needled him. "Better hurry up and talk to her, Bob," he said. "She probably wants to know if you're alive."

On the phone, RFK learned that a woman had crashed her car into a tree in front of their Hickory Hills home and was now sitting in their living room, hysterical. He said he would be right there. As he was leaving, Hoffa said, "Tell your wife I'm not as bad as everyone thinks I am."[40] Bobby laughed, then left to drive home.

Once Kennedy was gone, Hoffa turned to Cheyfitz and spat out, "He's a damn spoiled jerk."

Cheyfitz had hoped that the intimate dinner might bring the two strong-willed battlers closer together—perhaps even begin to feel comfortable with the other, the influence peddler's ultimate goal. If anything, the dinner had the opposite effect—having met in person, the two men learned that they truly disliked each other. On his way to Hickory Hills, RFK reflected on how much Hoffa had talked about his toughness, how he destroyed employers, and how he hated policemen. The aggressive talk led him to decide that Hoffa "was a bully hiding behind a facade."[41]

The Rackets Committee hearings, as the press nicknamed them, quickly captured the public's imagination. Walter Winchell, the country's most influential news figure, with his syndicated newspaper column and rat-a-tat-tat delivery over a nationwide radio network, followed the hearings and trolled for the sensational. On a February 24, 1957, broadcast, he announced: "The Senate's probe of the Teamsters Union will disclose that many records are missing. The most wanted records — payments to party girls for pro-union politicians." The Winchell item hinted at a dark secret about Hoffa's operation. He and certain Teamsters leaders weren't beneath blackmail to get what they needed. Hoffa once confided to a Teamsters official he trusted that he had compromising photographs of half the members of Michigan's congressional delegation.[42]

RFK and his committee staff worked out of room 101 of the old Senate Office Building on Capitol Hill. Angie Novello, the top stenographer on the investigations subcommittee and Carmine Bellino's sister-in-law, became his secretary, and LaVern Duffy, an investigator who had worked with RFK on the McCarthy committee, also came on board. Kennedy took a chance on Pierre Salinger, a portly bon vivant and magazine writer for *Collier's*. Salinger had written an investigative series on Hoffa and Beck that had been ready for print when the magazine folded in December of 1956. Kennedy asked him for his story and notes, and he turned them over and was hired shortly thereafter. Witty, a good storyteller, and able to "grasp the importance of a document better than almost anyone on the staff," he became a Kennedy intimate. Kenny O'Donnell, RFK's old townie friend from Harvard, where they bonded on the football field, served as chief of staff.

The supremely organized Carmine Bellino set up a filing and indexing system to keep control and manage the investigators' memos as well as all the financial records, court documents, correspondence, and tips that had begun to pour in to the committee. It was similar to the FBI's system. For each investigative subject or company, clerks opened a file and assigned it a case number. Each new document for the file was noted with a case number, given a page number, hole-punched, and assembled into the files. Each name in a memo that needed to be indexed was underlined and then cross-referenced by case number and page number on three-by-five-inch cards. Those index cards alone would eventually fill five ten-drawer file cabinets.

Congress approved an initial $350,000 for the committee to accomplish its work over the following year. To chase all the leads, Kennedy and McClellan continued bringing in investigators, accountants, stenographers, and typists. On paper, the senator approved all hires, but that method proved too slow for Kennedy. Sometimes he hired staffers, then told them to meet with McClellan and let the old country lawyer believe he was having the final say—Salinger, for example, already had the job offer when he met with McClellan. (The gruff-voiced senator made it clear he didn't like ex-journalists being brought on staff. "If I ever hear you talking to the press, I will deal with you in the harshest manner," McClellan warned.) Former journalists and all, by the spring of 1957, the committee was staffed up and investigating Teamsters officials in Seattle, Portland, Los Angeles, Detroit, Chicago, and New York City.

Kennedy was the only staffer with a private office. Prominent on one wall was a picture of the destroyer *Joseph P. Kennedy Jr.* He had also hung a framed copy of a quote from Winston Churchill: "We shall not flag or fail...we shall never surrender." Bobby worked long hours, often having a sandwich and a glass of milk at his desk and getting home at 9:00 p.m., long after Ethel and their five children had finished dinner.

He pushed his staff just as hard—Angie Novello and others often worked on weekends and occasionally put in sixteen-hour days.

He was finally stepping into his own, finding this committee's work the most fulfilling he had ever known. He was truly passionate about smashing labor rackets and helping workingmen and -women, and the joy of dedicating himself to the cause changed his demeanor. "He wasn't frustrated during that period," Lem Billings would recall. "This is when he blossomed....He wasn't the angry young man anymore, and he was much more pleasant to be around because he hadn't this terrible feeling that he wasn't contributing."[43]

At this point, the committee's progress was almost giddying. After only a few short months, Kennedy believed he and the committee had nearly enough ammunition to make two enormous contributions to the cause: knock both Beck and Hoffa out of the labor movement.

CHAPTER 3

Jump Off the Capitol

OVER THE FOLLOWING THREE WEEKS, double agent Cheasty provided morsels of committee intelligence to Hoffa on ten occasions, all under the supervision of the FBI. He would phone Hoffa's secretary and say "Eddie Smith" was calling, and she'd connect him to her boss. On March 12, Cheasty planned to meet with Hoffa for the first time since he had agreed to spy for him. It was the next step in the sting. Using tweezers so he wouldn't leave any prints, Cheasty placed committee records in a brown envelope, called Hoffa, and said he had something for him. Hoffa told Cheasty to come up to his room at the Dupont Plaza.

It's too risky, Cheasty complained to Hoffa. Cheasty knew that a private meeting with Hoffa would make it impossible for agents to photograph the exchange.

Then come up to the hotel in a cab, Hoffa instructed, and he'd climb in.

Cheasty did take a taxi, only it was operated by an undercover FBI agent. They picked up Hoffa.

Got something for you, Cheasty said, unfolding a newspaper to reveal the brown envelope.

Hoffa told the driver to stop; he wanted out. Cheasty paid the agent-cabbie one dollar and walked with Hoffa back to the hotel. Cheasty told Hoffa he needed to return the file later that night.

Hoffa said fine — come back after 11:00 p.m. "I have a couple of thousand for you. Do you want it?"[1]

"Nobody ever said no to money," Cheasty replied.

From across Dupont Circle, FBI agents filmed the two men as they shook hands and as Cheasty's came away holding a roll of bills. The documents, selected by Kennedy and the FBI, listed the fruits of Carmine Bellino's financial sleuthing — all the personal goods and expenses that Beck had purchased with union dues. When Hoffa returned the files to Cheasty that night, he said, "If that's the kind of stuff they have on Beck, it looks like his goose is cooked."

The next day, March 13, Cheasty called Hoffa and said he had more committee documents. They agreed to meet that night. Cheasty handed off the package in front of the glass doors to the hotel. When Hoffa walked inside with the documents, FBI agents swarmed out and arrested him. Eddie Cheyfitz, his public relations man, happened to be in the lobby as Hoffa was led off. He thought that Hoffa was being taken for a ride by goons and in danger and called the FBI only to be told that his friend had been arrested by its agents.

RFK was waiting in his office when Hoover phoned to tell him about the arrest. Kennedy was thrilled. He called Ethel and told her to call Clark Mollenhoff and other reporters at home and give them the news. After doing so, she joined her husband downtown, not wanting to miss the excitement. Meanwhile, Cheyfitz called his law partner, Edward Bennett Williams.

Williams, exhausted from spending three days in New York trying to keep mobster Frank Costello out of jail, had just climbed into bed. Even so, he appreciated Cheyfitz's call. He owed a lot to the red-haired image polisher. They met in the early 1950s, when Cheyfitz was enhancing his résumé as a political matchmaker by taking night classes at Georgetown law school. Williams was then a part-time lecturer already in ascendance. The ambitious Williams not only enjoyed having Cheyfitz in class but also realized he could make use of Cheyfitz's charm and newspaper connections to promote his own courtroom accomplishments. Lawyers were not allowed to advertise, and to drum up business, they often relied on news stories about their victories—so Williams brought Cheyfitz into his law firm with the idea that he would talk up the firm's cases to reporters. But Cheyfitz became the firm's rainmaker as well, putting Williams together with Dave Beck, who used him to defend some Teamsters officials in Minnesota. Beck had Williams at his side when he went before the McClellan committee, and eventually Williams became general counsel for the International Brotherhood of Teamsters, pulling in huge, steady fees for the next decade.

Over at the courthouse, Mollenhoff tried to kid Hoffa. "Well, Jimmy, so you finally slipped and slipped good. I was beginning to wonder if anyone would ever catch up to you."[2] Hoffa was in no mood for gibes—he was furious. From a couple of steps away, the union leader glared at Kennedy with the poisonous stare that had already become Hoffa's trademark, waiting for him to turn away.

"He stared at me for three minutes with complete hatred in his eyes," RFK recalled.

"Listen, Bobby, you run your business, and I'll run mine," Hoffa growled. "You go on home and go to bed. I'll take care of things. Let's don't have no problems."[3]

Bizarrely, somehow the standoff turned into a discussion about physical fitness, which devolved into juvenile boasting about who could do more push-ups. (Hoffa said he could do thirty-five, and RFK said he could do more.) Williams arrived and broke into the tense scene, demanding, "What's this all about?"

RFK snubbed him, while Ethel said, "You'll find out soon enough, Mr. Williams."

He was irritated. "Shouldn't you be home with the kids?" he snapped.

Hoffa was arraigned around 2:00 a.m. Afterward, he told reporters, "I am not guilty of any wrongdoing....This is not the first instance when a labor leader has been unjustly accused." When a television reporter complained that the early morning arraignment was interfering with his sleep, Hoffa, by then comfortable enough to joke, said, "You never ran a picket line; that's your trouble."

Any fears that Kennedy may have had about the success of the Rackets Committee were lifted. After only a few months of investigation and a dozen days of hearings, he was certain that Beck was going to be ousted as president and in all likelihood charged with financial crimes. And now he and the FBI had Hoffa on a seemingly airtight case of bribery, with moving pictures of the payoff.

Two days later, Kennedy was asked the unthinkable by a reporter: What would he do if Hoffa were acquitted? Bobby replied with a smile, "I'll jump off the Capitol."

Hoffa's sensational arrest apparently gave courage to Michigan's attorney general, because the next day he wrote a two-page letter to Senator McClellan that would command Kennedy's interest. For six months, Thomas Kavanagh said, he and his staffers had been trying to pin down a story that a suspicious Hoffa had equipped his employees with hidden microphones when they testified before a Detroit grand jury investigating their boss.

Hoffa supposedly paid a private investigator from New York, Bernard Spindel, $9,000 to install an elaborate system of hidden microphones in his Detroit union offices in June of 1953 and equip him with Minifones, expensive, state-of-the-art concealable recorders. Kavanagh learned this from transcripts of Spindel's testimony to a New Jersey legislative committee that was considering laws to restrict telephone intercepts; he also learned that someone had then gone one step further. "Mr. Spindel informed the committee that, among other things, he was paid to strap Minifones to [the union] lieutenants before they went in to testify before a 'local grand jury,' that when these witnesses emerged from the grand jury chambers the wire records made by the Minifones were played back, and that 'the labor leader' was gratified to learn that all his aides were completely loyal," Kavanagh wrote. Spindel didn't name Hoffa in his testimony, but his account neatly matched events that had unfolded in Detroit in 1953, when a Wayne County grand jury called Hoffa and his lieutenants in for questioning.[4] What unfolds inside a grand jury is supposed to be secret, especially from the target of proceedings. Hoffa had in effect bugged the room.

Kavanagh said his office was looking into the "grave matter" of apparent violations of grand jury secrecy but had been "hampered by lack of subpoena power and other legal machinery. In addition, key witnesses are in other states, and this office is without authority to compel them to testify." He asked the Rackets Committee to investigate "as soon as possible."

This was the first time Kennedy and his staff received word about Hoffa and grand jury shenanigans, but Spindel was familiar to some of the investigators. According to author Jim Hougan, Bernard B. Spindel was "a legend within the spooks' milieu, a wireman of unequaled genius. He was, by all accounts, the Nikola Tesla of electronic eavesdropping, an inventor whose seemingly magical...and conceptual leaps revolution-ized the state of the art—time and again."[5]

Spindel was a dark-haired man, six feet tall, 210 pounds, with the fingers of a fine tailor, able to deftly solder wires to tiny circuits inside electronic spyware he designed himself. He tapped his first phone as a boy of twelve, a pay phone in a New York tenement hallway. He dropped a line to the build-ing's coal bin, where he put on earphones and could hear every conversation that took place in the hallway. "It began to give me a very peculiar feeling of power, to know what everyone in that building was saying and what they were doing," he would write in his memoirs. "I've never lost the feeling. I have knowledge that no one else in the world has about certain individuals."[6]

Spindel had been trained by the army's Signal Corps in radio, voice, and electronics during World War II and served as an intelligence officer. After the war, he'd applied to the CIA but was turned down. He became a private investigator in New York City, and he found success by exploiting the advances in electronics that had led to the development of stronger, smaller, and cheaper transmitters, tape recorders, and other components that could be wired and soldered and made into surveillance gear. Police detectives, the FBI, and state police all used the new devices freely until new laws caught up with the technology and restricted its use. Spindel's clients ranged from aggrieved spouses looking for dirt on phi-landering partners to accused criminals wanting to even the odds against law enforcement. Spindel also consulted for prosecutors and the New York City Anti-Crime Committee. In the mid-1950s he exposed a huge police corruption scandal, turning in cops and detectives who bought gear from the same supply houses he frequented and then used it to monitor bookies, numbers joints, whorehouses, and other criminals and criminal enterprises. The cops wanted to know how much business these rackets were pulling so that they, in turn, would know whether they were getting cheated out of the percentage they demanded for protection. He also appeared on the hit television game show *What's My Line?*, trying to stump celebrity questioners who were trying to guess his profession. (Correct answer: professional wiretapper. They failed.) Much of Spindel's work for Hoffa was defensive, removing bugs and telephones taps. Hoffa had heard of Spindel through Johnny Dio, who paid the wireman $125 a week to sweep his places of business. The details of Spindel's work for Hoffa were fascinating. Hoffa brought Spindel to Detroit in the summer of 1953, hoping he was the miracle worker Dio said he was. First, Spindel swept Hoffa's Local 299 offices for hidden microphones and telephone taps. He found seven active taps, including one on the public pay phone in the front lobby,[7] but he could not determine who had planted them.

Next, at Hoffa's request, Spindel hid tiny microphones inside the office telephones of the Teamsters business agents and other key people in the local Teamsters headquarters. Spindel wired the microphones to a switchboard inside Hoffa's desk. The Teamsters leader could turn these hidden mikes on and off remotely and then listen through his telephone handset to conversations in the various offices; to anyone who looked into Hoffa's office, he would appear to be on the telephone. Spindel would later insist that the setup was legal in Michigan because he had not tapped a telephone wire, which was illegal—he had merely hidden a bug in a phone and separately wired it back to Hoffa's telephone handset.

Spindel also installed wiretap detectors in the offices and advised Hoffa to house his building's main telephone-terminal board and junction inside a padlocked steel case. The locked case, he said, might prevent government or corporate spies from trying to install any more hidden microphones.

To help Hoffa with the Wayne County grand jury, Spindel sold Hoffa half a dozen Minifones. The German-made device was considered remarkably small at the time, about the size of a two-inch-thick pocket-size paperback book, but it still was hard to hide. It came with an adjustable holster so it could be strapped on under clothing and a cord with a button microphone that could be threaded up and disguised as a lapel pin. Hoffa made all his lieutenants wear the rig when they were called to the grand jury, a sort of audio chastity belt that ensured they would say nothing negative about him. It worked, and he avoided indictment.

Hoffa put other highly effective, fairly low-cost surveillance technology to broad use across the region. The Teamsters deployed it to gain an edge during strikes and bargaining sessions. In August of 1955, the owner of Kurtz Brick Company in Detroit, facing a strike by Teamsters Local 243, found himself squeezed out of customers because Teamsters picketers kept showing up at the right time and place when his company's nonunion drivers tried to make a delivery. He convinced police to investigate, and they found a wiretap into telephone lines from a rented garage in back of Kurtz Brick. The man who had rented the garage was employed by Local 243.[8]

Illegal wiretapping was a federal crime, and the evidence was mounting. When Kennedy urged Justice Department prosecutors to look into the accusations against Hoffa, he learned that the US attorney in Manhattan, where Spindel had his office, had already started building a case.

To build his cases back in Congress, particularly against Hoffa, RFK needed top investigators. In April of 1957, he made one of his most productive hires: Walter Sheridan, a fellow Roman Catholic from Utica, New York, where his father ran a small hotel called the Montclair and a restaurant called Sheridan's. He and Bobby shared the same birthday and, as Kennedy once put it, "the will to fight what is evil and a desire to serve."[9] They became close friends.

Sheridan was president of his high school senior class, quarterback of the football team, and he met his future wife, Nancy Tuttle, there. He served on a navy submarine during the war. Afterward he went to Fordham University in New York City on the GI Bill, tried law school for a year, then joined the FBI. After four frustrating years, he quit the Bureau, uneasy about what he described as J. Edgar Hoover's obsessive focus on rooting out Communists while ignoring the greater menace of organized crime. Sheridan became an investigator for the super-secret National Security Agency but felt adrift professionally. "You grow up with idealistic ideas," he would later explain, "but you realize more and more that you can never get them into action."

Sheridan had heard from a man in his parish about the committee's work—that it was supporting a good cause and needed investigators. He was told to talk to "Bob Kennedy, whom I knew only vaguely as the brother of the fellow who tried to be vice president in 1956." Sheridan waited for a couple of hours at the Rackets Committee offices. "Bob Kennedy came out looking very gaunt and just nodded at me, and I walked out the door with him." Striding out of the building,

RFK questioned Sheridan about his background. "He inter-viewed me for a job going up the stairs on his way home," Sheridan recalled. "He hired me just going up the steps."[10]

It did not take long for Sheridan to realize the magnitude of the committee's task—and of RFK's demands. Early on in the job, Bobby assigned him to interviews in Chicago. Spot-ting him in the office the next morning, Kennedy asked what he was doing. Sheridan said he had a noon flight. RFK quietly told him he never flew at noon. From then on, Sheridan made certain to travel first thing in the morning.

"I got out to Chicago and met Pierre [Salinger]," Sheridan said. "Typical Pierre, with a big cigar and his feet up on the desk. He was a very flashy dresser at that time, and he had a checkered yellow shirt and a checkered red bow tie." Sitting at another desk was a much older investigator, Edgar Parkhurst, who was working his way through a stack of long-distance phone-call records, entering them by hand into a spreadsheet, carefully noting the names, dates, times, and locations of the calls, then ordering them chronologically. The records had been gathered from hotel operators and telephone compa-nies. Sheridan had worked for the FBI for four years and had never seen the technique. That kind of work would have driven him crazy, and he wouldn't appreciate the value of the chronologies until much later.

Sheridan quickly became good friends with Kenny O'Donnell, who managed the Senate committee staff, approv-ing travel and reading all the investigators' memos, even though they were addressed to RFK. "Kenny O'Donnell would screen out or get down to the real important things," Sheridan said. "He would give those to Robert Kennedy."[11] O'Donnell also coordinated the investigations. When investigators in Detroit developed leads that might help those working in

New York, O'Donnell made sure to pass them along. Meanwhile, everything was indexed and cross-referenced on three-by-five file cards, which were stored in ever-deepening drawers. Investigators would schedule tentative witnesses, send out subpoenas and telegrams, arrange for accommodations, and prepare witness sheets with questions and expected answers. If a witness deviated from the facts the investigators had dug up, RFK could easily see who was lying to him.

"We worked at an unbelievable pace," Sheridan recalled. A letter to his wife, written from a Chicago hotel about a month into his new job, captured RFK's near-frantic operation.[12]

> My dearest Nancy,
>
> I didn't get back from Gary until 11:15. It is now midnight and I'm going to bed soon. Bellino is coming out Wednesday and then the pressure will really come on. There is an awful lot left to do. Kennedy may come with him. At least this is the last lap of this thing and it won't be too long now until I get home. I miss you all very much. I'm tired and I'm going to bed....Good night darling. I love you.
>
> *Walt*

The committee's frenetic hard work paid off when Dave Beck rolled into the Senate Caucus Room that spring with two lawyers, a bulging brown briefcase of financial records, and a cocky smile. He had avoided a Rackets Committee subpoena for more than a month, thanks to a suddenly scheduled vacation in Europe and other tactics, and finally arrived to face Senator McClellan, his eager chief counsel, Kennedy, and the glare of television cameras. Asked by a reporter if he was nervous, Beck blared, "Nervous? Me? Haw!"[13]

Before settling in at the witness table, Beck turned his three-diamond ring into the palm of his left hand, claiming, "I always wear it that way because the light flashes in my eyes." He clasped his hands to hide any trembling as Chairman McClellan read the committee's provocative opening statement. Investigators had uncovered information, McClellan said, that "the president of the International Brother[hood] of Teamsters, Chauffeurs, Warehousemen, and Helpers of America, the largest, most powerful union in our country, may have misappropriated over $320,000 in union funds."

When McClellan asked Beck for the subpoenaed financial records, the Teamsters president declared that turning them over would violate his Fifth Amendment right against self-incrimination. Since he was entangled in tricky legal maneuvers with the IRS over accusations of income tax fraud, Beck was taking a prudent path. In question after question, McClellan bore in on the matter of checks paid to Beck from the Seattle Teamsters local, and Beck pleaded the fifth. Then McClellan provoked him: "Do you regard your privileges under the Fifth Amendment as transcending your duty and obligations to the laboring men of this country who belong to your union?"

By that point Beck was red-faced, and he leaned toward McClellan and appeared to begin to mouth a reply. "Just in time, his sad-faced lawyer, Arthur Condon, drove [a] swift knuckle into the small of Beck's back," a reporter would later write. "Three times Beck started to answer; three times Condon's knuckle dug into his spine. Beck soon developed a sort of Pavlov's dog response to the knuckle."[14] Each time Beck felt the jab, he replied, "I must decline to answer...."

When McClellan turned the questioning over to Bobby Kennedy, RFK was ready with documents that Bellino and others had harvested from labor fixer Nathan Shefferman, the IRS, and Teamsters union ledger books. He patiently introduced every damaging scrap into the Senate hearings record, knowing Beck would plead the fifth, and irreparably tarred Beck's once-clean public image. Within hours RFK had "made public one of the most fantastic money merry-go-rounds in congressional investigation history."[15]

The outline of Beck's boodling was vast: from 1948 to 1953, he took $196,000 in Teamsters funds to pay a contractor for work on his home on Lake Washington. In March of 1954, after IRS agents started digging into his taxes, Beck decided to pay back the union coffers. To raise quick cash, he sought a $200,000 loan from a large Detroit trucking firm, Fruehauf Trailer Company. Its officers couldn't put together the loan, so they went to Brown Equipment, a New York trucking company. Brown sent four checks of $50,000 each to Beck. He in turn sent $200,000 to the Teamsters from his own Seattle company, B & B Investment.

When Brown sought repayment, Beck concocted another maneuver, according to Kennedy. Beck "had the idea of selling his house to the union, which, of course, had paid for [it] originally, or at least a part of it, and selling the furniture, which the union had paid for."[16] Teamsters headquarters paid $163,000 for Beck's compound—a large brick ranch home and several smaller houses occupied by his mother, a bodyguard, the vice president of a Beck-owned brewery, and others. Beck was allowed to live in the big house rent-free—for life.

The Teamsters president never recovered from the humiliation of the Rackets Committee's brutal, televised drubbing. His worst sin, in the eyes of the public and union members, was the revelation that he had drained thousands of dollars from a trust fund set up to aid the widow of one of his best friends. "From that moment, Mr. Beck's star sank," the *New York Times* said. A month later, Beck announced he would not run for reelection as president of the Teamsters. By that fall, Beck and his son were charged with federal tax evasion.

To Hoffa's delight, his earlier prediction to committee investigator Cheasty turned out to be right: Beck's goose was cooked. Now, with the Teamsters presidency in play, Hoffa was more determined than ever to make certain Bobby Kennedy didn't scorch him the way he had Dave Beck.

CHAPTER 4

Lucky Bastard

LATE THAT MAY OF 1957, JOHNNY Dio's lawyers' delaying tactics had run their course, and the garment district kingpin came to federal court to face conspiracy charges for the acid attack on Victor Riesel. Dio calmly faced US attorney Paul Williams. The key witness against him was ex-con candy-store owner Gondolfo Miranti, the only person to directly tie the crime to Dio. Miranti, in prison for his part in the crime, feared for his life. On May 20, 1957, as the trial commenced, Miranti flatly refused to testify. The judge threatened him with five additional years in prison for contempt, which would be added at the end of the eighteen years he already was serving. Miranti took the five.

Without Miranti, Williams had no hope of convicting Dio. He asked the judge to postpone the trial. "The government has done all it can do," Williams—who'd hoped to leverage the case into momentum for a run for governor—complained bitterly. "The majesty of the law itself is on trial, where underworld intimidation of witnesses causes the collapse of the government's case....This is an affront to the national conscience."[1]

The New York *Daily News* summed it up brilliantly in tabloidese:

LOCKJAW, its big headline shouted. UNDERWORLD IS VICTOR.

Before taking Hoffa's bribery case, Edward Bennett Williams insisted on three things in advance, as he did with each client: "I must have dictatorial control of the case. You can't try it by committee. The client must be completely candid with me. And of course we have to agree on economics. After all, I have a family to support."[2]

Who sat at the trial table, what witnesses to call, which prospective jurors to strike, whether to use race to appeal to certain jurors—Williams called all the shots. But Hoffa, who'd been investigated, arrested, and sued more than three dozen times, was hardly a passive client. He jousted with Williams over tactics on how to defend against the bribery charges. Hoffa didn't follow Williams's second rule, either—he didn't trust his lawyer enough to share his secrets or his freelance efforts to beat the government. Hoffa's suspicion was not unreasonable. When Hoffa first thought he had hired John Cye Cheasty to spy on the Rackets Committee, he told Cheasty to try to figure out why Bobby Kennedy was going to lunch so often with Williams. He didn't realize they were friends or that Williams was bound to honor attorney-client privilege. "When all is said and done, I'm my own best lawyer," Hoffa said.

In defending Hoffa, Williams faced a seemingly insurmountable challenge—FBI agents had filmed his client standing outside a Dupont Circle flower shop in the early evening light, accepting committee memos from Cheasty, then handing back a wad of cash. Daunting evidence demanded desperate strategy. Williams hired an ambitious ex-FBI counterintelligence agent he knew well, Bob Maheu, to dig up dirt on Cheasty. In his late thirties and nearly bald, Maheu had been on the debate team with Williams at College of the Holy Cross. He had excellent skills and connections as a private sleuth. Years later, he would serve as right-hand man for reclusive billionaire Howard Hughes as well as help the CIA plot against Cuban dictator Fidel Castro. As Williams's firm grew, it became one of Maheu's steady customers. In Florida, Maheu or one of his associates learned that Cheasty had been involved as a lawyer in the NAACP boycott of segregated buses. Perhaps Williams could make some use of that.

But first he tried to delay the bribery trial for several months. Hoffa insisted on being tried after the Teamsters national convention in early October, when delegates would select the union's general president. Hoffa had worked for this prize for years, and a conviction would destroy his chances. If he were convicted *after* his election, he might even be able to stay in office. If he needed to drag out his appeals for years, so be it—he just needed those appeals to follow a post-October trial.

But above all—and in the best-case scenario—he needed to avoid a felony conviction in the first place. Williams did his part, filing motion after motion, accusing the government of contaminating the case with unfair publicity and illegally wiretapping Hoffa (Williams had no evidence to support this) and arguing that Cheasty had entrapped Hoffa. All to no avail.

Then events turned in Hoffa's favor. The US Supreme Court released a decision in early June that gave Williams a chance to peek into the Justice Department's file drawers. *Jencks v. United States* held that defendants had the right to see any prior statements by witnesses who testified against them.

Government lawyers, *before* trial, now had to share all witness statements and certain investigative reports with the defense lawyers.

Williams quickly and successfully fought for access to FBI reports that detailed or summarized everything Cheasty had told the Bureau. Hoffa and his lawyer learned that after Cheasty first met with Hoffa and was paid $1,000, he spent nearly $300 on travel expenses, shoes for his children, Valentine's Day candy for his wife, and other items—all before contacting Kennedy at the Rackets Committee. This conflicted somewhat with Cheasty's account that Hoffa's bribe attempt offended him so deeply that he quickly contacted Kennedy. If the government prosecutor failed to have Cheasty explain his $300 spending spree, a savvy lawyer like Williams easily could use it to besmirch the government's prime witness. Other government reports turned over to the Hoffa legal team were Cheasty's statements to Kennedy and McClellan, which differed from his FBI statements in minor details, all of which would be useful to Williams.

The federal prosecutor, Edward Troxell, was a workmanlike litigator, skilled enough to handle a case that looked like a certain winner. "Anyone could try this case," he said. "When the case is prepared the way the Bureau has prepared this one, it is just a matter of putting it in the record."[3]

Williams knew this and prepared relentlessly. He hated to lose, but he predicted failure, perhaps as a way to motivate himself. "This is the worst case, the *worst* case," he complained to Maheu. "We can't possibly win. It's hopeless."[4] He even had his influence peddler, Eddie Cheyfitz, downgrade expectations with the press, telling reporters that the Hoffa case was a loser. But if Williams won, Cheyfitz boldly told reporters, then he'd rightly be in the legal pantheon with Clarence Darrow.

Williams decided that his best shot at getting Hoffa acquitted depended on two tasks: first, seat African American jurors and portray Hoffa as someone who cared about their concerns; second, destroy Cheasty's credibility.

When it came time to select the jury, Williams had Maheu and another investigator take a day or two to run background checks on each of the potential jurors in the pool. Prosecutor Troxell did not. Williams knew which prospective jurors had run-ins with the police—arrests for drunken driving, disorderly conduct, and the like. These were people he wanted on the jury because they might bear a grudge against the justice system. African Americans would also likely distrust a federal government that seemed uninterested in or even hostile to civil rights legislation and enforcement. Each side had sixteen challenges it could use to eliminate a prospective juror for any reason. Troxell used six challenges, which were evenly divided between black and white jurors. Williams used each of his sixteen challenges to strike white male jurors. Eight black and four white jurors were seated.*

The small courtroom was filled with reporters, spectators, and several of Hoffa's men, including Chicago crime figure Paul Dorfman and the gargantuan Teamsters business agent and enforcer Barney Baker, both of whom came to show their support and to provide Hoffa with any freelance help he might need outside the courtroom. The case hinged on whether the jurors would believe John Cheasty. The balding forty-nine-year-old suffered heart problems and carried nitroglycerin pills in his shirt pocket in case he experienced chest pains. But he testified for the government without problems.

Then it was Williams's turn. Cheasty had to be destroyed.

---

* Removing potential jurors solely on the basis of race, the US Supreme Court would rule years later, was unconstitutional.

It was Hoffa's only hope. Williams planned to chip away at his story by subjecting him to days of cross-examination.

Williams's research showed that Cheasty had been hired by officials in Tallahassee to look into an organized boycott of the city's segregated bus system. Early on in his cross-examination, Williams tried to inflame the black jurors by asking Cheasty if when hired by the city of Tallahassee to investigate the NAACP he had used a fictitious identity.

Cheasty said no, that Williams's implication was false. "My job was to see if Communism was rampant and stirring things up," he said.

You were investigating the NAACP to break up the bus boycott, were you not? Williams insisted.

Cheasty said no; in fact after he looked into the boycott he urged the bus company to hire minority drivers and stop segregated seating. "I recommended they cut the color line on the buses down there."[5]

Williams, stung by Cheasty's answer, demanded that it be stricken from the record because the witness was bringing in racial appeals that were prejudicial to Hoffa. The judge, exclaiming amazement, denied his request, saying that Williams himself had first brought up the issue.

No bother—Hoffa's lawyer had other ways to undercut the government's key witness. Cheasty was receiving disability payments from the navy based on a deteriorating heart condition, which also affected his memory. To function as a lawyer and an investigator, he "made a careful record each day of his activities and made voluminous notes."[6] Because of the *Jencks* decision, Williams got his hands on pages of Cheasty's notes, which not only recounted his visits with Hoffa and his work as a committee staffer, but also detailed his personal life. Armed with this knowledge, Williams asked Cheasty about a particular telephone call he had with his wife.

Q: *What did you tell her?*

A: I told her I'd be in Canada and wouldn't be able to get home that night.

Q: *And what did she say?*

A: She wanted to know if I had taken up drinking again.

The admission had little to do with the FBI's photos of the Cheasty-Hoffa exchange or whether the confidential committee documents were in Hoffa's possession when he was arrested. But it was a mark against Cheasty. Time and again, Williams was able to cross up Cheasty about his recall of irrelevant facts buried in the thick stack of notes.

Williams was also ready to cross-examine his friend Bobby Kennedy when he came to court on July 15 to testify against Hoffa. For months, the two men had taken shots at each other through press releases and interviews with reporters. This was their first face-off since the arraignment.

Hoffa and his lawyers were not aware that Kennedy, who had never tried a case, fought with prosecutor Troxell over tactics during witness preparation. As Troxell went through the timeline of events with the young committee counsel, he learned that Kennedy and McClellan met with Cheasty on February 18 and scheduled him to be sworn in as a committee employee on February 20. But on the day in between, RFK had provided Cheasty with the names of four witnesses against Beck and told Cheasty that he could pass them along to Hoffa. Later that evening, Bobby had dinner with Hoffa. Learning of this, Troxell told Kennedy he needed to explain the dinner and its timing to the jury lest Hoffa's lawyer enjoy the first chance to twist the meeting into something underhanded. But Kennedy objected, strenuously; the information might be misconstrued or make Kennedy look bad. Nevertheless,

Troxell insisted that it was not only good trial tactics to bring it out before the defense did but also that he had "a legal and moral obligation" to do so.

Before RFK took the witness stand, Hoffa needled Williams, saying he was going to take it easy on Kennedy because they were friends. Williams later admitted Hoffa's manipulation had worked, because he "overcompensated."

Williams's cross-examination of his friend was effective. He got Kennedy to admit that he had often let trusted reporters read certain committee memos that dealt with topics the committee was going to address in coming days. As a result, the committee benefited from two waves of favorable news coverage — advance stories about upcoming revelations (attributed to documents or unnamed government sources) and daily coverage of the hearings themselves.

Williams further made Kennedy reveal that he let Clark Mollenhoff and other reporters read through investigative reports. Then he made RFK list each reporter and publication he had rewarded with such inside peeks: the *Washington Post*, the *New York Times*, the *Detroit Times*, United Press, and Cowles Communications (Mollenhoff's employer) — nearly a dozen in all. Williams's point was obvious: the findings in the committee documents were hardly secret if Kennedy shared them with seemingly every reporter on the Hill with a notepad.

Ethel Kennedy, sitting in the courtroom that day, got upset at Williams for grilling her husband. "He has no right to ask him those questions," she complained.

Troxell later said he was caught by surprise by those damning revelations. Had he known about RFK's practice of showing files to reporters before the information was publicly revealed in hearings, he could have presented that fact to the jury himself as a way to control the damage. Troxell blamed

Kennedy for not telling him about the widespread leaks to the press corps.

At the end of the government's case, Williams demanded a mistrial, arguing that Cheasty was a "provoking decoy" who had entrapped Hoffa in twenty-three of the twenty-four charges against him. The judge ruled against Williams without comment.

Outside the courtroom, Hoffa resorted to a tactic he had relied on in the past—try to get to the jury. On July 6, a local weekly newspaper, the *Afro-American*, published "one of the most amazing advertisements ever to appear in a newspaper during a criminal trial in the nation's capital," syndicated columnist Drew Pearson later wrote.[7] The newspaper intended to sway black jurors to Hoffa's side. Its front page displayed a large recent photograph of Martha Jefferson, a black lawyer from Los Angeles, standing next to Williams and Hoffa. Jefferson had just joined the Hoffa legal team, the article noted. (In fact, Jefferson had been sitting behind Hoffa in court for the past few days, but did not take part in the trial.) The *Afro-American* article described Williams as the "Sir Galahad of the legal arena" and called Hoffa a "hard-hitting champion for the 167,000 colored truck drivers in America." As Hoffa's entourage knew, this portrayal of Hoffa as a civil rights hero was false. More than once, the Teamsters boss had told his lieutenants about not wanting "jig drivers" or any "goddamned niggers" in Local 299, his union in Detroit.[8]

"Many more persons of color have important positions with the Hoffa organization," the *Afro-American* went on. "Hoffa, long before the Supreme Court dreamed of its May 17, 1954, school decision, was on the desegregations firing line."

The newspaper ad pointed out that judge Burnita Shelton Matthews hailed from Mississippi, home of such segregationists as senator James Eastland, and that Senator McClellan of Arkansas, whose committee instigated the case against Hoffa, had battled against civil rights in Congress. Copies of the propaganda showed up on the doorsteps of the eight black jurors (their names and addresses had been published in local newspapers at the start of the trial). When she learned of the tampering, Judge Matthews was furious and sequestered the jury for the remainder of the trial.

Williams told the judge and anyone who would listen outside the court that he had nothing to do with the ad, nor did he know how the photo showing him with lawyer Martha Jefferson was going to be used by the *Afro-American*. His excuses, coming from a supremely prepared litigator who insisted on total control of a case, were hard to swallow, considering how well the racial appeal fit into his overall strategy.

Williams also brought boxer Joe Louis, the former world heavyweight champion, to the courtroom as a possible character witness. The son of an Alabama sharecropper, Louis moved with his family to Detroit when he was twelve and had known Hoffa for years — as well as some of the same shadowy figures who infest the mob-dominated fight game. Louis's personal lawyer, Truman Gibson, was a business associate of Frankie Carbo, known as "the underworld czar of boxing." Retired from the ring since 1951, Louis owed a fortune in back taxes and penalties and bounced from one ill-fated business opportunity to the next.

On the evening of July 16, Louis arrived in Washington and checked into the Woodner hotel, where he made three long-distance calls from his room, including one to Martha Jefferson's phone number. Paul Dorfman, the Chicago rackets figure, whose family would make millions handling insurance for the Central Conference of Teamsters, had persuaded Louis, resistant at first, to attend. He spent part of the next two days sitting in court, both days eating lunch with Paul Dorfman and others in the cafeteria of the nearby Teamsters headquarters. Hoffa was also at lunch with them each day.[9]

Before the afternoon session began on Louis's first day in court, he took a seat on the aisle. Hoffa walked into the courtroom as the jury filed in. As he made his way to the trial table, Hoffa slowed, greeted Louis, and, in an unmistakable show of friendship, put his hand on Louis's shoulder. The ex-boxer clamped his hand on Hoffa's arm, and they exchanged words for a moment. "It was a strange scene, and a strange meeting, between two men I had seen talking together in the court corridor only a few minutes earlier," Mollenhoff later wrote. "But the Hoffa-Louis exchange wasn't missed by some of the jurors.... One who didn't notice at first was elbowed by a neighbor, calling his attention to that touching scene between big Joe Louis and his little pal, Jimmy Hoffa, defendant."[10] It certainly did not hurt Hoffa to appear to be friends with one of the most admired figures in the black community.

Williams dug in, and as he approached the end of his witness list, a key question still hung over the trial: Would Hoffa take the stand?

Troxell told Mollenhoff he didn't expect Hoffa to testify. As they conversed, Mollenhoff was shocked to learn that the prosecutor was unaware of damaging admissions by Hoffa that might be useful for cross-examination: that Hoffa, under oath, told a 1953 congressional investigating committee that he routinely destroyed Local 299's financial records and that he defended giving union jobs to convicted felons. After the trial adjourned that afternoon, Mollenhoff quickly made copies of stories he had written about Hoffa's admissions before the House Committee on Government Operations, chaired by

Clare E. Hoffman, and took them to Troxell's office. Mollen-hoff also groused to RFK about what he saw as Troxell's lack of preparation. Bobby called the FBI liaison to the McClellan committee to sound the alarm. The FBI agent, Courtney Evans, reassured him that the Justice Department would be ready for Hoffa.

If Hoffa was nervous during the proceedings, he concealed it well. "Throughout the trial, little Jimmy Hoffa sat morosely in a red leather swivel chair, hands tightly clasped in his lap as he swung gently side to side, his black shoes (covering white socks) barely reaching down to the floor, his gaze wandering from the jurors to the spectators to the white acoustical tile of the courtroom ceiling," *Time*'s reporter at the trial wrote in a memo to his editor.[11]

To the government's surprise, Hoffa did take the witness stand. He clearly was well rehearsed. He presented a clever story: he indeed had hired Cheasty — but as a lawyer, someone to help him and other Teamsters prepare for their grilling before the committee. Hoffa swore he had no idea that Cheasty worked for the government. As for the documents that Cheasty passed to him, Hoffa said he hadn't looked at them closely. When Williams asked Hoffa whether he had asked Cheasty how he obtained the documents, Hoffa was ready, testifying that Cheasty said, "I got it from a fellow who is writing an article for the press.... It's old material and it has been released to the press."[12]

Prosecutor Troxell believed Hoffa was lying but knew his case had just been significantly weakened. Kennedy's sloppy practices with the press had provided Hoffa with a plausible alibi.

On and on Hoffa went, clear and confident, with an answer for everything.

When Troxell got his opportunity to grill Hoffa, he did

not ask about Hoffa's criminal record, the union's missing financial records, or the racketeers pulling down paychecks at Hoffa's Detroit locals. Williams had interrogated Cheasty for days; Troxell questioned Hoffa for thirty-two minutes. After he sat down, Mollenhoff would later write, "I was shocked, and I felt sick."[13]

Troxell must have known he had delivered a feeble cross-examination of Hoffa. When it came to closing arguments, he spent more time preparing, and by most accounts it was a better performance, plodding but methodical, and he scored some points. Hoffa's story of hiring Cheasty as a lawyer simply didn't make sense, he argued. Why was he in need of a lawyer? As the evidence shows, the phone number Hoffa's secretary gave Cheasty to reach Hoffa rang at Williams's law firm. Hoffa, Troxell declared, had no need for a new lawyer because he was surrounded by lawyers. "Hoffa at that time did not have to hire a man like Cheasty to be met on street corners for the purpose of getting legal advice," he added. Cheasty "was hired...to be a spy to destroy a committee of Congress."

Williams took two hours and thirty-five minutes to give a masterful closing argument. He savaged Cheasty and beatified Hoffa while moving back and forth in front of the jury box, shouting in anger, and then coming nearly to tears. Cheasty was "a deceiver," an admitted "falsifier" who lived a lie to ensnare Hoffa. Williams, a Catholic, noted that Cheasty carried a rosary in his pocket. "What kind of a man is it who, while carrying a symbol of truth, honesty, beauty, a symbol of faith some of us hold dear — the rosary — can deceive and falsify at the same time?"

Hoffa, the workingman's friend, was the victim of a conspiracy, Williams said. Mustering his emotion, he went on: "Jimmy

Hoffa has fought many battles for labor. He has fought for the people that he loves. He has fought with his head held high. He has fought with a mind and heart without fear, and he has never betrayed a trust....Now he is in a fight for his own life. I ask you to send him back to his good fight." Williams was white and shaken when he finished, and the jurors appeared moved.[14]

Troxell, who as prosecutor had the last words to the jury, would need to break Williams's spell. But as the minutes passed, Mollenhoff's hopes sank. Troxell plodded from point to point without any apparent structure or plan. He seemed to almost invite the jurors to return a not-guilty verdict: "Did Hoffa, when he was sitting on the stand, appear to be a truth-telling individual? If he appears to be, believe him and acquit him. And if you think he was not a truth-telling individual, and if you think Cheasty was telling the truth, believe Cheasty and convict Hoffa. But it is up to you to decide whether or not Cheasty is telling the truth. If you think he is, I think you can find the defendant Hoffa guilty, if you find him guilty beyond a reasonable doubt."

Mollenhoff, a lawyer himself, felt it was a weak closing argument. Afterward, the reporter encountered Williams in the courtroom hallway after the jury left to deliberate. Mollenhoff said he was afraid it was going to be an acquittal. Williams replied that he was hoping for a hung jury. "I thought Troxell would be grilling Jimmy for two days. I was reluctant to put him on but felt we had to take the chance."[15]

"The chance paid off," Mollenhoff said.

Bobby Kennedy was in the Senate Caucus Room, in the middle of an afternoon of hearings, when his secretary passed him a note that the jury had come back with its verdict. Kennedy turned ashen, clearly disturbed. Hoffa—not guilty.

When the verdict had been read, bedlam erupted in the

courtroom: applause, shouting, a bellowing from a Hoffa associate heard above the din — "God bless the judge and jury" — all while a US marshal hoarsely commanded, "Order! Order!" Hoffa's wife and daughter were crying as they left the courtroom. Jimmy shook Williams's hand and said, "Thanks a million, Ed."

Mollenhoff made it to the courthouse as Hoffa was leaving and told him, "Jimmy, you are a lucky bastard."

Hoffa winked. "I just live right."

Outside the courtroom, Williams told reporters, "I'm going to send Bobby Kennedy a parachute for when he jumps off the Capitol dome." They all included the quote in their stories.

Unsurprisingly, the news of Hoffa's acquittal was not well received in the Senate Caucus Room. Senator Ives of New York, vice chairman of the committee, was furious: "This verdict is a miscarriage of justice." He added, "Mr. Hoffa's troubles are far from ended. He has not, as yet, even appeared before the Senate Select Committee." His fellow Republican, Senator Goldwater, a Teamsters supporter, commented, "Joe Louis is a pretty good defense attorney."

In private, Bobby raged about Williams and his courtroom tricks. He blamed the Justice Department and Troxell for poorly prosecuting the case. Williams, who charmed Kennedy at lunch and had once asked him to join his law firm, was now persona non grata. With his clear views of good and evil, RFK said he could not believe that Williams, who went to early morning mass each day, could help such a demonic person escape justice. Ethel Kennedy took it upon herself to call the president of Georgetown University, where Williams was legal counsel, and urge him to fire Williams. "We're all sick to death about Hoffa," Ethel wrote Rose and Joe Kennedy. "But we are relying on Carmine, Clark Mollenhoff, and Bobby and Jack to hit one for the team. . . . Even Ena and Josie

[Ethel and Bobby's housekeepers, who were black] are ashamed of Joe Louis."[16]

Williams was stung by the blasts. He wanted to be viewed as belonging to a higher class of defense lawyer—not a mouth-piece, but a battler for the constitutional rights of the accused, a Clarence Darrow (as Cheyfitz had said to the press). Williams explained to reporters that he had wanted Joe Louis to testify as a character witness but then decided against it at the last minute. (Doing so would have allowed prosecutors to put on their own witnesses who could present the dark side of Hoffa's character.) Williams denied, unconvincingly, that he made any racial appeals at Hoffa's trial. "Any time you make a bald, crass appeal to a minority group, you alienate those with any intelligence."[17] But of course Williams had chosen just that strategy from the start.

Trying to undo the damage to Williams's reputation, Chey-fitz took the blame for bringing Louis to the courtroom, telling well-connected columnist Drew Pearson that it had been his idea. A Hoffa lawyer from Detroit said he had paid $5,000 for lawyer Martha Jefferson to come to the trial to help with writing briefs. Pearson, whose column ran in the *Washington Post*, followed the trial closely. He wrote: "As a final grand-stand play, Hoffa's astute public relations adviser, Eddie Chey-fitz, suggested that a famous Negro hero be brought to trial. At this point, Joe Louis' name came up."[18] Pearson reported that he had reached Louis by telephone and got the ex-champ to admit that the Teamsters paid for his hotel stay at a suite in the Woodner.

Pearson also heard a rumor after the acquittal that Hoffa had paid Louis $2,500 for his appearance, but the columnist could not pin it down, so he passed the tip to RFK, who quickly sent Walter Sheridan to Chicago to track down the boxer.

At the time, Louis was still a national hero, arguably the best heavyweight boxer of all time. In 1938, with the entire country rooting for him, Louis had crushed German boxer Max Schmeling in the "fight of the century." Millions of Americans cheered Louis's victory, feeling it was a blow to the emerging threat of Nazi Germany and its propaganda about Aryan superiority.

But in Chicago, Sheridan found Louis in a sad third-floor walk-up apartment on the city's South Side. The former champ was in debt to the IRS for nearly $1 million in back taxes. As he arrived, Sheridan overheard Louis being ordered around by a former manager who had profited handsomely from his career. Louis told the investigator he hadn't taken twenty-five cents from Hoffa, let alone $2,500. Before Sheridan left the apartment, he told Louis that Kennedy had asked for the champ's autograph for his son Joe. Louis said he'd sign his autograph for the boy but not for Kennedy. "He can go jump off the Capitol."

Five days after the jury found in his favor, Hoffa was already moving on: he announced that he would run for general president of the International Brotherhood of Teamsters.

Kennedy and his staff had not spent much staff time digging up dirt on Hoffa because RFK thought it would be a waste of time; Hoffa was going to be convicted. Now an obsessed Bobby pushed himself and his staff to get ready for their first opportunity to question Hoffa at the ongoing rackets hearings, which would take place over four days in late August. Hoffa had to be stopped, Bobby told his staff — if Hoffa became Teamsters president, he would be all the more powerful and difficult to dislodge.

The hearings would not involve a jury, but there would be an audience, a sizable one. Hoffa would be testifying before the Senate committee under oath for the first time. Kennedy and his staff had at least three goals: besmirch Hoffa before a national television audience, reveal him as a crook to his fellow Teamsters, and (assuming he didn't plead the fifth) trap him into committing perjury.

RFK had much to be worried about. Early on, Hoffa had mentioned to Cheasty that he had two spies connected to the committee. Who were they? Would Hoffa be able to outmaneuver and embarrass him, as he had, thanks to Williams, during his bribery trial?

The Kennedy brothers faced a dilemma. The political success of a committee was often measured by its results—by reforms and new laws—not just by headlines exposing a problem. The scandals and allegations the committee had dug up so far—kickbacks, undeclared cash, beatings, fraud—already were against the law. In creating sensational press clips and capturing the public's attention, the Rackets Committee unleashed forces of outrage that might not stop at laws that narrowly targeted union corruption; they might end up with legislation that weakened honest labor unions generally. That was the goal of Goldwater and other Republican lawmakers, the minority party in Congress, who planned to attach anti-union provisions to whatever bill resulted. "If the investigation flops," RFK told his close friend Kenny O'Donnell, "it will hurt Jack in 1958 and in 1960, too. A lot of people think he's the Kennedy running the investigation, not me. As far as the public is concerned, one Kennedy is the same as another Kennedy."[19]

Bobby had already drawn fire from a powerful special interest that he hadn't expected to provoke: the editorial board of the leading daily newspaper in the nation's capital, the *Washington Post*. Its publisher and owner, Phil Graham, was a friend, confidant, and an informal adviser to his brother Jack, and behind the scenes in national Democratic circles, he promoted JFK's presidential fortunes. But his editorial writers went after McClellan and RFK: "On a number of occasions Mr. McClellan and Counsel Kennedy have announced what they were going to prove before proving it. Given the quasi-judicial role of the Committee, it would be a great deal better, we think, to reserve judgment until all the evidence has been presented and until accused persons have had a chance to speak in their own defense. This is an investigation, not a prosecution."[20]

The popular image of Bobby Kennedy as a ruthless prosecutor, the unfair questioner in the mold of his former boss Joe McCarthy, was taking hold. But such perception didn't deter him, because he believed he was right—"driven by a conviction of righteousness, a fanaticism of virtue, a certitude about guilt that vaulted over gaps in evidence," in the words of his biographer Arthur Schlesinger Jr. He also understood what had to be done. If a witness tried to mislead the public or hide the facts, then the chief counsel needed to shake them loose. "The right to ask a question and the right to demand an answer are essential to the democratic processes," RFK would later write, citing the words of family friend Supreme Court justice William O. Douglas. "That is why the embarrassing question from the Senator or Congressman sitting at the end of the table serves a high function. His right to demand an answer spells in a crucial way the difference between the totalitarian and the democratic regime."[21]

By posing the right questions to Hoffa, Bobby hoped the committee might bring about a regime change.

CHAPTER 5

The First Face-Off

August 20, 1957

IT WAS STANDING ROOM ONLY in the red-carpeted great Caucus Room of the New Senate Office Building when Jimmy Hoffa swaggered in "like a crowing cock in a coop of capons," wearing a well-cut brown suit and carrying a large brown briefcase.[1] Some reporters, seeing him for the first time, noted how short he was, as did so many others who encountered the Teamsters boss and had likely imagined that such a threatening figure would be more imposing. Asked how tall he was, Hoffa replied five feet, five and a half inches, and added proudly, "One hundred and eighty pounds." When he took his chair, feet dangling, his white socks were hard to miss.

Newspaper reporters filled one side of the hearing room; seven television crews, with their bulky cameras and lights, took up the other side. Powerful oversize lightbulbs had been screwed into the huge cut-glass chandeliers, flooding the room with a bright glare. On a long table facing the crowd sat the senators, with RFK in the middle, next to the chairman,

Senator McClellan. Seated behind him were Bellino, Salinger, and Cheasty, who hadn't seen Hoffa since Cheasty had testified against him at the bribery trial in June. Photographers crouched along the floor facing the witness table, their backs to the podium, where "they popped up like soap bubbles, snapping Hoffa from incredible angles with bulky cameras burdened by bulgy eye lenses. Hoffa never twitched an eyelid."[2]

Hoffa ordered the photographers to take their photos of him all at once and then move to the side "so I can concentrate on what the senators want to know."

The questioning started, and it didn't take Bobby Kennedy long to land a jab. "Since you have been with the Teamsters union, you have been arrested a number of times, have you?"

"That is correct."

"How many times, approximately, do you think?"

"Well, I don't know, Bob," Hoffa said. "I haven't counted them up." Hoffa came up with a number, seventeen arrests, mostly for picket-line brawls, he pointed out, with three that ended in convictions.

Sitting near the edge of his chair, Kennedy repeated himself in his high-pitched voice, underscoring Hoffa's arrests: "But there are about seventeen in all, and you think you have been convicted on three?"

"I think you have the record, and you can count them." Hoffa was cocksure, giving the impression he had nothing to hide or fear, and for much of the day he seemed to control the room.

Senator Barry Goldwater (who would be the Republican nominee for president seven years later) gave Hoffa a break from Kennedy's grilling early the first day, attacking, without naming him, liberal labor leader Walter Reuther, head of the United Automobile Workers. Goldwater appreciated that the big, brawny Teamsters union broke with its labor brethren in

1956 and endorsed President Eisenhower for reelection. Beyond that, Goldwater believed Reuther, the Democratic Party's single strongest ally, to be Communist-influenced. In his remarks to Hoffa, the Arizona senator outlined a scenario in which an all-powerful union leader might endorse political candidates against the wishes of the rank and file.

"Mr. Hoffa, we have labor leaders in this country today, labor leaders who are not particularly friendly to you—labor leaders who, I am sure, would like to gain control of an organization like the Teamsters," Goldwater said. "If those individuals were successful in getting control of your unions and expanded this to include the entire transportation field, then I think you can see the dangers immediately of what I am talking about."

"Maybe better than you can, Senator," an assured Hoffa replied.

"I am certainly glad to hear you say that," Goldwater replied.

"Senator," Hoffa went on, "on this question, I don't propose as one person to become involved in a situation...where anybody is going to call me into a room and tell me, without talking to my members, 'This is what you are going to do' or 'This is what you are not going to do.' My experience is when you endorse a candidate on that basis, you just went out of business."

Goldwater guided the exchange along. "I think we both recognize that, in the writing in the clouds today, there is an individual"—everyone knew he was referring to Reuther—"who would like to see that happen in this country. I do not like to ever suggest to let you and him fight, but for the good of the union movement I am very hopeful that your philosophy prevails."

Hoffa concurred with the Arizona senator's preference: "I assure you," he declared, "that the American people will accept my philosophy and not the one of the other," making it clear he believed in business unionism. Though he admittedly used the threat of strike and picket-line disruptions as weapons during negotiations, he prided himself getting new contracts without strife.

Hoffa's answers put Goldwater at ease. At lunch breaks that day and during the three more days of Hoffa's testimony, Goldwater and other senators made friendly visits to Hoffa at the witness table.

Bobby was not so chummy. When the hearing resumed, he steered matters back to Hoffa's finances. "I hate to take you back from being a labor union leader to a businessman," he said, with some sarcasm.

"Go right back," Hoffa retorted. "Don't worry about it."

Kennedy had the benefit of Hoffa's federal tax returns — Bellino first studied them months earlier, and they had searched for vulnerabilities. They also quietly had obtained federal tax returns of two of Hoffa's lawyers, George Fitzgerald and Dave Previant, which was a highly questionable maneuver; it could be attacked as interfering with Hoffa's constitutional right to counsel. (The committee's overreaching into IRS records has remained hidden until now.)

Asked about his finances, Hoffa told the committee that only recently had he opened his first checking account. His business dealings, loans, and bill payments were all in cash. Without a paper trail of canceled checks, Hoffa was hard to pin down. His income was significantly higher than his $25,000 Teamsters salary could account for, but he explained his extra cash in a crafty way: his closest friend, Bert Brennan, president of Detroit's Teamsters Local 337, owned several racehorses, spent hours at the racetrack, and was known to be a savvy bettor. Hoffa said that each time Brennan placed a bet, he laid down an identical wager for him. Each had annual winnings that exceeded losses by five to ten thousand dollars. "[He] has some horses, and he places some bets, and we are fortunate to win some money," Hoffa said. He declared the gambling winnings on his personal IRS returns and paid the appropriate income tax.

But that was far from the end of the committee's pursuit. The weeks of investigation in Detroit and elsewhere by Bellino, Sheridan, and others had been productive. Under Kennedy's questioning, Hoffa named a dozen or more companies that he or his wife had an interest in, some under her maiden name: real estate, oil leases, a company that leased trucks to businesses that employed Teamsters, a girl's camp in northern Michigan, a trotter racetrack. Kennedy walked Hoffa through an even longer list of union employees from whom he had been given interest-free loans, usually ranging from $2,000 to $5,000. There were no signed notes. All were men who relied on Hoffa for their jobs. He had paid some of them back; others he hadn't. With all his ventures, he clearly was trying to build a fortune.

During the hearings, union president Dave Beck took the Fifth Amendment refuge 134 times, following the advice of counsel. Beck needed the protection because he faced federal income tax charges and had been indicted in Seattle for theft of union funds. But to the surprise of some, Hoffa did not hide behind the Fifth Amendment and seemed determined to tough it out. The Ethical Practices Committee of the recently merged AFL-CIO, the self-policing arm of the labor federation, which included the Teamsters, had decided that union leaders who refused to answer committee questions about how they spent union funds could face expulsion. George Meany, the cigar-chomping federation president, had no use for Hoffa, but he would need to find another reason to try to expel Hoffa from the federation.

Time and again during the hearings, when RFK tried to pin down Hoffa with a yes or no answer, he eluded him: "You cannot answer the question yes or no. There is no yes-or-no answer to it. If you want the answer for your legislative purpose, I will give it to you."

"I want that," Kennedy snapped back.

"All right," Hoffa assented before returning to the wishy-washy.

When RFK got tangled up, McClellan, an ex-prosecutor with years of cross-examination experience, stepped in to help. Clearly Hoffa had been able to unnerve Kennedy, using intimidation tactics that had helped the labor leader flourish in Detroit's rough-and-tumble business world. "[Hoffa] was glaring at me across the counsel table with a deep, strange penetrating expression of intense hatred.... It was the look of a man obsessed by his enmity, and it came particularly from his eyes. There were times when his face seemed completely transfixed with this stare of absolute evilness. It might last for five minutes — as if he thought that by staring long enough and hard enough he could destroy me. Sometimes he seemed to be concentrating so hard that I had to smile, and occasionally I would make note of it to an assistant counsel sitting behind me. It must have been obvious to him that we were discussing it, but his expression would not change by a flicker."[3]

RFK felt that one of Hoffa's vulnerabilities was his business ties with trucking company owners who employed Teamsters. One relationship Kennedy pursued became known as the Test Fleet case and would haunt Hoffa for years. Hoffa settled a wildcat strike on terms favorable to a big Michigan trucking firm, Commercial Carriers—but at a price. After the settlement, Commercial had to lease some of its trucks from a cutout company known as Test Fleet, which was incorporated in Nashville, Tennessee. Test Fleet's owners: Josephine Poszywak and Alice Johnson, otherwise known as Mrs. James Hoffa and Mrs. Bert Brennan, wife of Hoffa's best friend and head of Detroit's Teamsters Local 337.

Over the next nine years, Commercial Carriers, via Test Fleet, paid annual dividends of between $3,500 and $10,000 each to Mrs. Hoffa and Mrs. Brennan. To any neutral observer, the women, who performed no work for Test Fleet, were clearly cash conduits through which the trucking firm kept the two Teamsters happy with a steady flow of money.

In this case, Hoffa's defense was simple: lawyers advised him and Bert Brennan that the company be put in their wives' names. Kennedy asked Hoffa how much his wife made from Test Fleet. It was her company, Hoffa replied, but he could try to get the numbers.

"We have some figures here," RFK said.

A cocksure Hoffa instructed Kennedy, "Read them off, brother."

He did. The tally came to more than $62,000, or about $500,000 in 2015 dollars.

Hoffa defended the right of a union official to own a trucking company. "It is my firm belief as a labor leader that if you know the business that you are negotiating in, and if you have some touch of responsibility, you will be in a better position at the bargaining table to get more for your men when it comes time to bargain," he said. "My experience of knowing what can be produced out of trucks, by leasing equipment and paying union wages, has saved our drivers throughout the entire Central Conference from having any strikes." He'd been able to get "the prevailing wage scales, prevailing increases, in many instances much higher and better fringe benefits than the average union that takes the position that they don't want to know what the employers' business is about." Beck had made the same argument to explain why he had outside business interests.

Bobby's brother dug into the curious business relationship between the head of a Teamsters local, Eugene "Jimmy" James, and Hoffa's wife, Josephine. Hoffa and Bert Brennan had loaned $2,500 to James and provided him with a union charter so James could open a Teamsters local to represent jukebox servicemen. James then repaid the $2,500 by putting the wives of Hoffa and Brennan on the payroll for $100 a week with no work duties. James's repayments quickly dwarfed the original loan amount. Senator Kennedy asked, "There were no services performed, and yet the money, the $2,500, went up to $6,000 in — what, two years or three years?"

> **Hoffa:** I can't answer that, sir.
> **JFK:** When the original loan was only $2,500, why would it go to $6,000?
> **Hoffa:** I can't answer that, except for the fact I can't answer that.

His answers seemed silly and evasive, but after the first two days of hearings, Hoffa wasn't forced to take the fifth. He deftly parried the Kennedys and was able to catch his breath during soft questioning by Republican senators Barry Goldwater and Karl Mundt of South Dakota. "We'd rehearse what Kennedy would do," Hoffa later explained. "He isn't the brightest fellow in the world. And he's got to investigate for weeks and weeks to find out what we already know.... I know what I done wrong and what I didn't. I know what they'll uncover and what they won't. And that's two-thirds of the worrying. All my life, I been under investigation."[4]

RFK worried about losing his temper on national television. "My biggest problem as counsel," RFK admitted, "is to keep my temper. I think we all feel that when a witness comes before the United States Senate he has an obligation to speak frankly and tell the truth. To see people sit in front of us and lie and evade makes me boil inside. But you can't lose your temper — if you do, the witness has gotten the best of you."[5]

Hoffa, who had a volcanic temper himself, seemed to sense this weakness and used other techniques to intimidate. At the witness table, the Teamsters leader continued to stare at RFK until Bobby noticed, then locked eyes with him. After a frozen moment, the unblinking Kennedy, embarrassed to be playing this childish game, would look away. Other times, Hoffa would catch RFK's eye, smile, and even wink. "It would drive the bastard crazy," Hoffa said.

Things took a turn when committee staffers set up speakers and a tape player and Robert Kennedy sat down with a stack of transcripts of telephone conversations Hoffa had with the man accused of masterminding the acid-blinding attack on labor columnist Victor Riesel.

"Mr. Hoffa," Kennedy asked, "do you know Johnny Dio?"

Hoffa said yes, and suddenly he seemed to lose his starch.

Bobby Kennedy had sometimes been an ineffective interrogator in the early days of the McClellan committee. But when the topic turned to Dio, he began his most effective questioning of the four-day Hoffa hearings. This time, RFK followed the time-honored two-step of a good cross-examination: first, pin down the witness on everything he says he knows and doesn't know about a situation, then present evidence to the contrary.

"Did you ever have any conversations with Dio about his coming into the Teamsters?" Kennedy asked.

Hoffa said he had talked about it with president Dave Beck. As for talking to Dio, "I don't know whether I did or not. I was trying to get the cab union into the Teamsters, and when Dave had said John could not come in, then I don't see any reason why I would have had a discussion. I can't recall one."

Hoffa was walking into a perjury trap. Kennedy had recordings of wiretapped conversations between Hoffa and Dio, obtained legally by the office of New York district attorney Frank Hogan. RFK had already alerted Hoffa's lawyer, white-haired George Fitzgerald, that the committee would play recordings of certain telephone conversations. But neither Hoffa nor Fitzgerald knew anything more specific about what was discussed. When Kennedy began to play the first wiretap recording and handed its transcript to Hoffa, Fitzgerald jumped up, florid-faced. He insisted the recorded calls broke a federal law that said intercepted telephone conversations could not be revealed publicly. To play them, he declared, was unfair to Hoffa.

In 1957, about half the states in the country, including New York, allowed police, with court review, to wiretap telephone lines as a way to intercept personal calls. Wiretaps by the FBI and other federal agents were not allowed as evidence in federal courts. But there was a loophole: conversations from state-approved wiretaps were allowed to be introduced as evidence in federal courts. Congressional hearings enjoyed even looser rules than federal courts about what could be introduced. McClellan overruled Fitzgerald's objection and allowed Kennedy to play the first phone call. Ever the lawyer,

McClellan cited a recent decision by a federal appeals court that refused to overturn a federal gambling conviction against underworld boss Frank Costello (represented by Edward Bennett Williams) that relied on New York State wiretaps.

The recordings were devastating. Despite Hoffa's testimony minutes earlier, he clearly was friendly with Dio. The wiretap recordings revealed that the two men had talked by telephone at least four times in the spring of 1953 as they schemed about bringing New York City cab drivers into the Teamsters.

As the first tape started to play, Hoffa, realizing his legal jeopardy, reminded the senators, "Let the record show that I said it was to the best of my recollection."

The room hushed, and people listened closely to the scratchy sounds. "Johnny, how are you?" Hoffa said in greeting Dio.

"Aw, Jesus, I been worried about you," Dio replied. "I been following you up there every day in the newspapers." At the time, Hoffa was being questioned in Detroit before the House committee chaired by Clare Hoffman, an antilabor Michigan Republican.

"Yeah, well, I didn't call because—"

"I know," Dio replied. "All I wanted to know was how were things. That's about all. I finally called Dave yesterday.... He said everything so far so good."

After this first tape was played, McClellan turned to Hoffa and asked: "Does this refresh your memory?"

Again, RFK asked him whether he was trying to get Dio into the Teamsters. This time, contradicting his answer from minutes earlier, Hoffa said, "I could have been, if that was necessary to clear up the cab situation."

You have changed your answer, Kennedy accused him.

That's your interpretation, Hoffa shot back.

Hoffa stumbled time and again as he tried to explain away his own words in the taped phone calls with Dio. As the days went on, Hoffa warily eyed the wiretap transcripts stacked at the senators' hearing table, completely spooked about how to answer Kennedy's questions. At times, Hoffa seemed almost punch-drunk. "To the best of my recollection, I just on my memory, I cannot remember," he answered at one point.

RFK, appearing to look incredulous, mocked Hoffa by repeating his words. " 'To the best of my recollection, I just on my memory, I cannot remember' — that is your answer?" Spectators laughed, and McClellan said, "Let's have order."

Hoffa knew he looked foolish, but he had no choice but to press on. On the fourth day of his questioning, he gave variations of "I don't recall...I just don't remember...To the best of my recollection" more than one hundred times.

Kennedy continued to hector him. "You have had the worst case of amnesia in the last two days I have ever heard of."

Then the chief counsel pushed into an area that captivated the press — the claim that Hoffa had equipped his union subordinates with tiny recorders, Minifones, when they were ordered to answer questions at a 1953 Detroit grand jury looking into Teamsters misconduct. Kennedy and Hoffa's exchange at the hearing resembled a "Who's on first?" comedy routine, but Bobby, frustrated with Hoffa, saw no humor in it.

> Kennedy: What did you do with the Minifones you purchased?
> Hoffa: What did I do with them? Well, what did I do with them?
> Kennedy: What did you do with them?
> Hoffa: I am trying to recall....
> Kennedy: You know what you did with the Minifones.

Hoffa: What did I do with them?

Kennedy: What did you do with them?

Hoffa: Mr. Kennedy, I bought some Minifones, and there is no question about it, but I cannot recall what became of them.

Kennedy: You wore a Minifon yourself.

Hoffa: I cannot recall doing it, and I may have.

Kennedy: Did you wear one?

Hoffa: You say "wear." What do you mean by "wear?"[6]

New York Republican senator Irving Ives, normally mild-mannered, had enough. He told Hoffa that he had "one of the most convenient forgettery of anybody I have ever seen.... By golly, you have not taken the fifth, but are doing a marvelous job crawling around it."

Hoffa spent seventeen hours at the witness table over four days before Senator McClellan wearily announced: "We have reached a point where it seems to be useless and a waste of the committee's time.... We have proceeded to the point where the witness has no memory, and he cannot be helpful even when his memory is refreshed."

McClellan told Hoffa he was still under an active subpoena, banged his gavel, and dismissed the combative labor leader.

At the end of the hearings, RFK talked privately with Hoffa about the way he screamed and swore at committee staffers who were assigned to look into him. "Told him I did not want him to talk to our investigators as he had been doing," Kennedy noted in his journal. "Told him if he wanted to hate anyone to hate me. He agreed. His eyes were bloodshot. The last two days of hearing he was a beaten man compared to the beginning.

His tone was subdued and no longer did he give the hate looks that he enjoyed so much at the beginning."[7]

Hoffa and Kennedy may have ended this round seemingly calm and under control, but under the surface of each there was building rage. Pierre Salinger had watched Bobby Kennedy easily take down Dave Beck and, at the end of the day, almost feel sorry for the buffoonish labor leader. It was far different with Hoffa, Salinger would recall. "Jimmy Hoffa had gotten to Bob Kennedy, had deeply offended his innate sense of honor and decency. Thus began a blood feud."[8]

CHAPTER 6

Hoffa for President

IN PRIVATE, STAFF INVESTIGATORS AND journalists close to committee members admitted that, other than exposing Hoffa's sleazy maneuver with Dio and the paper locals, Kennedy was ill prepared to pursue Hoffa. The chief counsel had caused the cocky Teamsters boss to become unglued by playing wiretaps of Hoffa's chummy chats with the famous hoodlum. But with Hoffa on the ropes, Kennedy had nothing else to throw at him. "It's a shame we didn't have this stuff to hit Hoffa with when he fell apart," an investigator admitted.[1]

With Hoffa's likely election as union president a month away, RFK felt compelled more than ever to stop him — "for the good of the country," he would say. He and a large team of investigators — Salinger, Bellino, Sheridan, and others — traveled to Detroit and continued the hunt.

The committee's mission was to investigate labor racketeering and, if need be, propose reforms. Kennedy interpreted that charge to include using the Justice Department to try to trip up Hoffa. RFK pushed to have perjury charges brought against

Hoffa for lying under oath about not being able to remember the details of his dealings with Johnny Dio. "We weren't just asking him what he had for breakfast four years ago," Kennedy later explained. "Some of these things were just a couple of months ago." Chairman McClellan, after reviewing the hearing transcripts, agreed with him that Hoffa's claims of ignorance were an act.

On September 3, 1957, McClellan called the Justice Department's second in command, William Rogers, and urged him to go after Hoffa for perjury. The senator also sent an official letter, along with transcripts of Hoffa's testimony, to US attorney general Herbert Brownell and urged him to "determine whether any violation of federal law is revealed within. It is my personal opinion the record clearly discloses the witness committed willful perjury on several material facts."[2]

Prosecutors opened a criminal investigation.

Chairman McClellan dismissed Hoffa as a witness on Friday, August 23. By Monday, Salinger and investigator Jim Kelly had already interviewed confidential informant D-1, their first in Detroit, who gave them tantalizing leads.[3] While Kennedy's investigative staff was camped in Detroit, chasing every anonymous tip, Hoffa and Beck, in separate command performances, each struggled to present his best defense to the Ethical Practices Committee of the AFL-CIO.

Even though Hoffa had seemed the victor, the pounding Hoffa and Beck had taken before the Rackets Committee and in the news industry left a stain that was spreading to labor in general. Polls taken in late 1957, many months into the Senate labor hearings, showed that positive attitudes toward unions had slipped. Several congressional committees had targeted labor racketeers in the postwar years, but with the growing reach of television news, the popularity of the film *On the Waterfront*, and a Cold War sensitivity to a sinister internal menace, these rackets hearings captured the public's attention. Now the labor federation, under president George Meany, intended to clean house, including possibly the expulsion of the Teamsters Union from the federation.

At a private hearing of the ethics committee, Hoffa defended his outside business deals and his loans from underlings and explained in detail his relationship with Dio, but he was unable to sway the AFL-CIO leaders. On September 16, the AFL-CIO reported as fact that Beck abused union funds for personal use and that Hoffa promoted the fortunes of well-known labor racketeers. The Teamsters union was "dominated or substantially influenced by corrupt influences." Meany made it clear that if the truckers' union elected Hoffa president, he would push to have the union expelled. The Teamsters, if it became a labor-movement outsider, would lose political power and be subject to raiding by other unions. Fearing this, 60 percent of the rank and file thought Hoffa should be dumped, according to a Gallup poll conducted that month.

In late September, McClellan kicked off four days of hearings into Hoffa and his associates by announcing a new focus: cash kickbacks to Hoffa from Detroit business agents. McClellan planned to call Hoffa as a witness on the weekend of September 28 and 29, only two days before the Teamsters convention opened in Miami Beach. RFK was wary about dragging Hoffa away from his campaigning; he said such a move might backfire, making Hoffa a martyr. And then there were the local critics. The *Washington Post* editorial board wrote that the committee was "improper to intervene in the Teamsters election." The senators, the board said, had no business campaigning for or against a particular candidate for union office or for corporate office.

The next day, the Justice Department piled on, indicting Hoffa for perjury. The charges stemmed from a September grand jury investigation by the US attorney in New York City that looked into Hoffa, Bert Brennan, and Bernard Spindel on suspected wiretapping charges. When asked at the grand jury if he'd first heard of Spindel through Johnny Dio, Hoffa said, "No, not to my knowledge." Prosecutors, who had the benefit of the Dio-Hoffa telephone tapes, said that answer was a deliberate falsehood. The Justice Department's timing with these charges was transparent: try to stop Hoffa by piling indictment upon investigation, thereby giving Teamsters leaders at the Miami Beach convention more reason to vote for someone else.

Fitzgerald, Hoffa's lawyer, pleaded with Kennedy and McClellan to postpone interrogating his client until he got past his criminal cases. Indictments, subpoenas, and AFL-CIO accusations "were dropping around us like confetti at a county fair," Fitzgerald said. "Frankly speaking, I am only one man." They agreed to wait on questioning Hoffa.

The hearings ran at top speed, with Kennedy rushing through witnesses. He did not slow down to badger witnesses who pleaded the fifth, as he and McClellan had done in the past. Their most revealing testimony about Hoffa came from a former friend of the Detroit labor leader, Robert P. Scott, a small, balding fifty-one-year-old man who came to the hearings with his wife despite having received two threatening phone calls the week before warning them to back off. Scott, who had been cultivated as a source by investigator Walter Sheridan, was a rarity: a witness who knew Hoffa well and was willing to detail dirty deeds, even though in doing so he implicated himself. Scott had been in the labor movement for a decade before Hoffa installed him as an official at Teamsters Local 614 in Pontiac at a rigged election. Three years later, Hoffa maneuvered to have him elected secretary-treasurer of the Michigan Federation of Labor. Scott traveled the state as a Teamsters lobbyist and Hoffa emissary, making political contacts and taking on special assignments. By then, Hoffa was one of the most powerful men in heavily unionized Michigan, with strong connections among police, judges, elected officials, and state commissioners. Scott was taken aback by some of Hoffa's assignments but followed orders — at first. In 1948, when Hoffa's ex-convict brother, Billy, was being sought by Detroit police for armed robbery, Hoffa ordered Scott to hide him. Scott hustled Billy, along with his wife and kids, to Pontiac and stashed them in the Roosevelt Hotel for a couple of months. The union paid Billy $75 a week and picked up the hotel bills. When Billy's wife abandoned him, running off to Reno, Nevada, the union paid several thousand dollars to find her and have a Teamsters business agent bring her back.

Another time, in the early 1950s, Hoffa told Scott to try to learn the names of witnesses who had or would testify before a Detroit grand jury looking into Hoffa and other Teamsters leaders. Scott knew an investigator in the Oakland County prosecutor's office, an old friend from school, who agreed to pass along witness names and, if he knew them, the outlines of their testimony. This is how Scott learned that one witness, a bar operator facing shutdown for liquor violations, had testified to the grand jury that he had given Hoffa $5,000 to bribe a Michigan liquor commissioner friendly to the Teamsters. Scott passed the information to Hoffa, who arranged for the witness to disappear to California and avoid testifying at trial.

After a fight with Hoffa over his tactics with the Michigan

federation, Scott quit. An unhappy Hoffa "threatened to break both my arms and my legs," Scott told the committee. But Scott's testimony didn't get the explosive results Kennedy expected.

This time, after the two weeks of hearings ended, Kennedy was disappointed with the press and the public's reaction. Most of the committee's revelations about Hoffa involved complex financial dealings that resisted easy headlines, could not be explained in a sentence, and didn't have a sympathetic victim at center stage. "People don't get as shocked at somebody stealing a half a million dollars as they do at a mink coat," Bobby complained.[4]

Down in Miami Beach, Hoffa operated the public face of his campaign for Teamsters president out of a hotel suite in the Eden Roc. He and his staff had thought of everything: buttons, banners, an election newspaper called *The Grass Rooter* — Hoffa's wife, Jo, even carried a big Hoffa banner through the fancy hotel's lobby. He was set up for clandestine meetings as well, having borrowed a powerboat, *My Gypsy Melody*, from a businessman in Dearborn, Michigan, and hauled it to moorage near the hotel. Believing that Kennedy staffers, the FBI, or private wiretappers might bug hotel rooms, Hoffa wanted secure quarters for meetings with certain confidants, and he knew it would be difficult for even the most talented wiretapper to bug his floating meeting room. As part of his own counterintelligence program, Hoffa used wireman Allen Hughes, who mostly worked for private investigator Robert Maheu, to sweep key hotel rooms and suites for bugs and wiretaps.[5]

On Sunday night, with no obvious concern for the views of the *Washington Post*'s editorial board, Senator McClellan sent a telegram to Teamsters delegates in Miami Beach, warning them that half of them might have been chosen illegally. Labor secretary James P. Mitchell also warned the delegates to think carefully about the charges against Hoffa before casting their votes.

When the convention was called to order on Monday morning, September 30, Hoffa claimed to be feeling tense and uncertain. "There were three thousand people sitting out there, and I didn't know what's going to happen. I didn't know if somebody was going to get up and say, 'You dirty louse, what's this I read in the paper' or what."[6] But instead he got a standing ovation from the delegates, who were either unimpressed by the McClellan charges or enraged by the Senate committee's meddling. Hoffa's sales pitch was simple: he had made the union more powerful and richer, and together they would continue the economic climb. Lest anyone not get his point, he had men dressed as clowns, wearing ragged clothes, wandering around the convention with signs saying they were the face of the Teamsters' future without Jimmy Hoffa. He had others dressed in white silk top hats and tails to symbolize the financial promise of his presidency.

His victory was never really in doubt. Most of the delegates were union officers, not rank and file, and they owed their jobs to him or to others who owed their jobs to Hoffa. At the vote later in the week, most of the crowd roared in delight as the tally put Hoffa over the top in a landslide. He called his wife, Josephine, to the stage and pulled her close and kissed her. She was in tears. When he addressed the delegates, Hoffa said he was so full of emotion that he couldn't talk to them as he normally would but instead had to read a speech. It was well crafted and cast their lot together against a common enemy.

To say that I do not feel deeply about the charges that have been made against me would be untrue. To say that it has not been tough would be untrue. I am a family man. I have a wife and children. I am proud of my family, and they are proud of me. They know how I believe in the cause of labor. They know this is my life's work, and I am not ashamed to face them at any time for anything I have done. I will fight to defend myself and to keep the name of Jimmy Hoffa as a symbol of good trade unionism and as a symbol of devotion to the cause of labor.

He didn't need to name his foe to be understood.

When a congressional committee concentrates on a personal attack or misuses its power, it can be dangerous for all of us. Something is wrong when a man may be judged guilty in a court of public opinion because some enemy or some ambitious person accuses him of wrongdoing by hearsay or inference. What is happening to our historic principle that a man is innocent until proven guilty?... The use of the lawmaking function to smear a man's reputation without the protection of judicial processes is one of the greatest threats to freedom and the rights of the individual that America has faced in our lifetime. I want to say that great injustice has been done to the individual members of the Teamsters union. You are the people whose good name has been smeared.[7]

It appalled Kennedy and his staff that an election within the nation's biggest union might have been stolen in banana-republic fashion — that is, by allowing Hoffa forces to hand-pick the delegates in violation of the union's own rules — and

Bobby could not let it stand. The committee subpoenaed key documents about the election from the Teamsters Credentials Committee, which had approved, man by man, those delegates who would be entitled to cast votes.

On the Sunday two days after Hoffa's election, an attorney from Williams and Cheyfitz's law firm telephoned Kennedy with some upsetting news. All the credentialing documents had been thrown down an incinerator chute at the Eden Roc hotel.

Who was responsible? Kennedy asked.

The night maid did it.

What is her name, so an investigator can interview her?

Well, she suddenly died of a heart attack.

Then how could you know she threw out the documents?

Nobody else would do that sort of thing.

The lawyer said they were trying to recover the documents from the trash before they were destroyed.

McClellan was furious when he found out the next day and lashed out in a press release that evening. He and the committee were going to find out if this latest incident of wayward documentation was "just another of many strange coincidences" the committee had encountered while trying to get the union's records or if it was "willful defiance" and "an attempt to obstruct its investigation."[8]

In fact, the lawyer's story about the fate of the missing paperwork quickly began to fall apart. Hotel staff recovered the documents at the bottom of a laundry chute, not an incinerator chute. Dumping something down the wrong chute was not a mistake that a hotel maid would make—but it was certainly one that a hotel guest might make.

CHAPTER 7

Mafia Conclave

ON A GRAY NOVEMBER DAY not far from the tiny town of Apalachin, in upstate New York, a state police sergeant named Edgar Croswell stopped in at the Park View Motel. Dressed in plain clothes that day, he was looking into reports about bad checks being passed at the motel when he spotted Joe Barbara Jr. park his Cadillac and head toward the front desk.

Croswell had been keeping an eye on the young Barbara's father for years. Joe senior, a fifty-two-year-old beverage distributor, owned a large horse farm that spread over 130 acres. Sicilian-born, a former bootlegger, a suspect in several mob murders in the 1930s, Barbara outwardly had "gone legitimate," living quietly, supporting local charities, and running a successful beer distributorship and a Canada Dry bottling plant.[1]

Croswell hung back and overheard Joe Jr. tell the front desk he wanted to reserve six rooms, saying his father would pay. Later that day, when Croswell spotted guests arriving in fancy cars with out-of-state plates, he knew something was afoot. The next morning, November 14, 1957, he and another state policeman and two federal Alcohol Tax Unit agents drove out in a light drizzle to the rolling, heavily wooded Barbara estate. They crept through the woods to get a closer look at the eleven-room stone manor, which also had a guesthouse and a barbecue area well hidden from the road. With binoculars, they could see dozens of men enjoying a midday steak dinner in a forty-by-twenty-eight-foot great room in the guesthouse, all of them dressed in suits and ties. Croswell arranged for backup, and later a large team of uniformed police and agents put up a roadblock around the area. Then, around 1:30 p.m., some of them moved onto the property and began writing down the license plate numbers of the big shiny cars lining the drive. When Barbara's guests spotted the police, about a dozen of them panicked and headed for the woods. Others ran to their cars and drove off the farm — only to run into the police roadblock. Meanwhile, officers pursued middle-aged men in fine suits and pointed shoes through the mud and underbrush on the farm. "It looked like a meeting of George Rafts," Croswell would later say, referring to the actor who frequently played gangsters in Hollywood films. "In fact we would have had a harder time getting them if it weren't for the fact that they were such city slickers.... Those city boys didn't have a chance. With their fancy shoes and hats and coats snagging on the tree branches we could grab them easily."[2]

All told, sixty men were rounded up and processed by early the next morning at the nearby police station. There was nothing to charge them with — no drugs or guns were found. In custody, they were polite and refused to be provoked. Only nine had no criminal record. Among them were ten crime bosses, including Vito Genovese and Joe Bonanno from New York, Sam Giancana of Chicago, and Santo Trafficante Jr. of Florida and Cuba. John C. Montana, Buffalo's man of the year and a city councilman, provided the most amusing alibi: his car had broken down, and since he knew Barbara had a mechanic on site, he stopped there for help. Others insisted that they had come from across the nation to visit their old friend Barbara, who had been sick. Together, their wallets held some $300,000 in cash. To no one's surprise, the "masterminds of crime" (as one headline writer described them) refused to explain their actions to the officers who detained them.

The front pages of newspapers across the country recounted the story of how dozens of suspected mob chieftains had been rousted at a Mafia conclave in a remote New York town near the Pennsylvania border. The astonishing event forced the public to consider a troubling truth: the criminal underworld was organized and national in scope, with tentacles reaching into labor unions, businesses, and politics. "The lid had been blown off our world," Bill Bonanno, son of the New York crime boss, was to say, "and there was no way to put it back."[3]

It was only the day before the mass arrests that Bobby Kennedy wondered aloud whether the Mafia truly existed. A specialist with the Bureau of Narcotics (later the Drug Enforcement Agency), Joseph Amato, testified at Rackets Committee hearings that an officer in Teamsters Local 813, Vincent Squillante, was a member of the Mafia. RFK appeared to be skeptical. The chief counsel even asked Amato if he was certain that the Mafia did in fact exist or if it was "just the name given to the hierarchy in the Italian underworld." Amato said that an organized secret society known as the Mafia existed nationwide "and in fact, international[ly]."

FBI director J. Edgar Hoover for years had denied the existence of a national criminal syndicate, calling the idea "baloney."[4] What a difference a day made. Kennedy seized upon the Apalachin news and asked the FBI and other federal agencies for background information on the sixty men. He was shocked to find out that the FBI "didn't know anything about organized crime." Despite his vaunted reputation and secret sources of information, crime-fighting legend Hoover seemed foolish or flat-footed after Apalachin.

Indeed, the FBI had "not even the slightest piece of information" on the well-dressed men who'd run through the woods or been snagged in roadblocks. RFK recounted in amazement that the Bureau might have "perhaps some newspaper clippings, but nothing beyond that.... The FBI didn't know anything, really, about these people who were the major gangsters in the United States. And that was rather a shock to me."[5] Across the street from FBI headquarters were the file cabinets of the Bureau of Narcotics, in the Treasury Building. When Kennedy asked its director, Harry Anslinger, for intelligence on these mafiosi, the agency was able to provide files "on every one of them." Seven of them owned trucking companies, nineteen were garment manufacturers, and twenty-two were labor consultants or officials at unions. In one fell swoop, the McClellan committee's list of investigative targets grew even longer. Hoover's effective publicity machine fell silent, and journalists filled the information vacuum with speculation. The purpose of the Apalachin meeting, wrote the well-sourced syndicated columnist Drew Pearson, was "to carve up the empire of recently slain Albert Anastasia, 'Lord High Executioner' of Murder Inc. But others wondered if the crime bosses were seeking a way to counter increasing pressure from the congressional probe of rackets" — Kennedy and the McClellan committee.

The bust turned out to be a well-timed gift, an opportunity that Kennedy and his staff seized. It needed to be investigated, explained, and exposed as widely and quickly as possible. Within weeks, the Rackets Committee was "preparing sensational charges that the underworld has been muscling into the labor movement for ten years," Pearson wrote. "The committee will attempt to link the recent gangland conference in Apalachin, New York, with certain segments of labor."[6]

To help make that link, Kennedy counted heavily on Walter Sheridan, who was chasing a promising lead in Hoffa's home state. In early December, Sheridan traveled to the Michigan Reformatory in rural Ionia, 130 miles northwest of Detroit, to meet with an inmate named Harry "Chinky" Meltzer, "an old-time racketeer," according to one of the committee's Detroit informants, "who could furnish considerable information on Hoffa." Besides the informant's tip, the committee had also received a letter from a Michigan prison employee who wrote that an inmate named Meltzer talked a lot about his shady dealings with Hoffa. The Kennedy brothers, the McClellan committee, the Justice Department, the AFL-CIO — all had deployed an arsenal of weapons against the Teamsters boss, but he seemed only to be getting stronger. If anyone on Kennedy's staff could wheedle useful information out of Meltzer, it was Sheridan. He desperately wanted to get something useful from Meltzer. With his angelic face and a low-key, persistent manner, Sheridan had a gift for recruiting informants and getting them to talk. "He was the best," said his friend John Seigenthaler, who would work with him and RFK a few years later. "Walter could see through the dark side of an informant and winnow truth from falsehood." Also motivating him was the fact that he had become close to RFK. They had much more in common than being born on the same day. Each possessed a strong idealistic streak and saw the world in black and white, because, as Sheridan would say, "to a certain extent, that's the way things are."[7] Working for Kennedy and going after Hoffa and organized crime gave Sheridan tremendous drive and energy. "It was all very exhilarating and worthwhile," he said.

From a distance, the Michigan Reformatory looked more to Sheridan like a college administration building than a prison. Built in 1877 from brick and limestone, it had high arches over its entryways and two domed steeples rising from a slate roof. But driving closer, Sheridan could see low, blocklike dorms arranged around an open yard, all of it ringed by barbed wire and watchtowers.

Sheridan made his way to an interview room to meet with Meltzer, a dark-haired man in his late forties. He had been at the Michigan Reformatory since 1950, serving fifteen to twenty-five years for "placing explosives with intent to destroy" during a union dispute at a grocery store in Detroit. Meltzer had deep knowledge of Detroit's organized crime; in 1930, his father opened the Oakland Health Club (also known as the Schvitz), a bathhouse that had served as a hangout for elected officials, sports figures, and members of Detroit's notorious Purple Gang.

Meltzer hoped that cooperating might improve his chances with the parole board, and he let on to Sheridan that he could provide a lot of dirt on Hoffa. He'd even be willing to testify at public hearings, but only after he was paroled, which wouldn't be until 1959. If he testified while still in prison, his life wouldn't be worth a nickel, he told Sheridan. On the outside you can run, but "in here they can carve you up in a minute." Plus, Hoffa had enough influence with Michigan's parole board to keep him in prison for years—or have him taken care of.[8]

Meltzer had a lot to say, talking wistfully of the rackets in the prewar days, when Jewish and Irish and Italian racketeers coexisted. Then "the Italians moved in, formed a national syndicate, and took control of everything," he explained to Sheridan. He looked down on the Mafia's methods. "We used to do our own killing, but these guys use torpedoes." A torpedo, he told Sheridan, could be a shoe clerk who one day gets summoned by the mob, is handed $10,000, told to go kill someone, and then does it. Meltzer respected their ruthlessness but disliked their style. "We used to use finesse, whereas these guys just come in and shoot up the place," he said.

He said he had known Hoffa for twenty years and explained how one of their schemes worked. In the 1940s, he had introduced Hoffa to Jack Bushkin, a "labor consultant" for grocery stores. "The Teamsters union would put the squeeze on supermarkets," Meltzer told Sheridan. "And then they would be given the word that Bushkin could solve their troubles. They would retain Bushkin as a labor relations consultant, and their troubles would be over. Hoffa would get a cut out of Bushkin's take." Meltzer said he had shaken down many scrap-metal dealers and other employers with Hoffa's knowledge, always giving him a cut of the proceeds. Between the first and fifth day of each month, he recounted, he would visit Hoffa at home and hand him $3,000 in cash. Jimmy "raked in quite a pile," Meltzer said, but the man was "power crazy." Meltzer had also introduced Hoffa to Detroit Mafia figures Angelo Meli and Pete Licavoli.

As they talked, Sheridan became excited. It was clear that Meltzer had the potential to be a breakthrough witness at the hearings. At the time, no midlevel organized-crime figure had ever come forward with names and dates and wholesale descriptions of how the rackets worked. If he did cooperate, Meltzer said, he "would go all the way and would give dates, places, police officers, politicians, and everything." But first, he insisted, he would have to be out on the street, with enough cash "to get out and get away fast."[9]

Sheridan wrote a three-page memo about his Meltzer interview and sent it to RFK and Carmine Bellino. One of them was so excited after reading it that he wrote at the top, "This is it!"

Hoffa had more important things to worry about than an old-school Purple Gang associate who'd been locked up for nearly the past decade. He faced yet another Justice Department attempt to put him in jail, this time a federal court case in Manhattan: the charge was one count of conspiracy to commit wiretapping. In November of 1957, Hoffa and his entourage moved into the Tuscany hotel in midtown Manhattan and prepared a defense. The stakes were lower this time: the charge was a misdemeanor that carried up to a year in jail and a $10,000 fine. His two codefendants, facing the same charge, were Bert Brennan, his close friend and the president of Teamsters Local 337, and private investigator Bernard Spindel, whose fortunes would remain entwined with the Teamsters over the next decade.

Despite being renowned for his electronic wizardry and spycraft, Spindel seemed torn about his occupation. He appeared before legislative committees to warn them about Big Brother and potentially criminal aspects of the new technology, while at the same time he made a good living in the field, which was growing. He was steeped in the laws about telephone privacy and eavesdropping, and he felt he knew enough to be able to banter and spar with detectives and lawyers who wanted to wheedle information from him about his private investigations and notorious clients. Sometimes he traded information with detectives or investigators if he found an angle to play. Spindel also cycled from bouts of stamina and strength to exhaustion and torpor, which he blamed on a childhood thyroid condition.[10]

As he well knew, federal law was clear—intercepting both sides of a phone conversation by wiretapping was a crime. Electronic surveillance, or bugging—using hidden microphones to capture conversations in a room—was allowed in most instances, as long as the person doing the bugging did not trespass or break in to plant the bugs. Back in 1953 in Detroit, Hoffa did not need telephone wiretaps to figure out who might be betraying him—he could listen in on his underlings simply by quietly picking up his office phone and punching a button to connect to one of the many office lines at Local 299. But Hoffa had wanted unguarded talk, so he paid Spindel to build an eavesdropping system.

The Justice Department's criminal case hinged on whether Spindel illegally wiretapped the union's telephone lines or instead had legally bugged the rooms with microphones hidden in phone handsets that then relayed room sounds over a line back to a master switchboard hidden in Hoffa's desk. Spindel, cleverly, had rigged his microphone system so that Hoffa could listen to conversations in different rooms through his own handset. Lawyer Ed Williams wouldn't take his wiretapping case, so Hoffa instead hired a highly regarded New York lawyer, Sol Gelb, fifty-eight years old. A short, sturdy man who grew up on the Lower East Side of Manhattan, he was the seventh of eight children. Like Hoffa, he dropped out of school after eighth grade to go to work. Unlike his defendant, though, Gelb read for hours at night in libraries, eventually earned his diploma, and went on to law school. As a former assistant to New York district attorney Thomas E. Dewey, Gelb was known for a sharp mind and a tendency for courtroom histrionics, which helped him win the conviction of mob boss Lucky Luciano as well as other racketeering figures.

Gelb's opponent was US attorney Paul Williams. Kennedy hoped that Williams and his team would do a better job than the Justice Department lawyers had done in the Hoffa bribery case. Bobby asked Carmine Bellino, the committee's documents wizard, to give the US attorney in New York helpful intelligence on Hoffa, including a detailed chronology that charted the labor leader's whereabouts, practically day by day and city by city, assembled from sheaves of telephone records, hotel receipts, airline tickets, and newspaper articles.

The indictment itself came about by a fluke, not by design. Spindel's admissions to the New Jersey committee ended up getting passed around and assigned by the FBI to agent Terence F. McShane. Spindel felt he had nothing to hide and cooperated with McShane, opening his books and talking to the FBI agent more than twenty times. McShane was trying to figure out, technically, exactly what Spindel had done, because the wireman insisted he knew the law and hadn't committed a crime. McShane had another reason for the many visits: he hoped to persuade Spindel to turn on Hoffa.

Much of the government's case was built on the testimony of Spindel's ex-assistant, Rudolph Doelicke, thirty-one years old, an aspiring actor and former New York state trooper. Doelicke had worked off and on with Spindel for a couple of years, helping him install the electronic equipment and hoping to learn enough to make a career of it. He even borrowed $1,000 from his mother and loaned it to Spindel, who said he needed it to develop advanced recording gear. Eventually, Doelicke went to court to force Spindel to repay him.

By the time Doelicke testified for the prosecution, the out-of-work actor had little good to say about Spindel. He told the court that in July of 1953 he had traveled to Detroit with Spindel and helped him finish the last stages of an elaborate installation of hidden microphones and recorders. Spindel had a key to the Detroit Teamsters building so they could enter at night, when it was empty.

Unfortunately for the feds, there were easily detectable problems with Doelicke's testimony. Under oath, he said that he and Spindel didn't meet with Hoffa when they first arrived because the Teamsters boss was suffering from injuries sustained in a horseback-riding accident. Then Doelicke testified that three days later, on July 9, he and Spindel met with Hoffa and Brennan and instructed them how to use the microphones, telephones, and recording system.

But Hoffa had been in Seattle on July 9 — something that should have been clear if prosecutors had studied Bellino's timeline of Hoffa's whereabouts — and it was Brennan the horseman, not Hoffa, who had taken a spill on July 4, ended up in the hospital, and hobbled around on crutches for the following ten days.

Lawyers rarely get such easy targets during cross-examination. Gelb asked if Doelicke would change his mind about seeing Hoffa in Detroit on July 9 if he knew the Teamsters leaders had been registered at a Seattle hotel that whole week.

"No; I know I saw Mr. Hoffa in his office the morning of July ninth."

"If it came to your attention that he attended a banquet in Seattle the night of July ninth, would that make any difference?" Gelb asked.

"No."

"If he attended a union executive board in Seattle that week, would you admit you made a mistake?"

"No; I won't retract my statement," Doelicke said.

Gelb asked the would-be actor about Brennan. Was he on crutches on either day that you met him? No, Doelicke insisted.

"If it was brought to your attention that Brennan had such an accident July fourth, was taken to the hospital, and was on crutches for ten days, would that affect your recollection?"

"No."

When Gelb presented the defense side of the case, he brought in records and testimony that destroyed these parts of Doelicke's testimony.

After a day of deliberations, the jury was sent home. The next day, jurors asked for portions of Doelicke's testimony to be read to them, which took place over three hours. They told the judge in the early evening that they were unable to agree, but he ordered them to keep trying. Three hours later, they said a verdict was near but they needed instruction from him on the conspiracy charge.

At midnight the judge sent a question to the weary jurors: Would you benefit from another overnight stay and another go-around the next morning? They sent a note back:

"Positively, absolutely no."

The jury was hung, eleven to one for conviction. The holdout was juror 9, Earle T. MacHardy, a vice president of a sugar brokerage in Yonkers that employed a few Teamsters.

A conviction in this case wouldn't have required Hoffa to step down as president. The single count of conspiracy to wiretap was a misdemeanor. Still, when the judge announced that the jurors couldn't reach a verdict and were being sent home, Hoffa jumped up, jubilant. He called Josephine in Detroit and said he'd take a flight back in the morning. It was December 20, and Hoffa had an early Christmas present.

In room 101 at the New Senate Office Building, news of the persistent holdout juror raised the suspicions of

Kennedy and the investigators. They opened an investigation into MacHardy and his company.

Likely because of Hoffa's good fortune, reporter Clark Mollenhoff sent RFK a Christmas letter certain to cheer him up, lavishly praising him for his work on the Rackets Committee: "You have carried a candle that has been a beacon to hundreds of reporters and editors, thousands of politicians and labor leaders, and literally millions of the rank-and-file labor union members and their families.... You may go ahead to higher office than committee counsel, but it is doubtful if anything you do will have greater force for good government and clean labor than what you have done this year."[11]

RFK appreciated the sentiment enough to save the note. But he was not satisfied. Hoffa was part of an evil conspiracy, had a knack for getting off light, and in a world of black and white he had to go.

CHAPTER 8

Keep the Pressure On

IN THE MONTHS AFTER HIS election, Hoffa surrounded himself with his own lieutenants and settled into the sumptuous Washington, DC, offices vacated by Beck. After years of hard work and politicking and scheming, he enjoyed running the show from the union's five-story glass-and-marble headquarters on Louisiana Avenue, just across from the Capitol. Opened in 1955 at a cost of $5 million, Teamsters headquarters was the nation's grandest union hall, with a massive marble-finished lobby, bronze-framed floor-to-ceiling picture windows, an auditorium that seated 474 people, and a dining room serving cuisine overseen by a French chef whom Beck had recruited from Seattle's Olympic Hotel. Hoffa, a fitness buff, added his own touch: a $50,000 gymnasium with a steam room, weights, and a Swedish masseur.

Hoffa worked from the president's office suite on the third floor. The huge chamber had a nine-foot mahogany desk, a large television and stereo system, a forty-eight-line intercom system, and a hidden built-in bar that popped up with the press of a button. Click another switch, and drapes would open, revealing a huge picture window and a stirring view of the Capitol dome. On his desk, a small sign bore the mock-Latin motto ILLEGITIMI NON CARBORUNDUM — "Don't let the bastards wear you down."* His secretary was Miss District of Columbia of 1948. "Nothing's too good for the Teamsters," Hoffa would tell visitors.

Adjacent was the office of his executive assistant, vice president Harold J. Gibbons, his key adviser and a well-paid loyalist. Like Hoffa, Gibbons had grown up in poverty. The youngest of twenty-three children of Patrick Gibbons, a coal miner from a hamlet in northeastern Pennsylvania, Harold dropped out of high school and worked for a while as a dishwasher and short-order cook. He knew he was smart and was determined to rise above his roots — to be rich and respected. At twenty, he won a YMCA contest to go to an industrial workers' summer school at the University of Wisconsin, and later he studied Keynesian economics at the University of Chicago. Concluding that he was a Socialist at heart, he transformed himself into a commanding public speaker, able to be fiery or persuasive or inspirational depending on the audience. By the 1930s, Gibbons, based in Louisville, Kentucky, was organizing textile workers in five states and pulling in a livable $35 a week. Companies fought back with threats and violence, aided by friendly law enforcement, and he went from the picket line to jail scores of times. "We were outlaws," Gibbons would recall. "If you could have seen the way the cops treated us in those days you'd understand a little more about why we became so cynical and disgusted about law and the establishment."[1]

Gibbons was hired as an organizer by the new Congress

---

* The phrase appeared in the first line of a popular Harvard fight song, almost certainly familiar to the Kennedys. It's unclear whether Hoffa knew the provenance.

of Industrial Organizations and led strikes for taxi drivers, schoolteachers, and textile workers, among others. In 1941, the CIO warehouse workers' union assigned him to Saint Louis to tame one of its rebellious locals whose members clashed with their union officers. Gibbons won the workers over with his brains, charisma, and hard work. In the late 1940s, he merged the Saint Louis local with eight-thousand-member Teamsters Local 688 and soon took over as its ambitious president. He turned Local 688 into the most socially progressive local in the country. He set up a health maintenance organization, which had fifty-seven part-time doctors, completely paid by employers as a worker benefit. Members received free nursing services and drugs, eyeglasses, and dental work at cost, along with privileges at a nonprofit food co-op. He preached the religion of union democracy and expected all union members to attend meetings. In 1951, for the first time, Gibbons successfully bargained for pension benefits. Membership soared to sixteen thousand.

In 1952, Gibbons's operation attracted the unwanted attention of gangsters controlled by East Saint Louis syndicate kingpin Frank "Buster" Wortman. They had already muscled into control of three Teamsters locals across the Mississippi in Saint Louis, and now they told Gibbons to put some of their men on his staff or he'd be killed. Gibbons sent his wife and children into hiding, then traveled to Detroit to talk to someone who had dealt with the mob for years: Jimmy Hoffa. Meeting Gibbons for the first time, Hoffa said not to worry, just put the men on his payroll and nobody would get killed. Of course, he added, in six months Gibbons would likely be taking orders from them. The other choice, Hoffa said, was to buy a pistol, "and the first son of a bitch who walks in the door, you shoot him in the head." Gibbons said he wanted to fight and went back to Saint Louis and bought some guns and holsters with union funds and armed his key aides.[2]

Gibbons would later explain that Hoffa gave him more than advice. "Jimmy offered to help. He came into town with his boys. You see, he had the okay of the Chicago mob and the Detroit mob to get rid of the Wortman gang. And he told them that whatever they tried to do to us, he'd do double to them."[3] Gibbons said Hoffa saved his life. But most things Hoffa did played into something bigger, and in this case, even more important to Hoffa was that he had fixed his grip on another Teamsters barony, one more stepping-stone on his path to eventually securing the presidency.

The two men were a mismatched pair. Hoffa was a Republican, a capitalist. Gibbons, the Socialist, pushed for antidiscrimination drives and open housing in segregated Saint Louis in 1952, two years before the US Supreme Court decision *Brown v. Board of Education* struck down legal segregation in public schools. Gibbons's Local 688 members boycotted drugstores that wouldn't serve blacks and stores that wouldn't hire them. At the time, Hoffa objected to African American long-haul drivers picking up cargo in Detroit.

Yet Gibbons's Socialism gradually became informed less by Proudhon and more by prime rib. Tall and lean, with dark good looks, he dressed in bespoke suits and had developed a taste for fine expense-account dining, pricey drinks, and womanizing. A nightclub habitué, he cultivated Frank Sinatra and Hollywood stars, some of whom admired his early stands in Saint Louis for desegregation. Hoffa was unimpressed with showbiz types, didn't drink, and hectored Gibbons about cutting back on his heavy cigarette habit.

Gibbons was savvy enough to know that Hoffa, popular with Republicans, could benefit from some political ballast, particularly against the Kennedys. Gaining support from the black community would also help Hoffa. Furthermore, Gibbons believed the steps needed to win such support were morally correct. A little-noticed letter by Hoffa that year to all Teamsters locals revealed Gibbons's hand. "As you know, the Teamsters International Union has a policy of nondiscrimination because of race, color, or creed," Hoffa wrote. "This is based not only upon our constitution, but also upon the traditional belief that the labor movement is in the brotherhood of man....As Americans, we should be opposed to bigotry and racial discrimination and do everything possible to make the Bill of Rights a reality for every citizen."

In May of 1958, Ethel L. Payne, Washington columnist for the *Chicago Defender*, an influential black weekly, called Hoffa's letter one of the most significant news stories of the year, though, as she noted, the letter went "almost unnoticed by the general press." Payne also remarked that "Hoffa's new mellow attitude on the race question is in sharp contrast to 1946 when he bluntly told lawyers for the FEPC [Fair Employment Practices Commission] that he had no intention of changing the policy against [the] assigning of Negro truck drivers on cross-country runs." With his letter, Hoffa "quietly paid back a debt he owed for beating the rap in the government's bribery charge against him."[4]

On some days, RFK felt that he was the one who installed Hoffa in "the marble palace" (as some mockingly referred to the Teamsters' lavish headquarters). The Rackets Committee had easily knocked off Beck, which cleared the way for Hoffa's ascension. Other Teamsters exposed at the hearings lost status or were charged with perjury, but Bobby's two best chances to take down Hoffa had failed: the bribery case involving John Cye Cheasty and the embarrassing revelations, in Hoffa's own voice, of his business intimacy with publicly reviled Johnny Dio. Hoffa had skated past both sorties and seemed stronger than ever.

If he was going to drum Hoffa out of office, RFK knew he needed more time and more ammunition. In late March of 1958, the Rackets Committee issued its first interim report — a summary of the past year's work, including recommended legislation such as requiring unions to have regular elections of officers, secret balloting, and complete financial disclosure. Under McClellan's name, the committee warned — some said it threatened — that unless unions and businesses "clean up situations" within their ranks, Congress would likely impose laws "in manners not yet contemplated." Hoffa and the Teamsters were distinguished by their own special section in Senate report 1417, which took care to describe Hoffa as a national menace running a "hoodlum empire." Former president Beck and vice president Harold Gibbons were slammed as well.[5] By that point, McClellan, with Senate approval, had secured a one-year extension for the wildly popular hearings and $790,000 in funds, up from the previous year's $500,000.

Though Hoffa had spent days jousting with Kennedy in the previous year's hearings about his document-deficient business deals and personal finances, RFK decided to dig back in, explaining that Hoffa had failed to give Congress a complete picture of his business affairs. In doing so, the chief counsel changed tactics. Previously, he told investigators that Josephine Hoffa was not to be targeted, that she couldn't be expected to know about her husband's business affairs. Perhaps his attitude had been shaped by notions of chivalry, or perhaps he thought about how little his mother knew of her husband's business dealings. (The ambassador conducted business largely in secret, out of earshot of his wife and children, using telephones that had a specially cupped mouthpiece that made it more difficult to overhear his side of conversations.)

Bobby's initial hesitancy had presented an obstacle to investigators striving to make a case—any case—against Jimmy Hoffa. Business documents and tens of thousands of dollars in checks bore his wife's maiden name, Josephine Poszywak, which was how she endorsed the checks. Then, in late May, Kennedy and his team started fishing for any gifts to the Hoffas from business owners. The Taft-Hartley Act of 1947 was intended to end such abuses—employers slipping bribes to union organizers—by making it illegal to give unions a "thing of value," a vague proscription. Under the auspices of assistant counsel Jerome Adlerman, the committee sent Hoffa and his wife an unusual letter—one that listed all Josephine's fur coats and pieces of fine jewelry—apparently the result of obtaining insurance company records under subpoena. The letter listed dozens of items, among them a "silver-blue mink cape," a "royal pastel mink coat," "a platinum-cultured pearl-and-diamond ring containing 38 round diamonds," and a pair of matching "pearl-and-diamond drop earrings containing two cultured pearls and 24 round diamonds."[6] The committee wanted to know from the Hoffas how much they paid for these furs and jewelry, where they were purchased, and from whom, hoping that the Hoffas wouldn't have ready answers or would admit that the luxuries were gifts from employers.

The IRS had been combing through Hoffas' income tax returns, but the process was moving too slowly to please Kennedy.[7] He was determined to go after Hoffa on his income at the upcoming Rackets Committee hearings. This was not the moment for patience.

That spring, several dozen Rackets Committee investigators and staffers spent weeks in a small, secure room at Internal Revenue Service headquarters, inspecting and hand copying hundreds of federal income tax returns. By law, Congress could review tax returns for a "legislative purpose" — to address tax-related problems that lawmakers needed to solve — but even then they needed to first obtain an executive order from the president. Tax returns were not to be used simply as tip sheets to provide criminal leads for investigators; Kennedy, Bellino, and the committee apparently found the restrictions worth ignoring.

By the summer of 1958, the committee had sent IRS officials 130 letters asking to inspect some 3,500 individual tax returns for several hundred taxpayers — astonishingly high numbers. Kennedy's team cast a dragnet, working backwards from suspicions about people and companies connected to Hoffa, the Teamsters, and mob figures. The IRS would not allow committee investigators to make photostatic copies of the returns, so they made do with another method — tediously copying them entirely by hand. The numbing work tied up staff and eroded morale. John A. Terry, a researcher, was assigned so often to copying duty that he complained in a memo to Kenny O'Donnell, grousing about Carmine Bellino in particular. "Bellino alone has requested the tax returns of 101 individuals and corporations from 1950 to [the] present, which amounts to between 500 and 600 returns," Terry, a Yale grad and law student at Georgetown,* wrote. He and other staffers had complained previously. "Since one person can copy an average of about twelve to fifteen returns a day, working all day long, it will require a terrific number of man-hours to make the desired copies. I personally feel it is grossly unfair for one solitary investigator, no matter who he is, to

---

* Terry was appointed a judge in the District of Columbia Court of Appeals in 1982.

make such excessive and unreasonable demands on the time of other staff members." There was a four-month backlog, he told O'Donnell, and unless someone was assigned permanently, "the information contained in those returns may never be utilized by the Committee as fully as it should."[8]

RFK put more than sixty committee staffers on the list of those who could inspect the tax records, and some sloppy practices ensued. A couple of months later, when the Chicago crime boss Anthony Accardo was called before the committee and refused to answer scores of questions, citing his Fifth Amendment right, Kennedy and his staff put into the hearing record that Accardo reported $904,654 in income from 1954 through 1956; unsurprisingly, those figures made it into the next day's *Washington Post*. The IRS's general counsel, Nelson Rose, was alarmed and quickly met with RFK and other staffers to warn them that such a disclosure was a crime, albeit a misdemeanor. Investigators and staff were allowed to see income tax data only because they had promised to keep it confidential, he reminded them. Kennedy reassured Rose that he would instruct his staff to follow the IRS's rules.[9]

Committee investigators also attempted to locate the Hoffas' safe deposit boxes so they could subpoena the ledgers that recorded the names of whoever accessed them and the dates and times they did so. If need be, the committee could obtain a judge's order to inspect what was stored inside. Investigators would use all this information—details about savings accounts, war bonds, business and real estate holdings, insurance policies (in Hoffa's name and in his wife's maiden name), plus hotel and travel receipts and long-distance phone records—to construct elaborate chronologies. At the end of such a thorough financial sweep, they hoped Bellino and the committee accountants could come up with a reasonable estimate of Hoffa's net worth. If he had wealth that couldn't be explained by his history of wages, investments, or inheritances, the IRS could go after him for tax fraud.[10]

Kennedy and his staff had underestimated how tough it would be to dislodge Hoffa; he matched and sometimes trumped the committee with his resources — from superb lawyers (paid by union funds) to powerful members of Congress eager to trade their support for Teamsters clout and campaign cash to journalists on the take.

The Teamsters were working defense on all angles and had no qualms about slipping cash to reporters to buy their loyalty and favorable coverage. Dave Beck had hired *Business Week*'s labor editor, Merlyn Pitzele, as a $5,000-a-year adviser in the early 1950s, funneling Pitzele's payments through labor fixer Nathan Shefferman of Chicago. When Pitzele's deal was exposed at the rackets hearings in late 1957, Pitzele claimed he merely had volunteered to advise the union about its publications for free but was turned down because Beck, as a matter of principle, insisted on paying for any advice. "This was an unusual union and they were unusual people," Pitzele tried to explain.[11]

Once reporters took the cash, the Teamsters held blackmail power over them, as Hoffa well knew. In January of 1956, he gave a $1,000 check for "professional services" to Owen Deatrick, the Lansing bureau chief at the *Detroit Free Press*, and sent him to Miami Beach for a week in early January, far from the Michigan cold. The guise was that Deatrick would study why Miami unions were having difficulty signing up hotel workers. Deatrick, who covered the state legislature in Michigan's capital, was questioned in 1958 by Carmine Bellino after he spotted the reporter's name on a Local 299 check ledger he had subpoenaed. When Bellino asked to see any memos Deatrick provided for the money, the reporter said he had given "Jimmy" "an oral report" about his week on the beach at the Bal Harbour hotel. When pressed, he said he took no notes and could not name anyone he had interviewed and added that the hotel had given him the room for free.

Kennedy had no time for this; the next time they brought Hoffa in for questioning might be their last good chance to stop him. In a memo sent out in midsummer, RFK ordered everyone — investigators, typists, stenographers — to work every Saturday through August and to be on call if needed for Sunday duty. Just so there would be no confusion, each staffer had to initial the all-hands-on-deck memo and pass it back. Yet most of Kennedy's staff were willing to endure the overtime — even the seemingly impossible workloads — without grumbling because they believed in the cause and had come to adore RFK, buoyed by the feeling that he cared about them and their efforts. Perhaps most important, he worked just as hard as anyone.

Kennedy wasn't above using the media for his own purposes, either. From late May through August of 1958, the committee staff subpoenaed a mélange of crooks, mob figures, and Hoffa hangers-on. Kennedy's strategy was to detail their sordid histories then push those details out to the public via cooperative news reporters. In attempting to besmirch Hoffa with the deeds of his brutal band of cronies, RFK hoped to turn rank-and-file Teamsters against their president.[12]

For days leading up to the mid-August round of hearings, Kennedy privately told reporters about a big gangster who was going be a showcase witness: Robert "Barney" Baker, an ex-boxer and ex-con turned union organizer. Baker not only reported directly to Hoffa but also had rubbed shoulders with Meyer Lansky and Bugsy Siegel, the homicidal gangsters who ran New York's notorious Murder, Inc., gang. Baker had avoided the Rackets Committee so far, even checking into two different weight-loss spas for his health, with the union picking up his $2,200 tab. (At 420 pounds, Baker had been an efficient "belly bumper," using his heft to keep picket lines strong or, depending on the assignment, break them down.) When Gibbons needed muscle after threats from the Wortman gang, Baker moved to Saint Louis and took an organizing job at the progressive Teamsters local.

As a result of Kennedy's salesmanship, the stately Senate Caucus Room was mostly filled to its capacity of three hundred the day Baker was sworn in. Sweating under the hot television lights, his dark hair glistening, the hulking union enforcer played the jolly fat man before his senatorial inquisitors. When Kennedy grilled him about his past associates on the New York waterfront, Baker ignored his lawyer's advice to plead the fifth and instead put on a show.

RFK: Did you know Cockeyed Dunne?

Baker: I didn't know him as Cockeyed Dunn. I knew him as John Dunn.

RFK: Where is he now?

Baker: He has met his maker.

RFK: How did he do that?

Baker: I believe through electrocution in the City of New York of the State of New York. [Loud laughter]

RFK: What about Squint Sheridan? Did you know him?

Baker: Andrew Sheridan, sir?

RFK: Yes.

Baker: He has also met his maker.

RFK: How did he die?

Baker: With Mr. John Dunn. [Laughter]

By his second day of testimony, the Caucus Room's capacity crowd grew to overflowing, lured by the antics of Baker, who apologized several times to the senators about his answers. "I am a ham at heart. I like to talk big. I drop names." Asked if he tried to choke a Chicago hotel manager in a dispute over a bill, he replied, "I don't remember nothin' in the choking department." Asked about doping a thoroughbred, he said, "I don't know nothin' about no horse races." His testimony didn't hurt Hoffa; if anything, it backfired on RFK. "A danger lurked in this. Kennedy and McClellan saw it from the start," *Time*'s Hugh Sidey said in a memo to his editor. "Barney Baker, despite one of the most unsavory lives yet exposed before the muckraking committee, was appealing in his comic sinisterism. Not even dour John McClellan could keep from bursting into laughter on occasion. And steel-mouthed Jimmy Hoffa literally broke up at some of the better antics of Barney.... For two days he kept the Senate Caucus Room laughing."[13]

Kennedy tried to recover the momentum once he ran out of questions and Baker was about to leave the witness chair. "I don't want you to leave the stand with the idea of being just the Teamster jokester," RFK lectured him. "You are associated with the scum of the United States. And you are just like them." RFK may have been telling the truth about Baker, but it struck some as petulant and bullying.

On August 21, during a break in the hearings, the Teamsters boss appeared cocky and unconcerned, while Bobby Kennedy found himself weary and bitter. For public consumption, he told reporters that the committee's most important work was to expose flaws in the rules about labor-management relations and then pass legislative reforms — in particular, laws that would create criminal penalties for defrauding union pension funds. It was a clear attempt to lower public expectations that the Kennedys and the committee would knock

Hoffa from office. But in private, with Sidey, a trusted friend, RFK raged against Hoffa the man and the need to destroy him and all he stood for. "It has become almost a religion with Bob. Eighteen months of hard work and frustrations have crystallized into a real bitterness," Sidey wrote in a confidential memo to his editor. "Hoffa sits at the apex. He is everything sinister. To somehow destroy Hoffa's gangster empire would be" — quoting RFK — "the 'greatest blessing this country could have.' "[14]

Kennedy slumped behind his littered desk in the basement of the New Senate Office Building one day as he talked to Sidey. "This is the most dangerous situation that exists in the country," he confided to the newsman. "We have witnesses and contacts that we can't begin to reveal. They don't dare come out. There is evidence in the files. There is not a gangster in the US that does not have a link with Hoffa and the four or five top men around him. There is not a region in the US where there is not corruption in the Teamsters. We have five times as much material on Hoffa corruption as on anything or anybody we have had before us in the last eighteen months including Dave Beck. I feel Hoffa's hours are numbered. Any man as totally corrupt as him cannot last very long. Everything he does is corrupt. He has surrounded himself with corrupt people. Wherever he goes he spreads corruption. When he has been on trial he has tried to obstruct it. When he has been before the committee he has tried to corrupt them. He has bought off newsmen. He has used union funds to elect and control judges and prosecutors. It is this utter contempt for humanity that really gets me."

RFK told Sidey there were five ways to nail Hoffa. Number one, he said, was still "income tax."[15]

Backed by Bellino's analysis, RFK subpoenaed a few of Hoffa's business associates to the Rackets Committee later that summer, hoping to get to the bottom of the $60,322 in income that Hoffa's accountant had described as "collections" in Hoffa's federal tax returns from 1948 to 1956.

A year earlier, at his first committee go-round with RFK, Hoffa said with a straight face that the money had come from racetrack earnings, thanks to the betting savvy of his Detroit business partner, Bert Brennan. For specifics Hoffa had suggested that Bobby talk to Brennan.

Now, in the summer of 1958, when Brennan was called to the witness chair and asked about his and Hoffa's gambling winnings, he politely told the senators he was being investigated by the IRS. Sorry, but his lawyer had told him to plead the fifth.

But Senator McClellan pressed: Mr. Hoffa gave you his permission to explain his winnings. He promised that his questions wouldn't move into Brennan's personal matters. Brennan again declined to testify.

McClellan did not hide his disgust. "Is the taking of the Fifth Amendment one of the prerequisite qualifications for advancement [in the Teamsters]?" he asked.

Brennan looked to his lawyer, got the signal, and answered McClellan by pleading the fifth.

RFK's spirits were lifted by information developed by Pierre Salinger from a new witness, Sol Lippman, the general counsel to the Retail Clerks International Association. Lippman said that in 1956 Hoffa had threatened to kill him after he opposed his union's merger with the Teamsters. Bobby reinterviewed Lippman, wanting to assess him himself. The high-ranking lawyer could be an important witness. Kennedy quickly decided that Lippman was telling the truth.

The day Hoffa threatened him, Lippman recalled for Kennedy, he had bragged that if Lippman complained to authorities, it would be a waste of his time. "If I did it, no jury would even convict me — I have a special way with juries," Lippman recalled Hoffa as saying.[16]

When Hoffa took the witness chair in early August of 1958, RFK badgered him relentlessly on Lippman, as if asking the same question over and over would make him admit fault.

> Kennedy: What did you say to him about having him killed?
> Hoffa: Killed?
> Kennedy: Yes.
> Hoffa: Sol Lippman? I wouldn't even waste my time talking about it.
> Kennedy: What did you say to him at that time?
> Hoffa: I didn't say anything about it.
> Kennedy: Will you swear under oath that you did not say anything to Sol Lippman in your office about having him killed?
> Hoffa: I did not.
> Kennedy: Did you say anything about the fact that you could have him killed in that office and nobody would know about it?
> Hoffa: I did not.
> Kennedy: Did you say anything to the fact that he could be walking down the street and could be shot one day?
> Hoffa: I did not.
> Kennedy: Did you say anything to the effect that juries treated you very well?
> Hoffa: What did you say?
> Kennedy: Did you say anything to him to the effect that juries treated you very well, that you could have him

killed, and that you thought that you could do very
well before a jury?

Hoffa: Now, you know, that is pretty ridiculous.

Kennedy: Did you say anything generally on the subject
of having him killed, murdered, shot?

Hoffa: Mr. Kennedy, if you want to make this dramatic, all
right, but the answer is no.

Kennedy: Nothing along those lines?

Edward Bennett Williams broke in, objecting. "I don't see
that repetition has done any good. He has answered the question fourteen times, by my count here," he said to McClellan.

RFK was annoyed. "I have information directly to the
contrary."

"Bring Lippman around here," Hoffa said, throwing down
a challenge.

Over the lunch break in the hearings, Kennedy and Salinger telephoned Lippman. They wanted him to testify publicly
about the threats he had told them about privately.

"Sol, can I get you to come over here and testify?" Kennedy pleaded with the union's lawyer. "It would make a real
difference."

Lippman would not go public. The retail clerks depended
on the Teamsters in so many ways — from boycotts to picket
lines, he told Bobby.

RFK listened for a minute, then asked Lippman, "[Are
you] going to let him stand up here and kick everybody
around? Just because you can't make a deal with him for six
months or a year?"

Lippman reiterated that the union couldn't risk angering
Hoffa.

Kennedy implored him: "The fact he threatened you and
made these statements to a leading union official like you—

everybody would know you're telling the truth. Hell, I talked to you [and] within twenty minutes...I knew it was the truth."

Lippman stood firm.

"Okay, Sol." Kennedy hung up the phone and turned to Salinger. "Shit."[17]

As RFK and the Rackets Committee's second extended interrogation of Hoffa neared its end, Bobby wrote a note in his journal. "I am mentally fatigued—more than any other hearing. We have been going on for a long time without a break & I have about had it. I shall be happy when Hoffa is finished next week. McClellan also very tired. This year seems to have been tougher than last. Plodding grind...I feel like we're in a major fight. We have to keep going, keep the pressure on or we'll go under."[18]

RFK was completely discouraged. The reporters at the hearings who were on his side could see that he had been bested. Ethel Kennedy, his wife, who attended often, would remember Hoffa as "confident, almost flip. He seemed to know he was winning."[19]

At one point, McClellan suggested to Bobby that they continue questioning Hoffa at a night session. Bobby replied that he was "bushed."

Hoffa overheard his honest reply. He knew Kennedy prided himself on his toughness. The young lawyer had provided a tiny opening for the master of intimidation. Just as he would at the bargaining table, he exploited it.[20] "Look at him, look at him!" Hoffa said derisively, making sure Bobby heard him, hoping to humiliate him. "He's too tired. He just doesn't want to go on."

CHAPTER 9

Promising Leads

THE KENNEDYS WERE DISAPPOINTED THAT they hadn't knocked Hoffa out of the Teamsters, but they kept trying. So did the Eisenhower administration's Justice Department, which began convening grand juries to look into misconduct by Teamsters and other union officials across the country. Using the sordid McClellan committee revelations, Republicans had taken up rackets-busting as a campaign theme in 1958, promoting themselves as the workers' protector and savaging Democrats as pawns of union leaders.

Bobby Kennedy pressured the Justice Department to take up cases that originated at the McClellan committee hearings. Several referrals were for perjury, a particularly difficult crime to prove. It required proof that a witness such as Hoffa was posed a clearly worded question, that his answer was unambiguous, and that he knowingly lied. With coaching from his lawyers and his awareness of the perjury trap and Kennedy's inexpert questioning, Hoffa had made himself tough to pin down.

Attorney general William Rogers, a moderate Republican,

knew something about the rackets. Crusading district attorney Thomas E. Dewey had assigned Rogers in 1938 to his sixty-man task force aimed at routing out New York City's mob influence in the garment district, shipping docks, and in prostitution. He enlisted in the navy during the war, saw action in the Battle of Okinawa, and rose in rank to lieutenant commander. He joined the Justice Department as a deputy attorney general and developed a friendship with Vice President Nixon. By 1958, Rogers had put together a group of three or four prosecutors to look into the Hoffa materials they received — "were bombarded with" might be a better term — from the Rackets Committee. Among his team were George MacKinnon, the former US attorney from Minnesota, and Jim Dowd of Texas, both under the supervision of William Hundley. They were, in fact, the first Get Hoffa squad.

Many of the career criminal prosecutors at the Justice Department considered the Kennedy referrals to be something of a joke — promising leads on their face, but not strong enough to enable prosecutors to bring charges. The referrals needed much more investigation and careful case construction to increase the likelihood of getting a conviction. Kennedy, who was not a trial lawyer, was frustrated by what he felt was Justice Department laziness, passivity, and lack of passion in its pursuit of an enemy whose dangers should have been clear to all. "He was always impatient that they weren't doing anything with them," Walter Sheridan would later say.[1] "We'd have meetings with the Department of Justice about it, and he was always pushing them to do something." Sheridan gave the Justice Department lawyers the benefit of the doubt. "They weren't used to a Robert Kennedy, because they had never encountered one. They weren't used to somebody who dug that deep, generated stuff that fast, and wanted something done about it yesterday. So a fellow like Bill Hundley, who was head of the organized crime section at that time at Justice—you know, Bill Hundley is as good and honest and able a man as you can find...but RFK blamed Hundley because it was Hundley's area."[2]

Kennedy complained publicly about what he saw as a lack of action. But Hundley wasn't the kind of person to be bullied or swayed by Bobby's insistence on bringing some kind of charge against Hoffa. In many respects, Kennedy and Hundley were very much alike: the same age, Roman Catholic, each interested in pursuing and punishing lawbreakers. "I'm just a little Irish kid from Brooklyn," Hundley liked to say, underselling himself as a way to disarm his opponents and gain advantage. But in other ways Hundley was Kennedy's temperamental opposite. In his teens, Hundley finagled his way into the army despite terrible vision in one eye, and he served as sergeant in a machine-gun section at the Battle of the Bulge. A smoker, red wine drinker, and not particularly observant Catholic, he possessed an easy, joking manner that put juries at ease. He seemed to like everyone he met, earning himself the description "a legal Will Rogers."

If Hundley and Kennedy shared a defining trait, it was that both were intensely competitive. "Even when the facts are bad I want to win the case, and I play very, very hard to win," Hundley once said.

Hundley personally liked Sheridan (another Fordham grad), Kenny O'Donnell, and Carmine Bellino, but none of them was a lawyer, and their boss was not a litigator; it had become increasingly clear to Justice that Kennedy did not yet have the experience to know how to build a criminal case that would stick—especially one that might be contested by a lawyer as brilliant as Ed Williams. Kennedy "sent over lots of what I thought were terrible cases on Hoffa," Hundley would later say. "I was the Justice official that was turning him down. I'd go see him, and I'd try to explain that he didn't have the evidence. Although he never said it, some of the people around him felt that I should indict Hoffa and get the evidence later."[3] Sifting through the dross, Hundley picked those few Rackets Committee leads that showed promise and sent those referrals to IRS or FBI agents for more investigation.

Hundley's most contentious exchange with Kennedy occurred when he admitted to Bobby that some of the documents and witness statements carefully collected by committee investigators showed that Hoffa almost certainly was guilty of wrongdoing but that the Justice Department either had no jurisdiction or no likelihood of winning a conviction. Kennedy sent over several cases in which he was certain Hoffa had lied as he dodged around the chief counsel's questions, but the prosecutor's burden of proof was high. "Sometimes there would be obvious instances of wrongdoing that wouldn't measure up to a federal case," Hundley would later say. "And in a lot of instances, he would just say that, 'Well, goddamn it,' he thought there was a case....On one occasion he said something to the effect that: 'When you admit to me that' — he had a pretty good temper—'there's obvious wrongdoing here and you tell me on top of that that you can't make a case out of it, it makes me sick to my stomach.' And I remember one day saying, 'Well, you know, I can't be responsible for your gastric juices.'"

Hundley instantly regretted his cutting remark. "He hung up on me. He was really sore that day." Twenty minutes later, Bobby called back and apologized. Hundley apologized as well.

The cases may not have "measured up," but as Hundley would later admit, the Eisenhower administration wasn't making an extra effort to develop the Rackets Committee's cases against the Teamsters because, at least indirectly, successful prosecutions would advance the political fortunes of the ambitious Kennedys, masters of news conferences and strategic leaks to favored journalists. "I don't think at that time the FBI or the Internal Revenue Service was breaking their back trying to make cases for Bobby Kennedy," Hundley admitted. "There wasn't the all-out effort on the part of the Department of Justice to make Bobby Kennedy look good."[4]

As general counsel for the International Brotherhood of Teamsters, Edward Bennett Williams often got involved early in such cases—once witnesses or documents were subpoenaed but before RFK's staff referred the matter to the Justice Department. Williams told Hugh Sidey that of the three dozen or so cases of which Williams claimed to have knowledge before Kennedy referred them to Justice, only five or six were accepted by prosecutors for further workup. Williams, by now the most famous defense lawyer in the nation, complained privately that Bobby was not only an inept investigator but also a lousy lawyer. Bobby's flaw, Williams said, was that he turned each case into a personal cause. "He divided everyone up," Williams said. "There were the white hats and the black hats. If you weren't for him, then you were against him. There was no middle ground."[5] Kennedy, Williams said, failed to understand the lawyer's role—that every man deserved a defense if the system was to work—indeed, the Sixth Amendment guaranteed it. Lawyers who battled each other by day in court should be able to enjoy each other's company at night over beers in a bar.

Perhaps that was easier to say when you were being paid by the hour. The two men had once been friends, attending weekday mass together. Williams even had offered RFK a job with his firm before Bobby's Rackets Committee fame. Williams had done his best to cultivate Kennedy, knowing well the commercial value of connecting his firm to a famous, wealthy family. Williams failed. Bobby rarely drank and avoided the boozy, smoke-filled bonhomie of Duke Zeibert's and the other DC haunts that provided a rowdy outlet for the busy, high-powered litigator. And instead of a future colleague and friend, Williams, by rescuing Hoffa from a bribery conviction and a certain prison term, had created a powerful enemy, one who possessed "burning vindictiveness" and, the attorney complained, went out of his way to hurt him professionally.

"If Jack Kennedy is elected president," Williams once joked, "I guess I better apply for a passport."

Despite all the setbacks, Kennedy and his staff still held on to hope in late 1958. Bernard Spindel was upset with Hoffa over money. Hoffa had given the wireman $34,500 in cash over the previous year and a half, most of it for the lawyers who defended Spindel in the two wiretapping trials he, Hoffa, and Teamsters official Bert Brennan endured in Manhattan federal court. Spindel had been satisfied at first. He would come to Washington, DC, and pick up envelopes of cash from Hoffa, or a trusted Teamsters official in New York would make the delivery. When Hoffa filed his federal tax return in 1958, he declared a $21,000 expense for cash given to Spindel. In turn, Hoffa ordered Spindel to report the $21,000 as income to the IRS — Hoffa, who had been under IRS scrutiny since the early 1950s, needed his tax returns to conform to Spindel's. The eavesdropper said he wasn't planning on declaring it: Spindel could report the money as income, but, according to his calculations, he would need an additional $6,200 from Hoffa to pay for state and federal taxes.

Over the years, Hoffa had treated Spindel the way he treated lawyer Ed Williams and other professionals whom he paid handsomely to help him — with disrespect. The self-made Spindel, who considered himself a savvy operator and sharp inventor, hated the degrading treatment. He never considered Hoffa a friend.

On November 5, 1958, Spindel met Hoffa at Teamsters headquarters, where they argued over the extra payment. Hoffa refused to pay the $6,200. "You're responsible for the trial," Hoffa told Spindel, furious. "If you hadn't spoken to the FBI, I would not have been in this trouble. Go and get yourself a job somewhere."[6]

Instead, five days later Spindel telephoned an old colleague, former New York City police detective Jim Kelly, with whom he had worked on the New York City Anti-Crime Committee. Kelly now worked as an investigator, based in New York, for the Rackets Committee. He respected Spindel's skills and had even tried a few times to get the wiretapper to testify before the Rackets Committee. Realizing that Spindel could be a breakthrough witness — perhaps even provide the basis for the Justice Department to pursue another criminal case against Hoffa — Kelly spent many hours over several days debriefing Spindel, who coughed up sleazy details on more than a dozen cash handoffs. In early September of 1957, for instance, Spindel met with Hoffa and his lawyer, George Fitzgerald, at a hotel near LaGuardia Airport in New York City. Later, as Spindel was crossing the parking lot, Hoffa and Fitzgerald pulled up in a car and the lawyer tossed Spindel an envelope from the window, saying, "This should hold you for a while." It was $5,000. When Spindel told Hoffa in April of 1958 that he needed money for medical care for his father, who had been hospitalized after a severe stroke, Hoffa ordered a New York Teamsters official to funnel Spindel $3,400.[7] That was the generous Hoffa, though it was clear that such gestures also served to underline the message that Hoffa was the source of assistance when you did what he wanted. And if not, beware.

Kelly urged Spindel to tell his story publicly at upcoming committee hearings, but the wireman refused. "As a result of about 12 hours of conversation with Spindel, he was willing to supply information concerning Hoffa's activities but was fearful of the consequences if it were learned that he was the source," Kelly would later write in a memo.[8]

On December 11, 1958, at the Carroll Arms Hotel in Washington, Spindel met with Kennedy, along with Bellino, Kelly, and O'Donnell, to see if they could close a deal. The eavesdropper was playing a dangerous game just in meeting with Kennedy. Why would he risk sharing off-the-record details about Hoffa? One possible reason surfaced that day: Spindel revealed that he hadn't filed a federal tax return for 1957 — the one Hoffa was so concerned about — nor was he going to file one for 1958 unless Hoffa came up with the disputed $6,200. In being helpful to Kennedy, Spindel may have been angling for well-connected help with any future federal tax problems. Months later, Kelly arranged for them all to meet again in New York, this time at the Kennedy family's apartment at 277 Park Avenue. When Spindel arrived, Kennedy said the meeting would have to be cut short because he needed to leave right away to catch a flight. In order to have a chance to talk, Spindel drove RFK and Carmine Bellino to the airport, with Kelly along for the ride. Unknown to them, Spindel would later write, he had a hidden tape recorder in his car, which he operated as he shuttled his passengers, capturing the conversation.

In the car, Spindel noted, Kennedy was persistent. Will you testify against Hoffa in a public hearing? Kennedy asked.[9]

Spindel declined, saying he could not afford to testify publicly. It would dry up future assignments from Hoffa and other clients.

What will it take to get you to cooperate? RFK asked.

A loan of $850,000 to start up an electronics firm in Puerto Rico, Spindel said. Kelly could tell that Spindel was joking, but RFK responded clearly.

"Now, Bernie," he replied, "you know my brother is going to be the next President. You don't have to worry about anything." Jack Kennedy officially hadn't announced he was running, but political columnists made it seem like a foregone conclusion. Spindel took Bobby's blandishments to mean he would be awarded with any federal job he'd like.[10]

Spindel was one of the committee's most promising leads yet, but through the entire process he had only been stringing Kennedy along. "For the two years his agents and staff were busy wining and dining me in the hope that I would be a witness against Hoffa, I was actually working as a double agent," Spindel would later write. "I immediately reported all of my contacts with Kennedy and his staff to Hoffa.... Kennedy's staff would never say exactly what it was that they wanted me to testify about. I tried to determine what possible information Kennedy wanted me to provide and, at the same time, I was able to analyze which information he did not have in his possession."[11]

For months, Kennedy, Bellino, and others had come to believe that Spindel would be an effective weapon against Jimmy Hoffa. Spindel's deviousness became clear to them in July of 1959, just before they brought Hoffa back for what would be his third interrogation before the Rackets Committee. Now they realized they had wasted scores of hours and hundreds of dollars flying Spindel back and forth that spring from Puerto Rico, where he recently had moved.

Spindel was finally subpoenaed to testify, but before doing

so he found an opportunity in the hallway of the New Senate Office Building to ask Kennedy if the rumor was true that he had forwarded an investigative file on Spindel to the Internal Revenue Service.

"I sure did," Kennedy said, "and I hope they get you. They are certainly going to try."[12]

When Spindel appeared on July 15, 1959, before the committee, then in its thirtieth month of investigating labor racketeering, he invoked Fifth Amendment protection. Frustrated, RFK burned him as a source, putting into the public record the fact of their off-the-record negotiations from earlier that year. "I have had some conversation with Mr. Spindel," Kennedy revealed to the crowded hearing room. "Mr. Spindel wanted material that we had obtained from him kept confidential.... At the same time, of course, I wanted him to testify. He made a statement to me at that time that it would be possible that he would consider testifying if it would be possible for me to make arrangements to have him set up in business in Puerto Rico."[13]

Spindel, from the witness chair, shot back, "That is an absolute lie, and he knows that!"

Chairman McClellan apparently didn't like where this exchange was heading, telling the chief counsel, "Let's not get into this now."

After he was dismissed, Spindel would recall, he stepped out of the hearing room and headed down the hall to talk to Teamsters official Bert Brennan. After a moment, Brennan looked up and warned Spindel, "Look out!" He turned and saw Bellino charging toward him, fists clenched. The investigator swung at Spindel, who, with time to react, ducked the punch and landed a solid blow of his own.

None of the press accounts that day made any note of fisticuffs, and Kennedy associates years later said they doubted that Bellino would try to sucker punch a witness, even one who had tricked him and made him feel foolish. Spindel later wrote that Hoffa's hangers-on were so impressed with his moxie that "that night, at the hotel, the Teamsters threw a dinner party for me in honor of the occasion."[14] A celebration was in order—and despite their fights, despite the wireman's reckless conduct, Hoffa had some new work for Spindel.

With help from indebted politicians and top-notch attorneys, private eyes, and publicists, Hoffa believed he knew how to outmaneuver federal authorities. He had far less faith that his local Teamsters officials could do so, especially by the fall of 1959, when the number of federal grand juries targeting Hoffa and company had climbed to a dozen. "The panels are probing alleged wrongdoing ranging from tax evasion and extortion to violation of antitrust laws," the *Wall Street Journal* reported. "At least 14 Teamsters were indicted last week alone....No one in government will admit, in so many words, to the plan to 'get Hoffa' by cutting off the base of his power."[15]

In November of 1959, Hoffa assembled top Teamsters officials from across the country in a conference room at the DC headquarters and closed the drapes across the room's picture window. He then lectured them about the importance of never discussing internal union affairs where somebody else could overhear them. Many of the men believed Hoffa was being persecuted by the Justice Department as well as by Bobby Kennedy. Even so, some believed that Hoffa was overly cautious, even paranoid. For these doubters, Hoffa sauntered to the window about forty-five minutes into the meeting, "looking like the cat that swallowed the canary," according to one account, then pulled back the drapes. Off in the distance, two men could be seen waving back at them.

"Take a good look at those guys, and then remember what I have been trying to tell you," Hoffa told his colleagues.

Who are they? he was asked.

"Fortunately, they are a couple of our boys," he replied. "They'll be over in a few minutes with a surprise for the whole lot of you."

After the two men joined the meeting, one of them displayed a small recorder. At Hoffa's command, they played a tape. The officials appeared aghast as they listened to their own words played back to them. How?

"Very simple," Hoffa told them. "I had a small broadcasting device that requires no wire of any kind hidden in my inside coat pocket and broadcast it to the recorder three hundred and fifty yards away." There were murmurs of amazement.

"I think I made my point," Hoffa finally said. "In the position we're in today, the best thing our people can do is keep their mouths zippered."[16]

CHAPTER 10

Primary Opponent

IN SEPTEMBER OF 1959, Robert F. Kennedy sent a letter of resignation to Senator McClellan, saying he was stepping down as chief counsel. It had been a remarkable run for Kennedy and his staff: some three hundred days of testimony over three years, more than fifteen hundred witnesses, the compilation of the most extensive files on racketeering, more than twenty thousand pages of testimony in the printed record. Now that Congress had passed "effective labor legislation," Bobby wrote, his job was over.

But it wasn't the bill he and his brother wanted. John F. Kennedy had counted on the McClellan committee hearings to lead to a major labor reform act that would carry his name, an accomplishment to boost his gravitas as a presidential candidate. The Kennedy-Ervin bill passed the Senate, but Republicans and southern Democrats in the House added business-friendly provisions that limited picketing and boycotts. Kennedy took his name off the consolidated bill before it passed as the Landrum-Griffin Act. The law did address union abuses exposed during the rackets hearings: after the law was passed, union members would have the right to vote by secret ballot, making it harder for racketeers to take over through intimidation; locals had to file annual financial reports with the Labor Department, revealing how officers were spending union dues; union leaders also had to disclose any conflicts of interest, such as having business deals with officials of the companies they were bargaining against, a provision that forced Hoffa to change his conduct.

But, more significant, the law rolled back union power, making it harder to organize new members. Hoffa and his forces blamed the Kennedys for what he called a union-busting bill and vowed to remind voters of this when Jack Kennedy ran for president.

Officially, Bobby was unemployed, but even after resigning from the Rackets Committee, he still would not admit publicly what his family, friends, colleagues, and favored journalists knew as fact: his brother Jack definitely was running for president in 1960. After he sent in his resignation letter, RFK was asked by a wire-service reporter whether he was working on his brother's campaign. Bobby smiled, stretched the truth, and said no, but "if he runs for something I probably will."

The flimsy subterfuge didn't fool Hoffa. Years earlier, in the early days of the Rackets Committee, he had accused Senator Kennedy of running for president on the backs of the Teamsters. In the summer of 1957, investigators Carmine Bellino and Pierre Salinger had arrived in Detroit to examine documents they had subpoenaed from five Teamsters locals. Instead of being shown the records at the Teamsters hall, the two men soon found themselves summoned to Hoffa's office. With his minions looking on, Hoffa exploded in rage, waving the subpoenas in a clenched fist, Salinger would recall. "What are you trying to do to me?" Hoffa had demanded, so angry he mangled his words. "You tell Bobby Kennedy for me that he's not going to make his brother President over Hoffa's dead body!"[1]

To have a Kennedy in the White House was unthinkable to Hoffa. He so far had survived the longest, most extensive congressional investigation in history, one that, at its peak, employed more than one hundred government lawyers, investigators, accountants, and support staff. He had been charged on four separate occasions in federal court: for bribery, perjury, and twice for wiretapping. Each time he beat back the indictments.

Publicly, Hoffa squared his shoulders and with a sneer dismissed Jack and Bobby Kennedy as "spoiled brats," soft-handed Ivy League types who had little understanding of the workingman. Privately, he knew that having an enemy as president of the United States meant he would face an even fiercer fight to hold on to his own presidency and to stay out of prison. He needed to find a way to stop senator John F. Kennedy.

Harold Gibbons argued for something more powerful and permanent than Hoffa giving individual contributions to lawmakers in exchange for favors, calling that effort a waste of money. Instead, he said, spend money building a multimillion-dollar political machine by organizing the Teamsters rank and file and their families into a national "community steward" network. It was a grandiose version of what Gibbons had accomplished on a smaller scale in Saint Louis in the early 1950s with his ten-thousand-member Local 688: there, a Teamsters union member in each neighborhood registered people to vote and told them how to get action on broken streetlights, ensure a quick police response, and deal with overflowing sewers — essentially the duties of a ward heeler. Gibbons's program had been praised by the liberal Americans

for Democratic Action and other political groups, but Hoffa
had his doubts.

Gibbons's plan would take an enormous amount of money,
as much as $5 million. Complicating Hoffa's decision was his
resentment of Gibbons. His top aide had been described in
the press as one of the "most articulate and literate leaders in
the labor movement." Gibbons, active in civil rights circles,
also let it be known that he had made progress pushing Hoffa
to support integration, arguing for it not on economic grounds—
Hoffa's guiding principle—but because it was morally right.
Hoffa and other officials had to have chuckled to hear Gibbons discuss morality: while his wife and family stayed home
in Saint Louis, Gibbons used his lavish expense account to
entertain attractive female companions.

Nevertheless, Hoffa went along with Gibbons's plan, believing that he needed to use every weapon at his disposal—
money, political muscle, political intelligence, public opinion—to
slow down the Kennedy campaign. Gibbons, excited to be
running the grassroots political campaign out of Teamsters
headquarters, called the effort DRIVE, an acronym for Democrat, Republican, Independent Voter Education. Gibbons and
lobbyist Sid Zagri focused their initial efforts on those pre-
cincts and congressional districts where national election
results showed Democrats and Republicans within five percentage points of each other. In theory, if the Teamsters could
sway outcomes in such swing districts, the union would
turn into a potent political player. And instead of tapping
existing Teamsters funds, the millions of dollars needed for
DRIVE would come from a national dues check-off campaign,
directed from headquarters, modeled after the one used since
the early 1950s at Gibbons's Local 688. About three-quarters
of its ten thousand members had signed cards allowing the
union to divert thirty-five cents a month from their dues to

fund its local political work. That same plan, applied across the International Brotherhood of Teamsters, would raise nearly $5 million a year—basically what Hoffa had estimated the program would cost.

The Teamsters made little secret of the ambitious plan. As Victor Riesel wrote: "Hoffa just knows that all the boys will sign such cards. To Hoffa, money means politics. It appears that he will be deep in both next year."[2]

It seemed as though both sides were gearing up. By late 1959, Justice Department prosecutors had waded through the Senate Rackets Committee referrals about Hoffa, done some spadework on their own, and narrowed their sights. Jim Dowd, a special assistant to the attorney general, believed the best chance to bring down Hoffa lay in the Sun Valley land scandal, a shaky real estate venture in central Florida in which Hoffa pushed retirement-home lots to Teamsters while secretly holding an option to buy nearly half the 2,475-acre project.

Hoffa was not a sophisticated investor. He favored risky ventures that provided steep rewards—racehorses, a heavyweight boxer, oil exploration—and in Sun Valley he was partaking in the scam-ridden Florida real estate boom. Thanks to air-conditioning, postwar Florida had become comfortably habitable year-round and a magnet for northerners seeking a cheap, warm place to retire. During the 1950s, the state's population nearly doubled as developers surveyed huge swaths of land and mapped out subdivisions. Unimproved lots were sold cheaply and bought on installment, sometimes through the mail, often sight unseen.

One land hustler was Henry Lower of Detroit, a Hoffa crony, who in 1954 put together a development in central Florida unimaginatively named Sun Valley. He started out with unsecured loans from the treasuries of several Detroit-area Teamsters locals, then snagged further financing arranged by Hoffa. First he transferred $500,000 in Detroit Teamsters cash to a Florida bank, where it mysteriously earned no interest; in return, a bank vice president loaned Lower the same amount. With the financing secured, Lower forked over $25,000 to Hoffa as a no-interest, no-note loan, to be repaid if and when Hoffa felt like it. Before long, Teamsters members in Detroit and elsewhere found themselves targeted by ads touting special Teamsters-only deals at Sun Valley, where lots could be had for as low as $150 and, for larger properties, as much as $1,000. (The cost to Lower, Hoffa, and other Sun Valley principal investors worked out to a mere $18 per lot.) "Every detail of your business transaction can be handled by your local business agent," went the sales pitch. "Your investment has every safeguard....Stake your claim in the Teamsters' model city of tomorrow."

Despite Lower's promises, roads weren't paved, lots were not on "high, dry, and rolling land," and the land was under water during the rainy season. Teamsters often were on the hook for routine assessments even before ground was broken for houses. But Lower had made his money early in the deal by essentially conning union members. Hoffa set himself up to make his own killing later in the game. Members had no idea that Hoffa, who had already pocketed the $25,000 "loan" from Lower, had a secret deal to buy as much as 45 percent of the Sun Valley development on generous terms, to be executed whenever he found it financially advantageous.

That wouldn't be in 1959. On December 7, after getting approval from his bosses, prosecutor Dowd opened a grand jury investigation into Hoffa on charges of misusing union funds in the Sun Valley scheme. Dowd lined up witnesses to put under oath, subpoenaed Teamsters records going back to

1953, and, as the Justice Department required, filed a letter with the federal court announcing his intent.

As his business partners in the Florida land deal found themselves called before the grand jury, Hoffa realized that the Sun Valley probe had turned serious. The Teamsters tried to quash a subpoena for union records, and, never one to rely only on lawyers to keep him out of jail, Hoffa quickly put his hopes behind a crafty counterattack that had him traveling to Miami Beach to meet with a close friend of vice president Richard Nixon.

On December 13, 1959, Hoffa made his way across the lobby of the luxurious new Americana Hotel, past its multistory, glass-enclosed tropical rain forest and the trendy, 500-seat Carnival Room nightclub, frequented by Sinatra and his Rat Pack pals when performing or partying in Miami Beach, "America's Riviera." Hoffa did not know the man whose hotel suite he was visiting, former two-term California congressman Oakley Hunter, a lawyer and smooth operator in the nation's capital. The meeting had been arranged by Hoffa's pal Irving Davidson, a Washington fixer whose clients included political candidates, Nicaraguan dictator Anastasio Somoza, and the Israeli gun industry.

As soon as Hoffa walked into the suite, he made a show of taking off his suit jacket "to indicate he was not recording our conversation," Hunter would later recount. The lawyer took off his suit jacket, too—the white-collar version of a weapons pat-down. The precautions indicated that slippery topics were going to be discussed.

Hunter was well suited to subterfuge and sensitive assignments. He joined the FBI after law school in 1940 and served four years as a special agent before signing up with the Office of Strategic Services, the precursor to the CIA, working in Germany and London during World War II. He was elected to the US House in 1950, representing a district in Fresno, California, and aligned himself with rising political star Richard Nixon. At some risk, Hunter stood up for vice presidential candidate Nixon during his "Checkers" speech crisis in the fall of 1952, when Nixon scrambled to stay on the Republican ticket after press accounts revealed that he had taken $18,000 from wealthy Republican backers for personal expenses. Hunter told reporters that, for his own part, he had accepted $4,000 from supporters. His admission was intended to reassure voters that there was nothing to be alarmed about — the practice was widespread and, in fact, necessary for those less-than-wealthy Congress members who had to maintain households in Washington as well as back home. With help from Hunter and many others, Nixon weathered the crisis.

In the privacy of the beachfront hotel suite, Hunter spoke carefully: he told Hoffa he was not meeting him at Nixon's request, nor could he speak for the vice president. Hunter said he was solely interested in his friend Nixon's political future and how the Teamsters might brighten it. Hunter flattered Hoffa, telling him that he and Nixon had a lot in common. "You were hated by experts, you were both self-made men, you were both dedicated to [your] respective fields, and you both had lots of guts."

Hoffa replied that he wanted no favors; he could fight his own battles. If he or any of his union members broke the law, they should suffer the consequences. But he wasn't getting fair treatment from the federal government, Hoffa insisted. "Hoffa was in a pleasant, an almost exuberant mood," Hunter would report back to Nixon in a detailed memo. "He feels he is being made a scapegoat and a whipping boy. He said he is cleaning up his union as best and as rapidly as possible, that this kind of thing cannot be done overnight."

Hoffa made an offer: he knew he was "hot," and therefore

to endorse Nixon would do the candidate more harm than good. But top Teamsters officers in strategic cities could openly endorse Nixon and assist the campaign, which would be of considerable political benefit. Much could be done by knocking Kennedy, Hoffa added.

Attorney general William Rogers knew that his good friend Richard Nixon faced a problem when it came to Jimmy Hoffa. The Kennedys were not only attacking Hoffa as a racketeer run amok but also blasting the Eisenhower administration for its lackadaisical pursuit of the Republican-leaning Teamsters leader. Such accusations did little to help Vice President Nixon in his pursuit of the presidency. So Rogers came up with a plan in the meantime, one that involved a friend from the 1952 Republican presidential campaign, George MacKinnon, at that time a lawyer in private practice in Minneapolis. Rogers invited him to Washington and told him that "the most troublesome problem in the Department of Justice was that they had not been able to come up with any criminal prosecution of Jimmy Hoffa," MacKinnon was to say. "He indicated that the Department was getting a great deal of heat on that matter."[3] Feeling pressure from the public and Democrats and Republicans alike, Rogers urged MacKinnon to accept an emergency assignment as a special prosecutor to go after Hoffa.

MacKinnon was uniquely suited for the job. He was a Republican, a former congressman elected in 1946 along with freshman lawmakers Jack Kennedy and Dick Nixon. He also helped write section 186 of the landmark Taft-Hartley Act, which dealt with bribery in labor unions. This section barred union officials from taking money or anything of value from an employer whose workers the union represented. MacKinnon also convicted Teamsters official Sidney Brennan, Hoffa's man in Minneapolis, for section 186 violations.

After giving Rogers's request some thought, MacKinnon replied, "Well, I wouldn't mind taking that on."[4]

MacKinnon arrived in Washington in early 1960 and took over all the Justice Department's Hoffa investigations except for the Sun Valley case, which was being handled by prosecutor Jim Dowd. They both reported to the criminal division chief, Malcolm Wilkey. The Justice Department's plan was to quickly bring a case against Hoffa and, they hoped, knock out one of Kennedy's key campaign issues.[5] MacKinnon read the Justice Department files and the McClellan committee documents on Hoffa, then spent a month in Detroit examining the US attorney's files and all Hoffa's tax returns at the Internal Revenue Service.[6] After weeks of study, he decided that the best strategy for building the strongest criminal case against Hoffa was to target him and Bert Brennan for accepting money from the owners of Commercial Carriers after the two Teamsters officials settled a wildcat strike against the company. Hoffa and Brennan, through their wives, pocketed dividends of at least $115,000, as far as MacKinnon could quickly determine.[7]

He needed help from the FBI to work up the Test Fleet case properly. He outlined what he needed in an April 1960 memo to J. Edgar Hoover. He especially wanted the FBI to secure the corporate books from the truck company's Detroit lawyer, Carney Matheson, who had incorporated the Hoffa-Brennan entity in Tennessee.

MacKinnon told Wilkey that the Test Fleet case "will take a massive investigation, particularly so if the results are expected in the near future. The McClellan Committee material is helpful but the evidence produced at the hearings in many respects is almost as harmful as it is helpful. Too often, the nature of the questions hurt. Too often, the question assumes facts to be true which are not true and the assumption helps Hoffa. If a clean question had been asked the witness we might have received a true and helpful answer. It seems that too often the interrogator wanted to use the question to show how much *he* knew about the answer before the answer was given."[8] It was clear he was referring to Bobby Kennedy. Still, MacKinnon was excited—he would later write, "The case had been kicking around for fifteen years and nobody realized what they had."

At his brother's insistence, in late 1959, Bobby officially took on a job title he'd been asked about many times before— campaign manager. Jack's decision stung his chief aide, Ted Sorensen, the brilliant, bespectacled young Nebraska liberal who was described as Kennedy's alter ego. Sorensen had spent months and months on the road with the senator, accompanying him to local Democratic clubs across the country, meeting county party chairmen, collecting the names and backgrounds of thousands of volunteers and loyalists and coding them in an elaborate index-card system. Sorensen had devoted himself to Jack Kennedy, putting in punishing hours, neglecting his family, completely entranced by the Kennedy cause. Still, Bobby was the smart choice. He worked relentlessly, was absolutely loyal to Jack, and he was more patient and astute than anyone else in dealing with their father, the campaign's shadow moneyman and behind-the-scenes meddler-adviser.

With Bobby in charge, Sorensen remained policy chief, chief speechwriter, and keeper of the senator's Washington office. Kenny O'Donnell and Pierre Salinger, from the Rackets Committee staff, also joined the campaign's inner circle; like the rest of the team, they had no experience running a national campaign. Their most experienced political pro was Lou Harris, who had done polling and consulting for numerous governors and US senators. He had begun working with JFK on his successful 1958 Senate run, and since then Joe Kennedy had come to believe that the pollster was key to a successful presidential campaign.[9] "His father had made up his own mind that he was going to spend a lot of money, if that was what it would take, to see that Jack had a real run at the presidency," Kennedy's closest friend in the Senate, George Smathers of Florida, was to say. He said Joe Kennedy used polling "actually in the merchandise business and, much before anybody ever thought about it, in politics." The Kennedys signed up Harris for a $100,000 guarantee, and by the end of the campaign his firm's tab came to more than $300,000, or $2.4 million in 2015 dollars.[10]

At this point, the Kennedys' main concern was which key midwestern primary to enter — Wisconsin or Ohio. They didn't believe they had the money or the time to compete and win in both states at the same time.

On its face, Wisconsin presented a pitfall for JFK: Minnesota senator Hubert Humphrey, a rival Democratic contender for president, was known as Wisconsin's third senator because of his support for farmers and unions, powerful interest groups in both states. Beating Humphrey in his own backyard would be a tough task.

But Jack Kennedy, with his family wealth and his father's business savvy, took full advantage of Harris, the first private full-time pollster in a presidential campaign.[11] At the time, candidates didn't have their own pollsters; the Democratic Party or Republican Party would commission a survey, or big firms such as Gallup and Roper would be paid to ask questions for candidates. Harris would give Kennedy a significant tactical advantage.

When Kennedy first ran for the Senate in 1952 against Henry Cabot Lodge Jr., Smathers told his good friend he had no chance. Only later, Smathers said, did he learn that JFK had inside knowledge based on voter survey data. "Yes, I'm going to beat Henry Cabot Lodge, and here's what percent I'm going to beat him [by]," Smathers recalled Kennedy saying. "I said, 'You've got to be crazy, man, you can't do it.' And lo and behold, he did it." By 1960, Kennedy's edge was even more pronounced. "I do know that in 1960," Smathers recalled, "when the race began to get started...Jack Kennedy had the insight as to what were the issues in these various states in which he ran in the primaries....In Wisconsin, he knew exactly what the issues were."[12]

Harris surveyed twenty-three thousand people in Wisconsin in late 1959 and early 1960, an astonishing and expensive task. He told Kennedy that by focusing on the right issues he could carry the state — he was pulling 63 percent of the expected vote — and win delegates in eight of the ten congressional districts, some of them largely Protestant. In one fell swoop, Kennedy could knock out a fellow northern liberal and knock down the argument that he couldn't win outside of heavily Catholic areas, such as those in Milwaukee. Indeed, Jack Kennedy *needed* to run against Humphrey in Wisconsin and was counting on his own knowledge of the state as well as on its "third senator" being lulled by overconfidence.

But that strategy would only work if the Kennedys didn't have to campaign at the same time in Ohio, a crucial swing state with sixty-four delegates. Ohio governor Mike DiSalle held the key. Time and again, he privately told Jack Kennedy that he supported him for president, but when asked to immediately announce his support, DiSalle begged off. He said that because he was Catholic, like Kennedy, it would be better for both of them if another big-state governor, a non-Catholic, announced first. DiSalle was being coy. He wanted to be on the ballot, alone, running as a "favorite son" in Ohio's May primary. He easily would win the popular vote, and come to the national convention with sixty-four delegate votes to trade for promises of patronage, pork, and Ohio-friendly policies from Kennedy or whoever the nominee turned out to be. Kennedy was leading in the polls in late 1959, but he might lose either to senator Lyndon Johnson, from Texas, or Stuart Symington, from Missouri. If DiSalle could put off Kennedy until after the late-January deadline for getting on the Ohio primary ballot, DiSalle could run unopposed in the primary.

JFK assigned Bobby to pin down DiSalle. "You are mean and tough and can say more miserable things to Mike than I can say," he told Bobby, as Kenny O'Donnell recalled. "And, if you get too obnoxious, then I will disown and disavow what you said and just say to Mike, 'He's a young kid and does not know any better.' "

Bobby was not amused and threw off a sarcastic "Thanks a lot."[13]

Still, Bobby would do as JFK asked. John Bailey, the seasoned pol who ran Connecticut's Democratic Party, accompanied Bobby in late December of 1959 on the DiSalle visit and reported back to O'Donnell about how the meeting went. "Bobby was awfully tough, completely unreasonable, rude, and obnoxious and totally demanded that DiSalle come out immediately and if he did not, threatened him," Bailey would tell O'Donnell. If DiSalle didn't publicly announce his support, Bobby told him, his brother would run in the Ohio primary, spare no expense, and win, thereby humiliating DiSalle in his own state.

"DiSalle called me after the meeting and was furious," O'Donnell would later say. "He said to me Bobby was the most obnoxious kid he had ever met. He said Bobby practically called him a liar and said we can't trust you; you will do what you are told." At his brother's insistence, Bobby had turned to cutthroat tactics and tough talk, which further inflated his reputation as a ruthless political operator.

But it paid off.

On January 2, in the midst of the marble and majesty of the Senate's Caucus Room, the setting for so many confrontations with Hoffa, senator John F. Kennedy of Massachusetts formally announced that he was running for president. Three days later, Governor DiSalle, boxed in and realizing it was his only option, publicly announced he supported Kennedy for president.

On January 13, RFK made an interesting comment to the media, telling reporters that he advised his brother not to compete in Wisconsin's presidential primary in Wisconsin. It was unfair to expect Senator Kennedy to compete successfully against Minnesota senator Hubert Humphrey in his own backyard, he said — his brother would be happy to face Humphrey or any other candidates on "neutral" ground, such as Oregon, Maryland, or Indiana.

The story was a ruse. By then, Bobby had already deployed campaign staffers to Wisconsin, and the Kennedys already had their operation in place there. Polling in Wisconsin showed Kennedy with 63 percent of the vote, a massive lead over Humphrey. But Bobby wanted to lower expectations so that when his brother eventually won, the victory would seem more dramatic and hard-fought. Also, he didn't want the Kennedy campaign staff to get overconfident. So he continued the charade five days later in a Boston television interview, at station WBZ. "I think he'd have a very difficult time winning in Wisconsin," Bobby said of his brother.

Then came the reporter's question: "Do you expect that Jimmy Hoffa and his organization might pose a serious campaign threat?"

"No, I don't," the younger Kennedy replied. "Jimmy Hof-fa's already announced and has been making statements all along that he's extremely opposed to my brother getting the nomination and that he's going to use all his means to destroy him politically. He's marked him for political oblivion. He's going to spend money.... He's got a lot of money, millions and millions of dollars, and that money will be used to defeat my brother. I don't think there's any question about that. I don't think the people in the United States are going to follow the leadership of Jimmy Hoffa."[14]

The interviewer didn't seem to buy Bobby's rosy interpretation, though, and pushed again. "Do you think his opposition will be meaningless?"

"I think the money," Kennedy admitted, "will have some effect."

Hoffa was in fact at work on the Teamsters' effect on the race. On Sunday, January 24, 1960, Hoffa took a private plane to Mauston, Wisconsin, a busy trucking junction and resting spot halfway between Chicago and Minneapolis–Saint Paul. He had Teamsters business to conduct, but that was a cover for his real purpose, one he embraced with passion. About eight hundred Teamsters, their spouses, family members, and others had been rounded up by officials of the local and gathered near a speaker's platform at the Dell View Hotel. There Hoffa attacked Jack Kennedy with his by then familiar appeal to the class differences between the blue-collar audience and the Ivy League presidential candidate. Kennedy, he declared, was "a millionaire playboy brought up by handmaidens and educated in the best schools." His concern for the working class was completely false, Hoffa insisted. "Phony liberals are worse than reactionaries. Reactionaries you watch," but phony liberals lie in wait, embrace you, then "stab you in the back....You are stabbed to death, and then it's too late." Replying to a reporter's question, Hoffa said he planned to travel back to Wisconsin four or five times over the next several weeks to reengage in battle against the senator.

That same day, one hundred miles away, in Fond du Lac, Bobby Kennedy complained to supporters that Hoffa had marked his brother for "political extinction."

When Jack Kennedy officially kicked off his Wisconsin campaign on February 16 in Milwaukee with his wife, Jackie, at his side, he said he would run a positive campaign and not attack Senator Humphrey. "I do intend, when his name is mentioned, to speak well of him. I request, moreover, that everyone working on my behalf in this state abide by the same principles." He made no such promise about his shadow opponent and went after Hoffa directly. "I regret, too, that Mr. Hoffa and others are coming into Wisconsin to challenge my legislative record, my integrity, and my competence for the presidency. But I prefer to leave that judgment, too, to the people of Wisconsin — and I shall accept their decision on April fifth."

Wisconsin's presidential primary was particularly susceptible to voter mood swings (and behind-the-scenes mischief by the Teamsters) for one simple reason: it was an "open primary" — on Election Day voters could pick either a Republican or Democratic ballot. Harris's early polling had already revealed a reversal of the state's usual voting pattern. His survey picked up heavy Republican crossover, with Roman Catholic Republicans saying they planned to abandon Nixon to vote for Kennedy in the primary. Indeed, Harris showed JFK getting 83 percent of the Catholic vote, which accounted for nearly one-third of the Wisconsin electorate. Humphrey, a Protestant, was doing well with liberals, Protestant Democrats, and farmers in the districts along the Minnesota border. But unlike Kennedy, Humphrey was not benefiting from corresponding crossover — i.e., Protestant Republicans who said they'd vote for Humphrey because they did not want a Catholic to win.

The Kennedys kept Harris's promising results within the inner circle; the public wasn't yet aware that the senator from Massachusetts was expecting to win the Wisconsin presidential primary based on huge numbers of Republican votes. "The danger, of course, is that at the last minute the religious issue will be stirred and when it does, it will drive Republican Lutherans over to the Democratic primary to vote against Senator Kennedy," Harris warned in a February 13 memo. The pollster urged Kennedy not be photographed with priests or nuns at Catholic venues or to give the slightest appearance of any pro-Catholic favoritism.[15]

"The religious issue" stayed in the background until deceptive campaign ads caused it to explode into public controversy only five days before the April 5 primary.

By late March, Jack Kennedy had benefited from a well-funded race, flying around the state on the family's private plane, *Caroline*, and running generous TV ads. His sisters, brothers, friends, and mother, Rose, gave speeches and held receptions across the state. He outspent Humphrey four to one, based on the itemized records of campaign contributions and spending reports the candidates were required to file. His father likely spent much more under the table.

Humphrey was the better stump speaker by far. As mayor of Minneapolis, he had landed a slot at the 1948 Democratic convention to talk about an issue that defined him to his core, civil rights. Looking earnest in a double-breasted suit, with his thinning black hair slicked in place, he had pleaded with the delegates to add a progressive civil rights plank to the

Democratic Party platform. It was an overdue but divisive plan, certain to anger the southern Democrats. By the end of his eight-minute speech, Humphrey had most of the delegates on their feet, cheering, many standing on chairs, some with tears in their eyes. Unexpectedly, against the party leadership, the delegates approved the liberal plank by a comfortable margin. Years later, after seeing Humphrey work his emotional magic in the Senate, Johnson paid the man known as the Happy Warrior the highest compliment: "Hubert has the greatest coordination of mind and tongue of anyone I know."[16]

But unlike the Kennedys, Humphrey was disorganized and old-school. He traveled the snowy roads by bus or car, not by plane. The Happy Warrior groused about the wealth of his opponent — referring to Jack's "jack," saying "I'm not the candidate of the fat cats" — and seemingly everywhere he turned he was running into one of the Kennedys. *New York Times* columnist Scotty Reston echoed the complaint. He wrote of the ubiquity of the "members of the Kennedy Clan, all handsome in those elaborately planned simple clothes that make them look slimmer and simpler than they are....There they find the cover-boy in person: not only glamorous but intelligent, earnest and literate....It is the challenge of a wholly new generation with different arguments and manners and new political techniques out of the university and the theatre. It is, in short, the Presidential debut of the Organization men, with their wide minds and narrow lapels, and lovely wives in carelessly beautiful scarlet coats."[17]

Hoffa, too, remained present in Wisconsin, as promised. He taunted Bobby directly, calling him a coward for refusing to debate about labor issues and for hiding from Hoffa to avoid being served with legal papers. A short time before, Hoffa had filed a libel lawsuit against Bobby, NBC, and Jack Paar, host of *The Tonight Show*, over remarks RFK made during a July 22, 1959, appearance on the popular late night show. He had been deliberately provocative because, at the time, he wanted viewers to call their congressional representatives to support his brother's labor reform bill. Asked by Paar who was worse, Hoffa or Dave Beck, Bobby replied: "Dave Beck is just a thief." Paar, worried about libel, laughed nervously and joked, "I hope you know what you're doing!"

"They feel they're above the law," RFK went on. "They feel they can fix judges and juries. Mr. Hoffa has said every man has his price. This country can't survive if you have someone like him operating. . . . All of our lives are too intricately interwoven with this union to sit passively by and allow the Teamsters under Mr. Hoffa's leadership to create such a superpower in this country — a power greater than the people and greater than the government. . . . Unless something is done, this country is not going to be controlled by the people but is going to be controlled by Johnny Dio and Jimmy Hoffa and 'Tony Ducks' Corallo." Bobby's remarks were not any more incendiary than those made at the Senate hearings, but this time his words weren't shielded by congressional immunity. Hoffa sued for $2.5 million, saying he was the victim of a conspiracy between Kennedy and NBC to target and degrade him with false and "vicious attacks."[18]

Hoffa's Wisconsin tactics were just as chin-first as Bobby's television performance. But whether the labor boss was improving Humphrey's chances was in doubt. "Sen. Kennedy should pay Hoffa's expenses," a *Racine Journal-Times* columnist wrote, "because the more speeches Hoffa makes, the better it should be for the senator."[19]

Jack Kennedy also figured out that Hoffa's personal attacks might be working in his favor. At the end of a March 11 news conference, Kennedy was asked by a reporter if he had anything more to say, and the senator slyly added: "I would like to make a statement addressed to Mr. Hoffa, who is making a lot of remarks to the effect that he has been looking for my brother Bob for the last three months with a subpoena but hasn't been able to find him. Tell Mr. Hoffa that Bob has been in the state for the last three weeks and will be here for a while longer. And tell him I'll personally arrange for him to meet Bob if he so desires. And tell him that Bob intends to continue saying the same things about Mr. Hoffa."[20]

Perhaps most slyly, Bobby took every chance, by public inference and innuendo, to link the union boss to Humphrey. These clever tactics enraged Humphrey's good friend and campaign strategist, lawyer Joseph L. Rauh Jr. "Bobby didn't play fair on this," Rauh said. "He would go around saying, 'Hoffa's against us.' Well, there was an implication in there that Hoffa was for Humphrey. That was just nonsense, and Bobby threw that implication all around. I don't think that was fair, but it did hurt us."[21] Off the record, Bobby told friendly reporters that Hoffa was in Humphrey's camp and that the Teamsters were going to spend $2 million to defeat his brother, and he wondered why the Minnesota senator hadn't denounced Hoffa as the Kennedys had.

Eventually, Humphrey lost his patience at being tied to Hoffa and lashed out, aiming his barbs at Bobby in particular. The Kennedy "boys" didn't deserve the reputation as rackets busters, he fumed—he had fought racketeers as mayor of Minneapolis, actions that held far more political peril than serving on a congressional committee. "You are looking at a man who has fought the rackets all his life," he shouted in one speech. "And I did so before some of the people who are doing all the talking about rackets were dry behind the ears.

Whoever is responsible deserves to have a spanking. And I said 'spanking' because it applies to juveniles."

By mid-March, Humphrey settled on another tactic that began to move some voters his way. He taunted Kennedy for refusing to debate or to directly talk about their respective voting records, particularly on farm issues. Humphrey insisted every chance he got that only he was "a consistent friend of the farmer." Drop the "razzle-dazzle, fizzle-fazzle" and debate, he demanded. But the front-runner refused to engage.

Then, five days before Election Day, the two senators finally did find something they could agree on publicly.

It was a political ad, only two columns wide and four inches deep, but it appeared in 256 weekly newspapers across the state and inflamed anti-Catholic sentiment. Mild by today's standards, the ad "brought the primary campaign to a new peak of frenzy and bitterness."[22]

"Let's give Humphrey a square deal," the ad read. "The Democratic party rose to its greatest heights with the New Deal and the Square Deal. How about a square deal for one of its greatest liberals? Is Humphrey getting a square deal? A leading political pollster reported, 'The solidarity of Catholic voters behind Kennedy shows up as far greater than that of Protestants behind Humphrey. Five out of six Catholics who were interviewed favored Kennedy over Humphrey. Included are many normally Republican voters who say they would back Nixon against any Democrat except Kennedy.' Should the Republican voters quoted above determine who the Democratic nominee for president shall be?"

Those words fed the backlash that Harris had warned of and that the Kennedys feared.

Small print at the bottom of the ad said its sponsor was the Square Deal for Humphrey Committee. The Wisconsin

Newspaper Association, which placed the ad with its member
weeklies for $1,450, said the man who paid for them by check
was Charles Greene. A former chairman of the state Democratic Party, Greene lived in Tampa, Florida, and had come to
Wisconsin to get involved in the primary.

Since the ad had his name connected to it, Humphrey had
to move quickly. He put aside his campaign schedule and
held an emergency news conference. Any ads "that raise the
issue of religion or the ugly fact of bigotry are not of my making," he said, his voice full of outrage and hurt. "I repudiate
them! I deplore them! And I denounce them." Whoever was
exploiting religious bigotry was only hurting him, Humphrey
said.

Campaigning in Milwaukee that day, candidate Kennedy
soon condemned the ad as well. He told reporters he knew
Senator Humphrey as a respected colleague and didn't believe
his opponent could be responsible for such ugliness. But JFK
said he certainly wanted to know who had put up the money
for the ad buy. It wasn't long before his brother blamed the
ads on his all-purpose whipping boy, Hoffa. When reached
by reporters, Greene denied that Hoffa had anything to do
with financing the ad.

It was telling that none of the weeklies in heavily Catholic
Milwaukee County were asked to run the ad, indicating the
ad was intended to foment Protestant fear and backlash,
which could damage Jack Kennedy. A little-noticed inquiry by
the state attorney general many months later confirmed the
Teamsters' hand. Greene, who was unemployed at the time,
had been given the money for the ad by his good friend
Leonard Bursten, a successful Milwaukee lawyer who knew
Hoffa and, like Greene, lived in Tampa. Bursten and Greene
were old Wisconsin political cronies; in the late 1940s, they
ran Democratic politics in the state when Greene served as

state Democratic Party chairman before being ousted by a more liberal wing of the party. He moved to Tampa in the late 1950s to work at an engineering firm Bursten partly owned. By then more businessman than lawyer, Bursten had plans to build a seaside resort on an island just off Florida's Gulf coast, but was unable to get conventional loans from a bank, in part because the venture required a costly bridge to the island from the mainland. Bursten turned to Hoffa and the Teamsters' Hoffa-controlled Central States Pension Fund, which had a history of funding risky deals. Bursten secured a $4 million loan from the fund, at the time Central States' second-largest loan ever. He certainly was indebted to Jimmy Hoffa.

In the three days before the controversial ad ran in the weeklies, Bursten made nine long-distance calls to Greene, who was in Milwaukee for the primary. Telephone toll slips would show that Bursten also talked to people at Teamsters headquarters — even reaching Hoffa himself on his private line.[23]

How much did the Teamsters' dirty trick hurt Jack Kennedy?

Two months earlier, JFK owned Wisconsin's crossover vote, nearly all of it Catholic Republicans. In late March, before the ad controversy, JFK and journalist Ben Bradlee each guessed how many of Wisconsin's ten congressional districts Kennedy would carry, and each wrote his forecast on a piece of paper and sealed it in an envelope. Bradlee's guess: seven. Kennedy's prediction — nine. In the final days of the campaign, Harris's polling showed Kennedy's lead dwindling. On April 5, JFK's original Catholic Republican support was nearly balanced out by Protestant Republicans crossing over and voting for Humphrey.[24] JFK captured delegates not in nine congressional districts but in six, barely above a tie.

Instead of the predicted kayo to the "third senator" from Wisconsin, the Kennedys knocked Humphrey down but not out.

If Hoffa expected his efforts to defeat Jack Kennedy, by late evening on Election Day he had to be disappointed. JFK took the state with 56 percent of the vote, and in winning majorities in six of ten Wisconsin congressional districts he earned twenty-one and a half of the state's thirty-one convention delegate votes. But if the Kennedys expected their efforts to knock Humphrey from future primaries, they, too, were disappointed. Humphrey vowed that night to fight on. As they watched results in a Milwaukee hotel suite, JFK's sister Eunice wondered how to interpret the disappointing numbers that were casting gloom on her two exhausted brothers. "What does it all mean, Johnny?" she asked.

"It means," he replied wearily, "that we've got to go on to West Virginia in the morning and do it all over again. And we've got to go on to Maryland and Indiana and Oregon — and win all of them."[25] That meant RFK would be going to all those places — and so, he expected, would Jimmy Hoffa.

CHAPTER 11

Nixon's Favor

THE KENNEDY CAMPAIGN DID GO on—to West Virginia and Maryland and Indiana and beyond. Jack Kennedy faced a daunting confluence of forces: anti-Catholic sentiment, Hoffa's hostility, and behind the scenes efforts by senator Lyndon Johnson to derail the Kennedy bandwagon by supporting Hubert Humphrey. But he won the vote, time after time.

Bobby played a key role in his brother's success. Direct, no-nonsense, and so in tune with his brother's wishes and temperament that he could make decisions on the fly, he worked fiendishly long hours on the road. At the "Kennedy for President" headquarters, a nine-room suite on the top floor of an office building near the Capitol, he led staffers by example—or, if that failed, by caustic tongue. A card tacked on the wall next to press secretary Pierre Salinger's desk captured the mood: "As soon as the rush is over I'm going to have a nervous breakdown. I worked for it. I owe it to myself, and nobody is going to deprive me of it."

RFK may have found himself in a familiar role—subservient, serving Jack's career, running another campaign—but now it was a starring role, one that was helping him put his brother in the White House. Bobby's star turn surprised his friend Kenny O'Donnell, whose campaign duties included dealing with the "professionals," everyone from clubhouse hacks to party bosses such as mayor Richard Daley of Chicago, John Bailey of Connecticut, and Pennsylvania's David Lawrence. "The first strength and the first card that was now showing was that Bobby was totally recognizable due to the McClellan hearings," O'Donnell would later explain. "Bobby was known and really had become a national figure and was now totally acceptable to the professionals....They felt they could trust Bobby. They liked the way he talked, and they rather felt they were talking to the candidate when they were talking to him....This was to become a great ace in the hole for us in the future. Bobby lent an awful lot of clout to this thing."[1]

Contributing to his clout and celebrity was the fact that RFK became a bestselling author — in large part because of Jimmy Hoffa — in the spring of 1960 with *The Enemy Within*, described by the publisher as "A crusading lawyer's personal story of a dramatic struggle with the ruthless enemies of clean unions and honest management." RFK was following the successful path marked by Jack with his *Profiles in Courage*; they shared the same publisher (Harper & Brothers) and editor (Evan Thomas II). *The Enemy Within* came out at a point in Bobby's political career when it could do him the most good, undercutting his image of youth and inexperience, projecting seriousness instead.

RFK was determined to avoid the problems Jack encountered with *Profiles in Courage*. JFK's 1956 book was well written, was a hit at the cash register, was glowingly reviewed, and won the Pulitzer Prize for biography. But scuttlebutt circulated that the book was ghostwritten by Ted Sorensen, the senator's "intellectual alter ego."[2] Columnist Drew Pearson, interviewed on an

ABC network news show in December of 1957, said he knew "for a fact" that Kennedy hadn't written the book. The charge was picked up and repeated, staining Kennedy's reputation and infuriating his father. The senator engaged Clark Clifford, the former White House counsel, to demand a retraction from ABC, but Joe Kennedy told Clifford he wanted blood instead. "I want you to sue the bastards for fifty million dollars!" he raged over the telephone to Clifford. "Get it started right away. It's dishonest and they know it. My boy wrote the book. This is a plot against us."[3] Jack told Clifford to ignore his father's demands; ABC soon made a retraction and apologized.

To help him with his book, Bobby had employed a friend, John Seigenthaler, the tough *Nashville Tennessean* reporter who had exposed Teamsters corruption and violence in his home state and who subsequently covered the McClellan committee hearings. He, RFK, and two secretaries worked as a team on *The Enemy Within* in the months before Bobby had to join Jack's campaign full-time. Kennedy filled up legal pads in longhand, then his secretary, Angie Novello, typed up the pages and gave them to Seigenthaler. The reporter restructured, edited, cut, and polished the typescript, then Novello or another secretary, Dorothy Frey, retyped it. Working in tandem, they toiled through the summer and fall at Hickory Hill, "all day and often long into the night." In the afternoons, RFK and Seigenthaler took long walks, the newsman said, and "I got to know Bob Kennedy...better than I got to know anybody during my whole life. He was completely candid with me about everything."[4]

Just as the book was coming out, Seigenthaler joined RFK and his father at a restaurant in Manhattan. Bobby made a show of signing a copy of his book for Seigenthaler and, while his father looked on, added a note: "Thank you for writing my book for me." The two men smiled as old Joe got mad at his son: Grow up; stop joking around; people might see that and take it seriously. You saw what happened to Jack.[5]

In a review in the *New York Times*, Washington bureau reporter Joseph Loftus, who wrote often about the Teamsters and Hoffa, called *The Enemy Within* "an exciting, valuable and honest book" and offered his opinion that "Mr. Kennedy exposed himself and his family to terrible danger for three years."

Certainly in his book Kennedy had insulted and belittled Hoffa, saying he was weak, unbalanced, crooked, and greedy. But he'd never accused Hoffa of threatening Ethel and the kids. Hoffa was enraged that Loftus implied that he was a danger to RFK's family. As president of the nation's biggest union, Hoffa no longer had to throw punches or swing a chain to accomplish his goals; his tough reputation often was enough. But Hoffa had relied on threats, intimidation, and violence to punish strikebreakers, bring rebellious Teamsters in line, and bend company owners to his will. And when he felt the need, he directed threats and violence from his office on Capitol Hill, on one occasion giving precise instructions over a long-distance phone call to organizers about how to ambush nonunion drivers and frighten them with gunfire while avoiding injury.[6] Yet as part of a personal code, Hoffa said he drew a line at threatening women and children.

When Hoffa next encountered Loftus on Capitol Hill, the labor boss "accosted me with great fury," Loftus was to say. "I just sneered at him and he walked away." But "the tone that he used at me was a threatening kind of tone," and Loftus was not without worry. "Knowing his background and his ability to get even, why, I was somewhat concerned."[7]

Hoffa had less to worry about with Loftus than he did with federal prosecutor Jim Dowd, who in the spring of 1960

Jimmy Hoffa grew up in rural Indiana. At age eleven he moved with his family to Detroit, after his father died when he was small. Here he rides a horse, the symbol of the Teamsters. A teamster was originally a person who drove a team of horses. (*Detroit News*)

Young Hoffa, on his way up the ladder in Detroit, made his mark as a tough, fearless organizer. (*Detroit News*)

Hoffa shooting dice with the guys in Detroit in the 1940s. (*Detroit News*)

Hoffa holds back a smile as he sits next to Teamsters president Dave Beck. "Who's in charge, Jimmy?" Beck once asked Hoffa in front of reporters. "You are, Dave," he replied. (*Detroit News*)

After Hoffa established the Central States Pension Fund, he staged a media event and handed out checks in front of cameras. (*Detroit News*)

Jack, Bobby, and Teddy Kennedy at the family's Hyannis Port compound on Cape Cod in 1946. (John F. Kennedy Library)

Hoffa resented that RFK came from a wealthy family. From left: Eunice, Jack, Rosemary, Jean, Joe Sr., Teddy, Rose, Joe Jr., Kathleen, Bobby, and Pat. (John F. Kennedy Library)

Undersized Bobby (No. 86) willed his way onto the Harvard football team, where he forged a lifelong friendship with Kenny O'Donnell (No. 22), who would later work with him on the McClellan committee in the Senate. (John F. Kennedy Library)

Bobby greets his father aboard the *Joseph P. Kennedy Jr.* on April 12, 1946. He went AWOL for two days shortly thereafter while the ship continued to be docked near Boston. (John F. Kennedy Library)

The former Ethel Skakel and Robert F. Kennedy at their 1950 wedding. (John F. Kennedy Library)

The happy Hoffa family after Jimmy's surprise acquittal on bribery, Washington, DC, July 1957. From left: children, Jim and Barbara, Hoffa, and his wife, Josephine. (*Detroit News*)

The confrontations between Hoffa and chief counsel Robert Kennedy at the Senate Rackets Committee hearings captivated the public. Here, the two face off during August 1958 testimony, as investigator Walter Sheridan (center) homes in on a document handed to RFK. (Corbis)

As chief counsel, Bobby worked closely with Rackets Committee chairman senator John McClellan, an Arkansas Democrat. (Associated Press)

Harold Gibbons, Hoffa's No. 2 in the Teamsters, takes a smoke break with his boss in a Capitol hallway outside the Senate rackets hearings. (Associated Press)

Lawyer Edward Bennett Williams, left, suffered abuse from his client Hoffa, but his law firm benefited by handling the union's legal work across the country. Here he and Hoffa tangle with questioning from chief counsel Robert Kennedy and the lawmakers on the Senate Rackets Committee. (Associated Press)

Electronic surveillance wizard Bernard Spindel, left, at his and Hoffa's trial for illegal wiretapping in 1957. The federal jury couldn't reach a verdict. (Library of Congress)

Despite support from the president, attorney general Robert Kennedy had less than full support from FBI director J. Edgar Hoover (center) to pursue labor racketeers and organized crime. (John F. Kennedy Library)

Bobby, Ethel, a few of their children, and some cousins sail off the coast of Hyannis Port, Massachusetts. (John F. Kennedy Library)

Ethel and Bobby playing touch football in 1961. (John F. Kennedy Library)

Robert and Ethel Kennedy and family on the front lawn of their Hickory Hill estate in McLean, Virginia. (John F. Kennedy Library)

The three Kennedy brothers at the White House in 1963, shortly after Ted took office as senator from Massachusetts. (John F. Kennedy Library)

Barbara Hoffa and her fiancé, Robert Crancer, met at the 1961 Teamsters convention in Miami Beach and married three months later. She later became a lawyer. (Associated Press)

Edward Grady Partin, a Louisiana Teamsters official with a long rap sheet, turned on Hoffa in 1962 to get out of jail. Partin's testimony in a 1964 trial in Chattanooga resulted in Hoffa's conviction, capping RFK's seven-year quest to put him in prison. (Library of Congress)

Louisiana Teamsters official Edward Grady Partin, left, wormed his way into Hoffa's camp at the 1962 Test Fleet trial in Nashville in order to find evidence of jury tampering. He walks outside the federal courthouse with Hoffa's lawyer, William Bufalino of Detroit, Hoffa, and Tennessee Teamsters official Ewing King, right. Hoffa and King were later charged with tampering with the Nashville jury. (Associated Press)

The Hoffa family leaves the Hotel Patten in Chattanooga to walk to the courthouse where Jimmy was on trial in 1964 for jury tampering. From left: Jim Hoffa and his sister, Barbara Crancer, Hoffa, and Josephine. (Associated Press)

Attorney General Robert Kennedy testifying before Congress, 1963. (Library of Congress)

was investigating Hoffa's shaky Sun Valley land deal. Dowd was not a fan of John F. Kennedy, either. He had told one of Hoover's top assistants, Cartha "Deke" DeLoach, that Kennedy might not possess the character to be president. A friend of Dowd's who worked in the Capitol had told him about a disturbing photo on JFK's desk, Dowd told Hoover's man. It showed Kennedy and his buddies on a yacht with "several girls in the nude." Security guards and the cleaning staff "were aware of the photograph and that Kennedy's 'extracurricular activities' were a standard joke around the Senate Office Building."[8] This hearsay account didn't explain why a man running for the White House would display such a photo, but DeLoach added mention of it to JFK's expanding FBI dossier.

Despite Dowd's dismay with Kennedy, he didn't let it interfere with efforts to indict Hoffa. By the summer of 1960, Dowd felt that the investigation into Sun Valley was ready to be presented to a federal grand jury. His Justice Department superiors reviewed his work and agreed that Hoffa and his associates should be indicted, so Dowd traveled to Orlando, the federal court district with jurisdiction over the case, and began to present evidence and witnesses to the grand jury. Then one day, nearing the end of his presentation, Dowd was called out of the grand jury room and, to his surprise, told by his superiors to suspend his work and return to Washington.

Dowd was upset that the indictments, for reasons he couldn't fathom, were being held up at the highest level of the Justice Department. He later unburdened himself privately to Rackets Committee investigator Walter Sheridan, Hoffa's determined pursuer. "[Dowd] was in the grand jury room summing up to get an indictment when he was called on the telephone, called out of the room, and told to come back to Washington," Sheridan would later say. "When he got back they raised all kinds of questions of why was he doing this? He told them he'd been authorized to do it. It was obvious to him that something was wrong." Dowd later learned that Hoffa, by reaching out to the vice president through Oakley Hunter, had made a deal with Nixon: if the Justice Department would lay off the Sun Valley case, the Teamsters would back Nixon for president and help him defeat Kennedy.

Prosecutor MacKinnon ran into the same problems and found his case "thwarted by colleagues in the Justice Department." Months into his Test Fleet investigation, the Justice Department made a surprising turn and decided it didn't want to aggressively pursue Hoffa. "The Criminal Division, for reasons unknown to me, took it upon themselves to prepare an opinion indicating that the Test Fleet case would not be sound legally, which was a pure farce," MacKinnon was to write. "I was so upset about that development that I decided to go back to Minneapolis."[9]

It took more than a year for MacKinnon and Dowd to learn the reason behind the Justice Department's puzzling hot-cold behavior with Hoffa. Muckraking columnist Drew Pearson provided the answer after he got his hands on Oakley Hunter's letters to Hoffa and to Nixon. The documents exposed the sleazy trade-off between Nixon and Hoffa as brokered by ex-congressman Hunter. It was astonishing that Hoffa had been able to influence justice at such high levels.

The burly labor boss also intended to influence the outcome of the 1960 Democratic National Convention, if he could. To Hoffa's dismay, Jack Kennedy had won each of the seven presidential primaries he entered and in early July headed to the convention in Los Angeles as the clear favorite. He was only a few dozen delegates short of the 761 needed to clinch the nomination. He arrived tanned, looking relaxed and out-wardly healthy, but he and Bobby were nervous. They believed they had to win on the first ballot at the convention, other-wise Senate majority leader Lyndon Johnson, with his dedi-cated southern delegates and strong ties to northern party bosses, might be able to start a stampede on subsequent bal-loting as voting blocs shifted, looking to coalesce around a winner.

Hoffa and his political director, lawyer Sid Zagri, were in Los Angeles, too, working to deny Kennedy a first-ballot victory.

Behind the scenes, Hoffa quietly set out some snares, hop-ing to entangle the Kennedys or their campaign staffers in misconduct. Well aware of JFK's reputation as a womanizer, Hoffa tried to see if an operative could spring a honey trap at the Biltmore Hotel (the convention's headquarters) or at some of the other hotels, bars, and parties connected to the politi-cal spectacle. The plan would be to hire call girls to try to seduce Kennedy and his associates and, if possible, gather evidence of the assignations with hidden recorders or cam-eras. Hoffa had relied on sexual blackmail in the past. (He bragged to associates that he had dirt about the extracurricu-lar sex lives of nearly half the members of Michigan's congres-sional delegation.[10]) He indicated that he used the information to keep certain lawmakers voting his way; he didn't use the dirt to destroy them. But with the Kennedys, it would be different.

Hoffa got in touch with Fred Otash, "private eye to the stars," a handsome, dark-haired detective whose client list included Frank Sinatra, mobster Mickey Cohen, and some of Hollywood's most celebrated movie stars. If anyone could dig up dirt on Jack Kennedy in Los Angeles, it would be Otash, a former vice cop who was determined to be the city's top private eye. Six feet tall, a solid two hundred pounds, an ex-marine and judo instructor, he joined the Los Angeles Police Department after World War II. He was promoted to the vice squad, where he acquainted himself with the city's hookers, touts, wiseguys, and gamblers, and eventually he became a player in this demimonde himself. By the early 1950s, Otash moonlighted in private investigation, drove a new blue Cadillac, and was dating Swedish actress and pinup star Anita Ekberg. He quit the force in 1955 after clashing with superiors who believed his business pursuits interfered with his police work.

Otash made a small fortune doing divorce work. In the days before no-fault divorce, he was able to easily provide grounds for divorce by taking advantage of the miniaturization of microphones and recorders and loose state laws against eavesdropping. He was on retainer for *Confidential*, the country's most popular magazine in the mid-1950s, a gutter-sniffing, sensational, gaudy gossip rag owned by Robert Harrison. With more than three million in monthly circulation, *Confidential* appealed to readers by promising Hollywood titillation and the political lowdown with such stories as "Why Sinatra Is the Tarzan of the Boudoir" and "The Real Reason for Marilyn Monroe's Divorce."

Besides Otash, *Confidential* benefited from a spy network of lesser private investigators, hack journalists, waiters, call girls, and "75-dollar-a-week starlets who were on the rosters of the major studios and were going nowhere except to bed anyone who might boost their careers."[11] One such operative was a beautiful but struggling actress named Francesca De Scaffa, who slept with movie stars and captured their pillow talk with a miniature recorder. She supplied *Confidential* with more than two dozen stories in the mid-1950s, making an estimated $40,000 for betraying her colleagues.[12]

Otash and his operatives staked out cheating movie stars, bugged apartments, and procured affidavits and surveillance photos as proof. He had little loyalty to his clients; Otash was known to sell incriminating photos back to *Confidential*'s targets for the right price or, failing that, deliver them to the magazine for an upcoming issue. He did work for Hoffa's lawyer, Edward Bennett Williams, who once used him to babysit mobster Frank Costello in a New York hotel room while Williams went to court to try to get charges against Costello dropped. According to Otash, he and the man called the prime minister of the underworld played cards and listened to baseball on the radio.

Otash had at least two burning reasons to help Hoffa: he needed the money and he hated Bobby Kennedy. In 1959, the third year of the Rackets Hearings, Otash clashed offstage with chief counsel Kennedy. RFK's investigators had been digging into the mob's jukebox and vending machine business in Los Angeles. Racketeers loved the industry's untraceable, easily skimmed cash and the ease with which they could threaten tavern owners and small businesses into using only the underworld's approved machines. Otash had done some legwork for a vending machine operator who was being muscled by a company connected to Mickey Cohen, the tiny, dapper LA mobster. When Otash arrived at a waiting room in the New Senate Office Building, he spotted Cohen, whom he considered a friend, and shook hands. Otash warned Cohen that he planned on testifying about the facts he had dug up on the competing vending machine companies; so if Mickey was going to answer questions, Otash appeared to be saying, it would be in his best interest to stick with the same facts or else one of them might end up facing perjury charges. Bobby witnessed the exchange and, not unreasonably, interpreted it as two slippery witnesses rehearsing their stories so they couldn't be played off against each other by Senate inquisitors. Kennedy yelled at Otash, telling him to shut up and not talk to any other witnesses. As Otash later recounted the incident, he replied, "Go fuck yourself!"[13]

That same year, Otash was investigated for conniving with jockeys, trainers, and bettors to fix horse races at Santa Anita Park, in Southern California, and Agua Caliente Racetrack, in Tijuana. He was convicted of conspiracy to dope a horse at Santa Anita, a felony, which was later reduced to a misdemeanor. But he lost clients as a result, and the state of California moved to strip him of his private investigator's license. Steady work for Hoffa and the Teamsters could save him.

Confidential already "was investigating a rumor of 'an indiscreet party' at Sinatra's Palm Springs home attended by Sen[ator] John F. Kennedy and actor Peter Lawford, a Kennedy brother-in-law," an informant had told the FBI. With any luck, Otash likely figured he could serve both the scandal sheet and Hoffa with this new assignment.

On the evening of July 10, 1960, the day before the convention officially kicked off at the Los Angeles Memorial Sports Arena, Otash got in touch with "a high-priced Hollywood call girl" he had cultivated.[14] He figured her to be a good candidate to question about salacious conduct by the Kennedys. He pressed her about whether she was ever intimate with John F. Kennedy. He also asked whether she ever had sex with actors Peter Lawford, Frank Sinatra, or Sammy Davis Jr.

Otash hadn't selected these three names by chance. Lawford was married to Kennedy's sister Patricia, and through Lawford, Kennedy came to know Sinatra and his crew of Hollywood drinking buddies. For three weeks in February, Frank Sinatra and these buddies, Dean Martin, Sammy Davis Jr.,

Joey Bishop, and Peter Lawford, spent their days in Las Vegas filming *Ocean's 11*, a caper flick about a group of veterans robbing Vegas casinos. At night, they performed onstage together at the eight-hundred-seat Copa Room in the Sands hotel and casino. Their show was a mix of tunes, impromptu clowning, and skits, with Davis dancing, a bar set up front and center, and teetotaler Joey Bishop writing the material. They called their act the Summit at the Sands, a play on their nickname for their group, the Summit, when they got together. (The newspapers and fan magazines would soon dub them the Rat Pack, but they didn't use that term at the time.) People slept overnight in their cars off the Strip so they could get in line to try to score a ticket to the Copa Room shows.

With informants everywhere, the FBI noted in its Kennedy file that "a steady stream of chorus-line dancers and minor starlets made their way to the Senator's motel room at the Sands casino." Otash and his call girl came up with nothing, though.

The next day, she traded up, calling the FBI's Los Angeles office and telling an agent that Otash was trolling for dirt on Kennedy and his friends. Within hours, agents visited Otash in his office.

He was not disturbed by the visit. An FBI informant himself, he was comfortable with the sleazy trading of gossip and dirt. *Confidential* was "looking for dirt on Kennedy or Lawford" for use in a series of articles to run before the November election, he told the FBI agent. He revealed that someone—he refused to name the person—was attempting to "spy on Senator Kennedy's hotel room." The client likely wanted a bug planted in Kennedy's room, and Otash had worked with the top wiremen in Los Angeles.

Later, Otash telephoned his call-girl source again and

asked if she could arrange to be introduced to Senator Kennedy. "He suggested that he would like to equip her with a recording device for taking down any 'indiscreet statement' the Senator might make," the FBI reported in a memo that went up the ranks to director Hoover.[15] She told the FBI that she refused.[16]

In another effort to deny Jack Kennedy the nomination, Hoffa joined forces with Senate majority leader Johnson, who was trying to stop JFK from winning on the first ballot. With no victor at that point, the convention would be "brokered," with another round of delegate voting after horse-trading by party leaders and powerful local pols, a situation that favored Johnson. Hoffa had already met with John Connally, Johnson's top adviser, and promised that the Teamsters would support the Texas senator with money and a voter-turnout effort if Johnson won the nomination. To help him reach that goal, Zagri, with Hoffa's blessing, told Los Angeles–area Teamsters officials to whip up turnout for an impromptu rally at the airport when Johnson arrived for the convention. A few hundred people showed up at the rally, displaying no overt signs that they were part of a Hoffa operation. But Sheridan, Bellino, and other former McClellan committee staffers now working for the Kennedy campaign had sources inside the Teamsters union, and it was impossible not to see Hoffa's hand. In a statement, Bobby called the airport rally "just another crude effort" by Hoffa to try to influence the nomination.[17] "The delegates to the Democratic convention can do without interference from Mr. Hoffa and Mr. Zagri."

Hoffa also backed a "draft-Stevenson" movement, a maneuver that essentially served as a front for Johnson. Former Illinois governor Adlai Stevenson, the unsuccessful Democratic presidential candidate in 1952 and 1956, was the sentimental favorite of Eleanor Roosevelt and other liberals. If nominated, he had little chance of winning. But he held strong ties to certain of those attending the convention, and if he won over only one-tenth of the more than fifteen hundred delegates, he would deny Kennedy his first-ballot victory. The Kennedy camp had its suspicions about Stevenson confirmed when senators Eugene McCarthy and Hubert Humphrey, believed to be Johnson supporters, arrived in Los Angeles and then unexpectedly announced their support for Stevenson.[18]

When Stevenson, a delegate, arrived at the crowded convention hall to sit with the Illinois delegation, novelist Norman Mailer, covering the political spectacle for *Esquire* magazine, described the scene: "The day before the nominations, he entered the Sports Arena to take his seat as a delegate — the demonstration was spontaneous, noisy and prolonged; it was quieted only by Governor Collins's invitation for Stevenson to speak to the delegates."

But the seemingly emotional outpouring for Stevenson was in significant measure staged with Teamsters union cash. The "draft Stevenson" forces had packed the convention with paid actors, college students, and others who would cheer for Stevenson on cue. To get around restrictions that only those with credentials could assemble on the main floor, the "draft Stevenson" workers smuggled out credentials from supporters already on the floor, relay after relay, to bring in successive waves of new pro-Stevenson demonstrators.

Hoffa provided the money for these ringers — $50,000 or more, according to delegate Dan Gilbert, a former Chicago police captain who, as head of the department's labor squad, was well connected in union and political circles.[19] The spectacle was managed by a key backer of the draft-Stevenson movement, Dore Schary, a former movie studio president, playwright, and liberal activist. "Schary was up in the balcony," Gilbert would later explain. "They had guys in sections all over the place to catch his signals and run the show. He sat down by Mrs. Roosevelt and put his legs over the rail of a front box [where] he stood out.

"Suddenly, all over the balcony, the signs came out and they raised hell. First Schary gave his section guys the up sign with the hands and the mob came up yelling. They had a time limit and he was obeying the rules. Pretty soon, he gave them the down signal. Down they went.... Schary played that mob like Toscanini."

Gilbert said his union sources told him that the "Stevenson show must have cost Hoffa from $50,000 to $100,000. They got those guys from the colleges around Los Angeles and all kinds of political clubs and the casting bureaus and modeling agencies."[20]

With the crowd whipped up (even some young Kennedy supporters took off their campaign boaters before clapping for Stevenson), some political operatives believed Stevenson might have a chance to throw the convention into a deadlock on the first vote.

Called to the stage of the sports arena, Stevenson made his way through the packed floor, took the stage as the crowd roared, and thanked people for the raucous outpouring, the first real public excitement of the convention, by then two days old. "I am grateful for this tumultuous and moving welcome," said Stevenson, known as an eloquent and witty speaker. "After getting in and out of the Biltmore Hotel and this hall, I have decided I know whom you are going to nominate." He paused. Would the reluctant candidate throw in his name, promise to fight, pump the emotion even higher? No. With a grin and a flip of his hand, he revealed the nominee: "It will be the last survivor."

Stevenson's prevarication "broke the roar of excitement for his presence. The applause as he left the platform was like the dying fall-and-moan of a baseball crowd when a home run curves foul."[21]

A less reluctant performance by Stevenson might have shifted enough delegates to vote his way, throwing the convention into a second round of balloting, in which the first-ballot promises to Jack Kennedy would be adrift and the party bosses and their delegates would coalesce around a different candidate. A New York newspaper columnist at the convention, a dedicated supporter of Stevenson, complained bitterly to Norman Mailer about the Illinois politician's balky response to the adoring crowds and just how close he came to making a difference. "If he'd only gone through the motions, if he had just said that now he wanted to run, that he would work hard, and he hoped the delegates would vote for him. Instead he made that lame joke."

And it would be Kennedy who won on the first ballot.

RFK, O'Donnell, Salinger, and others were exhausted when Jack triumphed on the first ballot. Even so, immediately after the convention Bobby jumped back into the national campaign without taking a break. He insisted it was time to get to work. If people wanted to rest, they could do so after the election. The candidate, with a bad back and weak immune system compromised by his Addison's disease, needed to take a short vacation, but a pause was the furthest thing from Bobby's mind. Jack Kennedy later marveled to a friend about his dedicated brother. "He's the hardest worker I've ever seen. He's the best organizer. He went right to work after the convention, he took no time off. He's fantastic."[22]

Over the next few months, Bobby cemented his reputation

for being a ruthless political operator. Disdaining hand-holding and pleasantries, Bobby offended old-school party bosses and their minions with his rude urgency. "All they did was sit around and talk," Bobby complained. "They never got off their asses." He dismissed their unimaginative, cookie-cutter strategy: hold a candidate rally, turn out a crowd, and get their photos taken with Jack Kennedy. "I don't care if they like me or not," Bobby said as the complaints came in. "Jack can be nice to them. I don't try to antagonize people, but if they are not getting off their rear ends, how do you say that nicely?"

The Kennedys were putting in practice a theory they had held for years, one shared by their father: one of the biggest problems with the Democratic Party was the lack of a tough guy at its core, someone who could and would say no. It surprised no one that after Bobby took on the tough-guy role, complaints that he was hurting the campaign made it into reporters' notebooks.

Jack Kennedy would have none of it. "People get mad but they get mad whatever you do," he said. "Whatever moves things, upsets someone. You can't make an omelet without breaking the egg. I don't pay attention to the beefs. Every politician in Massachusetts was mad at Bobby after 1952 but we had the best organization in history."[23] His father admired his son's toughness but said it was far from ruthless. "Ruthless?" Joe Kennedy said. "As a person who has had the term applied to him for 50 years, I know a bit about it. Anybody who is controversial is called ruthless. Any man of action is always called ruthless. It's ridiculous."[24]

Jack Kennedy did worry that Bobby was wearing himself out. "I don't think he's as patient as I am," he said at the time. "But he's overtired. First he went through the McClellan hearings. Then he wrote his book. And then he joined me. He's living on nerves." The candidate blamed a lack of sleep when Bobby criticized baseball legend Jackie Robinson after he endorsed Nixon for president. When Kennedy learned of his brother's stumble, he put his head between his hands and muttered, "We're not running against Jackie Robinson."

No — they were running against a newly empowered Nixon.

Shortly after the Democratic convention, FBI director Hoover, a Nixon supporter, had the confidential FBI files of the entire Kennedy family moved into his office for convenience and safekeeping.[25] He also had his staff prepare a dossier on JFK, summarizing the best intelligence about the presidential candidate sifted from Hoover's Official and Confidential files, the Bureau's juiciest information on prominent citizens. The Kennedy dossier, the synthesis of more than two decades of reports on JFK, his father, and their family members, made for fascinating reading. It noted the Kennedy family's long ties to Hoover, their friendly relations, the congratulatory notes back and forth between Hoover and JFK about each other's books. But under the section entitled "Miscellaneous," the FBI noted: "As you are aware, allegations of immoral activities on Senator Kennedy's part have been reported to the FBI over the years....They include...data reflecting that Kennedy carried on an illicit relationship with another man's wife during World War II; that...Kennedy was 'compromised' with a woman in Las Vegas; and that Kennedy and Frank Sinatra have in [the] recent past been involved in parties in Palm Springs, Las Vegas and New York City. Regarding the Kennedy-Sinatra information, *Confidential* magazine is said to have affidavits from two mulatto prostitutes in New York."[26]

Sinatra and Jack Kennedy were friends. The singer, active

in liberal causes (his mother was a Democratic ward leader in New Jersey), had adapted his popular song "High Hopes" so that it could be used as the theme of Kennedy's 1960 campaign. He publicly endorsed Kennedy for president in October of 1958, after having ingratiated himself with the Kennedys—particularly Joe Kennedy—years earlier. And he would soon invest with him in Cal-Neva Lodge, a casino in the Sierra Nevada foothills at the California-Nevada border. Hoover's Kennedy dossier also included details of JFK's intimate relationship with Judith Campbell, a frisky, brown-haired woman whom Sinatra introduced him to in Las Vegas on February 7, 1960. She also dated the Chicago mob boss Sam Giancana.

Later in the summer of 1960, Hoover slipped his salacious JFK dossier to candidate Richard Nixon.[27]

In the final six weeks of their race to the White House, Kennedy and Nixon faced off in four televised debates—a new twist in national politics, one that would forever change the face of future presidential campaigns. The first debate took place in the CBS studios in Chicago on September 26. Each candidate was allowed to make an eight-minute opening statement and then, after fielding questions from the moderator, a three-minute closer.

Speechwriter Ted Sorensen and Kennedy aides presented the senator with a draft of an opening statement that he rejected as "too rhetorical." In going over the draft, they had to decide whether Kennedy would specifically attack Hoffa by name in the opening remarks. The morning before the debate, JFK rehearsed with his team, working through a stack of three-by-five cards that displayed debate points and Nixon policy positions, flicking them to the hotel floor one by one once he felt he had mastered the topic. He had lunch with Bobby, Sorensen, and Lou Harris, who advised JFK to slow down when he spoke. Bobby insisted that Jack take an afternoon nap and be fully refreshed.

At the CBS studios, Kennedy was selected to go first. In front of a televised audience of seventy million viewers, the Massachusetts senator—tanned, confident—began in a slightly rushed tempo.

"This is a great country," he intoned, "but I think it could be a greater country; and this is a powerful country, but I think it could be a more powerful country." Then he listed ways he thought the country was falling short.

"I'm not satisfied when the Soviet Union is turning out twice as many scientists and engineers as we are.

"I'm not satisfied when many of our teachers are inadequately paid, or when our children go to school [in] part-time shifts. I think we should have an educational system second to none.

"I'm not satisfied when I see men like Jimmy Hoffa—in charge of the largest union in the United States—still free."[28]

It was a remarkable attack—a man who wanted to be president calling one of the most powerful figures in the country a criminal who should be in prison. Hoffa was the only public figure except for Soviet premier Khrushchev whom Kennedy named in his remarks—and he was tougher on Hoffa.

In the next day's newspapers, political pundits and editorial writers called the groundbreaking debate a draw. There was little comment then on what later would become conventional wisdom about the debates—that Kennedy, controlled and telegenic, clearly defeated perspiring, shifty-eyed, pasty-faced Richard Nixon.

What did draw attention was Kennedy's dramatic assault on the Teamsters leader, which went beyond what JFK had been saying earlier that year. A few days later, on NBC's evening news show, *The Huntley-Brinkley Report*, Kennedy was asked, "You said the other night you regretted Mr. Hoffa was still president of the union and still free. What did you mean by that, exactly?"

Kennedy didn't soften his words. "Because I think Mr. Hoffa has breached national law, state law. I don't think the prosecutions have been handled against him very satisfactorily. I think there is a great question of how effectively the prosecution presented and, in addition, whether all the available cases have been used." It was a familiar thesis—blaming the Eisenhower Justice Department—one that Bobby detailed in *The Enemy Within*.

Even so, some in the Kennedy camp believed Jack's slam on Hoffa was too harsh, so much so that it created sympathy for Hoffa. "I think John Kennedy's statement that Hoffa should be in jail was a mistake," said Walter Sheridan, the committee investigator working on the Kennedy campaign. "I think it cost him some union votes that [it] didn't have to."[29] Staffers in New Mexico, Oregon, and other states offered the same judgment.

But Jack and Bobby Kennedy knew that the downside to bashing Hoffa was limited, at least according to Harris, whose associates had done extensive polling of voters' attitudes that summer. He put his analysis in a strategy memo for the campaign. "In the document were two very strong messages," Harris would later explain. "One was about Jimmy Hoffa. It said: you've got to get rid of Jimmy Hoffa. He's bad news all the way. The America people think he is. He's a blight on the labor movement, [a] blight on the country, and it's got to be done. The other thing is Castro. You've got to get rid of Castro. Castro is—and this reflected public opinion; people want Castro and Hoffa gone. Now, the person who took that most seriously was Bobby. Because he'd always say, 'Lou, you're right. We've got to get rid of Hoffa.' "[30]

Despite the relentless demands of running an international union of nearly one and three-quarter million members, Hoffa spent considerable time and union treasure to influence the election. Hoffa was determined not to be cast out of his own office, and that fall, Hoffa kept his promise to the Nixon camp about using the Teamsters grassroots operation to savage Kennedy. Whether by press release, the monthly *International Teamster* magazine, or his own speeches and press conferences, Hoffa served as a one-man Kennedy wrecking crew, calling him antiunion, a spoiled millionaire, "a fraud on the American people," and misspelling RFK's name to make it seem girlish. He said the Kennedys wanted to do away with the union itself. "The Kennedys — Jack and Bobbie — repeat their chorus with predictable regularity, 'Hoffa must go.' They are embarrassed by their failure to destroy an individual and rip an organization asunder."[31]

To wage war more effectively, Hoffa enlisted several proxies. The union's education department, which had an extensive lending library of Teamsters-produced movies, distributed a short attack film for viewing by members at their locals, featuring popular Oregon senator Wayne Morse — effective propaganda because it didn't specifically defend Hoffa and because Morse was a Democrat who blistered Kennedy from a prolabor perspective. Stretching the truth, Morse called Kennedy the man "most responsible" for "one of the most antilabor bills" in history, the 1959 Landrum-Griffin Act. The AFL-CIO, which didn't want to do anything that would help Nixon, said it would not use the Morse film.

Hoffa also used his public relations apparatus to try to

exploit Bobby's occasional intemperate remarks. In an interview with a magazine reporter that summer, the weary Kennedy campaign manager revealed his belief that "the two hundred lawyers who take their money from the Teamsters are legal prostitutes....Most of them are criminal lawyers. They spend their time trying to keep Mr. Hoffa in office rather than representing the union membership."

It was a dumb comment, a distraction for the campaign, and Hoffa pounced. In an editorial that he sent out to Teamsters, he blasted Bobby's beliefs as unconstitutional and authoritarian: "Another example of the Kennedy family's arrogant and dictatorial philosophy is found in Brother Bobby's published reference to Teamster attorneys as 'legal prostitutes.' Later, Bobby endeavored to wiggle out of this one by saying he meant only those lawyers who defended the Teamsters in 'criminal' cases. This only compounds the dirty deed. For Bob Kennedy's hatred of the Teamsters Union and its officers is well known, thanks to his performance with the McClellan Committee. Apparently this hatred has moved Bob Kennedy—himself a lawyer—to entertain the strange notion that the Teamsters Union and its officers are unworthy of having legal counsel to defend themselves against his vicious charges. A lawyer who dares to defend a Teamster against the Kennedy family is a 'legal prostitute.' "[32]

At some point, Hoffa needed some cover with union members to explain his sudden, full-throated support for a Republican with conservative credentials. So he credited Nixon with a "break" from GOP orthodoxy. Without providing any specifics, Hoffa insisted that there had been "a deep and basic change in the Republican Party"[33] and pointed to the moderate Republican governor of New York, Nelson Rockefeller, as proof. Just four days before Election Day, when there was little time for a counterattack from the Kennedy campaign,

Hoffa crossed a line. He told members they "would be better off" voting for Nixon. "His background puts him in a position to understand what it means to be poor and to have to earn a living."[34]

The week before the election, polls showed Nixon leading by less than 1 percent. On Election Day, November 8, results poured in, but the race was too close to call by midnight, even in Hoffa's home state, Michigan. By early morning, Hoffa was more than disappointed. Kennedy had not only won but had also won across the board. The results were a stunning rebuke for Jimmy Hoffa and his team. Of the forty members of Congress the Teamsters had worked to defeat—officials whom the union had branded as public enemies of labor—only one incumbent failed to get reelected. Hoffa could call a strike or steer the fortunes of the nation's trucking industry, but his famous iron grip fell slack in the secrecy of the polling booth, and the Teamsters' million-dollar political operation had not made a dent on Election Day.

In mid-November, the president-elect leaked the news to the *New York Times* that he was seriously considering appointing Bobby as attorney general. It was an unorthodox, controversial idea, one that was pushed insistently by their father, who wanted someone absolutely loyal to the president in that job. Also, Bobby would be in charge, at least on paper, of the FBI and its director, J. Edgar Hoover, someone the Kennedys had cultivated but wanted to keep close because they did not trust him. At a news conference in Hyannis Port a day later, Jack Kennedy told the assembled journalists that if Bobby wanted a position in his administration, the public certainly would believe that he had earned it and deserved it. He was deliberately vague about his plans, wanting to see what kind of public reaction this startling cabinet selection might bring. Afterward JFK talked privately to reporter Marguerite Higgins, the *New York Herald Tribune* correspondent who'd won a Pulitzer Prize for her Korean War coverage, trusting her to protect a confidence. In the next day's newspaper, Higgins published a story in which she floated a trial balloon about Bobby as attorney general. "In the case of Bobby Kennedy, crime prevention has been a major interest and a major endeavor, even if Jimmy Hoffa is still boss of the Teamsters," she wrote. "If merit and fitness for the job are any criteria, there is every reason then why a person with Bobby Kennedy's experience should be considered for a government post such, for example, as Attorney General. In an open democracy, is it fair to deprive a man of public office merely because he is related to the President?"[35] Her framing of the issue was perfect from Jack Kennedy's point of view.

But his brother wasn't sold. After years of serving Jack's career, Bobby wanted a career of his own, something in the public service. With his bestselling book and the sensational rackets hearings, he had achieved fame, respect, and his own identity as crusader for the public good. He, Jack, and others in his family had long talked of his running for governor of Massachusetts. "It takes someone with Bobby's nerve and his investigative experience to clean up the mess" in the Massachusetts statehouse, Kennedy told historian and future White House special assistant Arthur Schlesinger.[36]

Bobby also knew that at thirty-five, with no trial experience, he wasn't ready to be the nation's top lawyer, in charge of some thirty thousand government workers. "Clearly, Bobby was not qualified by any traditional standards," Nicholas Katzenbach, who soon joined the Kennedy Justice Department, would later recall. "He was too young, too inexperienced, too political, too brash, too immature in every way. All of these shortcomings were obvious to everyone, including Bobby."[37] Everyone, that is, except for Joe Kennedy.

For his part, RFK said he wanted to do something beyond busting racketeers. Not long after the election, he discussed with his friend Walter Sheridan how he might contribute to his brother's administration. Jack indeed had asked him to serve as attorney general, and he had turned him down, Bobby told Sheridan. He talked about being the number two man at the Defense Department, where he could streamline operations, make the huge bureaucracy work more effectively, and serve as a roving troubleshooter. Or perhaps he could play a similar role at the State Department. "I just think he had a real vision of what the New Frontier was all about and the bureaucracy problems that it faced and that he had the facility for cutting through that kind of thing," Sheridan would later say. "I think he would have liked to have been kind of just a troubleshooter throughout the government."[38] Sheridan told Bobby he understood why he didn't want the attorney general's job but that he should take it.

Seeking guidance from outside his family, Bobby turned to others for advice, and nearly all of them told him not to take the job, albeit for different reasons: columnist Drew Pearson told RFK he'd be so effective as AG that he'd create problems and enemies for his brother; Supreme Court justice William O. Douglas, a family friend, suggested Bobby take time off instead and think about what path he wanted his career to take; RFK even called on Hoover, who told him to take the job, advice that Kennedy later said he didn't find sincere. ("I didn't like to tell him that," Hoover later told one of his division heads, "but what could I say?")

To try to budge his father, Jack Kennedy asked lawyer Clark Clifford, the Washington insider and the man to call on for delicate tasks, to explain to Ambassador Kennedy why it was a bad idea for Bobby to be attorney general. Clifford was perplexed by this strange assignment, he later said: Why couldn't the president-elect just tell his own father what he planned to do? Clifford gamely traveled to New York City and met with Kennedy père at Le Pavillon for lunch. There Clifford laid out a careful presentation on why Bobby would be the wrong choice. Afterward, Joe Kennedy thanked him politely and in a matter-of-fact tone said, "I do want to leave you with one thought, however, one firm thought.... Bobby is going to be Attorney General. All of us have worked our tails off for Jack and now that we have succeeded I am going to see to it that Bobby gets the same chance we gave to Jack."[39]

Meanwhile, Hoffa, fearing the worst, was reported to have made peace overtures to the president-elect through his father. The effort went nowhere, and Hoffa complained to friends: "I'll have to hire two hundred more lawyers to keep out of jail."[40]

Bobby "finally just deferred to the president, very reluctantly," Sheridan would later explain. Explaining his change of heart, Kennedy said he learned how hard it was to recruit good people to serve the new administration and came to understand the terrible loneliness of the job of the president. "I realized then what an advantage it would be for him to have someone he could talk to," he said, once again putting himself in his brother's service.[41]

On December 16, a cold day in the capital, with snow on the ground, reporters and photographers waited in front of Jack and Jackie's redbrick Federal-style home in Georgetown, as they had each day for nearly the past week, waiting to be handed news of significant appointments in the new administration. That day they were not disappointed. Jack and Bobby Kennedy, dressed in dark suits and ties, but with no coats, stepped out onto the small brick porch. This would be the president-elect's most controversial cabinet appointment. "Don't smile too much," Jack first advised his brother, "or they'll think we're happy about the appointment." Jack read from prepared remarks: "In every assignment he has undertaken, I believe that he has distinguished himself. His work with the rackets committee on which I served shows his intellectual energy, his courage, his integrity, and his organizing ability. In looking for an attorney general who must lead law enforcement, who must administer our laws without favor, and with matchless integrity, I have turned to a man in whom I have found these qualities." Bobby appeared sheepish at first, but soon he was smiling for the cameras.

A reporter pressed Jack Kennedy about a president having a sibling in his cabinet. "Do you know of any historical parallel for this?"

"No," Kennedy quipped. "We are going to start one."[42]

Bobby's appointment was greeted with outraged howls from across the political spectrum. The idea that RFK, the ruthless campaign manager, could now be expected to uphold the nation's law without considering how it might affect his brother's political fortunes struck many as preposterous. The leftish magazine *The Nation* called it "the greatest example of nepotism this land has ever seen." *Newsweek* called the appointment a "travesty of justice."

Senator Frank Lausche, the Ohio Democrat and Kennedy supporter, said he thought it was a terrible idea. Hoffa attempted to whip up fury among his rank and file. Senator Goldwater, who personally liked Jack but detested Bobby, arranged for the conservative magazine *Human Events* to publish a "thoughtful" letter the Arizonan had been sent by "a young practicing attorney who is a Democrat and was an ardent supporter" of JFK. The writer was in fact a forty-year-old lawyer who formerly worked for the navy and possessed inside knowledge that almost certainly came from the senator's staff. "It was common knowledge among the lawyers that young Kennedy was inept and unskilled in both direct and cross examination," the Goldwater man wrote. "He constantly argued and quarreled with the witnesses. His fumbling and stumbling frequently caused the proceedings to be reduced to a pier 6 shouting contest, rather than an orderly conducted Congressional inquiry."[43]

Anthony Lewis, who covered the Justice Department for the *New York Times*, felt personally affronted by the appointment. Lewis, who would continue to cover the department during the Kennedy administration, believed that Bobby was too inexperienced and shallow. They had had some contact as undergraduates at Harvard, where RFK struck Lewis as "callow," predominantly "a football player." Despite his misgivings, or perhaps because of them, Lewis sent notes to RFK with the names of lawyers he should hire for top Justice Department jobs — meddling by a beat reporter who within a few years would become a member of Kennedy's social circle.

Lewis wasn't off on the timing; Bobby soon started assembling a team at the Justice Department, with an eye to taking on racketeers — in particular, Jimmy Hoffa.

As it turned out, the very day the president-elect revealed his choice for attorney general outside his Georgetown home, Hoffa stood in front of a different clump of reporters nearly nine hundred miles away, inside the US district courthouse in Orlando, Florida.

The Justice Department had reactivated its indictment against Hoffa for the Sun Valley real estate scam. Hoffa, furious, felt double-crossed, but there was little he could do other than complain. Richard Nixon, the lame-duck vice president, had little power over his friend attorney general Bill Rogers; and Rogers, with only a month left in office, had little leverage over career prosecutors who were upset by the slowdown of the Hoffa case and had no reason to help him.

In a December 8 letter, Nixon operative Oakley Hunter tried to calm down Hoffa.

> Dear Jim,
>
> I was sorry to hear about the indictment against you in the Orlando matter. I know for a fact that your side of the case was put before the Vice President and that he discussed the case with the Attorney General, Bill Rogers.
>
> I do not know what was said by the Vice President to Rogers. I do know, however, that the Vice President has been sympathetic toward you and has felt that you were being subjected to undue harassment by certain parties.
>
> It would be my surmise that Bill Rogers acted as he did for reasons of his own. Mr. Nixon lost the election. I doubt that he has since been in a position to exercise any decisive degree of influence. As Vice President he had no authority to order the Attorney General to do anything.[44]

Hoffa wanted Nixon to at least publicly attack the indictment, but Hunter explained to an intermediary why such a move could backfire. "Regarding the 'big double-cross,' as you call it, it wouldn't do your friend any good to make the Vice President party to the matter," Hunter wrote, because such an attack would only force Rogers to publicly defend the indictment.

Hoffa stood at his arraignment that December 16, dressed

in a blue suit, his dark hair slicked back. The judge outlined the twelve fraud counts against Hoffa and two associates in the Sun Valley deal and asked the Teamsters boss for his plea. "Not guilty, Your Honor," Hoffa sang out.

Everybody has his price, Hoffa liked to say, and he thought he had met Nixon's. Instead he found himself in the dock, facing charges he believed he had kiboshed. And even worse, in a few short weeks, this criminal case—and his future freedom—would be firmly in the hands of his nemesis, the new attorney general, Robert F. Kennedy.

CHAPTER 12

Get Hoffa Squad

MOVING INTO HIS NEW OFFICES at the Justice Department, the attorney general took possession of what was in reality a small apartment inside the magnificent seven-story classical revival building. Dominating the complex of rooms was a huge conference room, with fifteen-feet-high arched ceilings, walnut paneling, a red carpet, a massive wood-burning fireplace, and two large murals at opposite ends. One was *Justice Granted*, which showed people coming into the new world with hopeful faces. *Justice Denied* displayed a stark scene of people being put under arrest by brown-shirted troops. Off this great room was a large office used by RFK's predecessors, a dining room, a kitchen, a bathroom, and, up a flight of stairs, a small bedroom. A private elevator enabled the attorney general to come and go, largely unseen. Unbound by convention, Bobby set his desk in the great room and converted the office into a small conference room. Before long, he had his children's crayon drawings taped across the walls.

Well before he settled in, Kennedy already had an ambitious plan to nail Hoffa. It had been honed in the trenches of the Rackets Committee, but only now, with his brother as president, did Bobby have the power to attempt it. He wanted to put together a sweeping interagency strike force against organized crime—the Justice Department, the IRS, the FBI, the Narcotics Bureau, the Marshals Service, the Secret Service, and others—all working cooperatively, sharing information, coordinating tactics. It would be a high-powered team designed to take down labor racketeers, the mob, and the corrupt judges, cops, and politicians who enabled them. On a local level, New York prosecutor Thomas E. Dewey, with his famous Rackets Bureau, successfully took down key figures in the Murder, Inc., underworld in the 1930s. And prosecutors had been declaring war on the underworld since the days of Chicago crime lord Al Capone in the Roaring Twenties. But a true national war on organized crime had never been attempted.

At his first Justice Department press conference, when RFK announced the antimob campaign, he made certain to point out that the president supported the effort wholeheartedly. But even together, the Kennedys faced a problem more intractable than bureaucratic inertia: FBI director J. Edgar Hoover. Robert Kennedy commanded thirty-two thousand Justice Department employees, but more than thirteen thousand of them were FBI employees who up until that point saw themselves as working for the director at the "seat of government," or SOG, as field agents had to refer to Hoover's office in their reports. For decades, Hoover had made it clear that the Bureau did not share information; it gathered it from everybody else. "The FBI has always been very, very jealous of prerogatives in working with any other agency," Nicholas Katzenbach, deputy attorney general, once explained. "An investigation is either theirs or somebody else's.... This has been the problem all along with the strike-force concept. Mr. Hoover simply didn't want it."[1]

But Kennedy had another powerful weapon at hand, one with the potential to be brutally efficient: the IRS, the federal agency that famously brought down Capone in the 1930s. Subsequently, tax agents and federal prosecutors nailed godfather Frank Costello and Los Angeles mobster Mickey Cohen. As committee counsel, Kennedy knew well the effectiveness of an IRS investigation once it gained momentum. He had watched as the agency tripped up two prominent gangsters targeted by the committee: Chicago mob boss Anthony Accardo and garment-district racketeer Johnny Dio. And former Teamsters president Dave Beck was on his way to McNeil Island federal prison for signing a false tax return.

Even so, RFK knew he faced problems in trying to unleash the IRS. The agency didn't target criminals; it believed its primary mission was to raise revenue. Certainly its agents would pursue solid leads, whether they came from congressional committees or local police, but the IRS wouldn't simply go after someone like Hoffa and see what it could find. Indeed, during the McClellan committee hearings, RFK had complained privately that the IRS moved too timidly on Hoffa. "Their philosophy was that their responsibility was to collect taxes, not to put people in the penitentiary," Courtney Evans, an assistant director and the FBI's liaison to the McClellan committee, would later explain. So Kennedy wanted an IRS commissioner who was not hidebound about going after organized-crime figures. His top candidate was Mortimer Caplin, who had taught RFK tax law at the University of Virginia School of Law. Forty-four years old, dark-haired, favoring bow ties, Professor Caplin was a smart, tough New Yorker who served in the war as a navy lieutenant and was decorated for his bravery during the Normandy invasion. He remembered Kennedy as "a tough-minded sort of fellow, taciturn, and he didn't really sparkle very much in class. But he was likable, in a tough sort of way."[2]

Before offering the appointment, RFK first needed to find out whether Caplin believed the agency could change course and join the fight against the mob. "One of the things I am going to do as attorney general is to take on organized crime in this country," Bobby told him. "How do you feel about the Internal Revenue Service getting involved in that?"[3]

Caplin needed time to think about it. He discussed the issue with the dean at his law school, who had taught tax law as well as constitutional law. In a letter to RFK, Caplin concluded that "part of our resources could properly be used to combat organized crime, but [the] IRS's role ought to have a specific tax orientation. We shouldn't be there just to help the Department of Justice investigate a drug dealer or gambler." Bobby liked his answer, and Caplin got the job.

Another key appointment was Kennedy's deputy attorney general, Byron "Whizzer" White, a Colorado native with stunning accomplishments: Rhodes scholar, professional football player with the Detroit Lions, Yale Law School, navy commander during the war. White helped recruit Nicholas Katzenbach (Yale Law School, US Army, University of Chicago Law School professor) as head of the Office of Legal Counsel; Burke Marshall (Exeter, US Army, Yale Law School, white-shoe firm Covington and Burling) to head the Civil Rights Division; Edwyn Silberling (Harvard Law School, a former assistant district attorney in Manhattan and a chief assistant to a New York State special prosecutor) to run the Organized Crime and Racketeering Section; and other top-notch legal talents. "It was the most brilliantly staffed department we had seen in a long, long time, and that was very impressive," said Alexander Bickel, a noted constitutional scholar at Yale Law School who a couple of months earlier had written in *The New Republic* that RFK was unfit for the job. "One immediately had the sense of a fellow who wasn't afraid to have able people around him and indeed of a fellow who had a vision of public service that would have done anyone proud."[4]

Not long after being confirmed as attorney general, Kennedy and his team compiled a list of the nation's top forty racketeers, then sought every shred of information about them in the possession of twenty-seven federal agencies, everyone from the Narcotics Bureau to the US Postal Service. They counted on getting little from the FBI. To make the intelligence quickly available, Winifred Willse, a nineteen-year veteran of the New York City police department's narcotics squad, and a team of clerks set up an alphanumeric indexing system, using three-by-five cards and folders, to organize the files, and investigators and prosecutors went to work.

Bobby then brought the heads of those investigative agencies to a Justice Department conference table for an information session and pep talk about the Kennedy administration's war on the underworld. At the top of the target list was Hoffa.

Despite any earlier reservations about taking the IRS job, Caplin was thrilled by the mob-busting campaign. In the afterglow of this unprecedented gathering, Caplin said in a February 15, 1961, directive to his staff: "I cannot emphasize too strongly the importance I attach to the success of the Service's contribution to this over-all program.... The tax returns of major racketeers to be identified by the Department of Justice will be subjected to the 'saturation type' investigation, utilizing such man-power on each case as can be efficiently employed. In conducting such investigations, full use will be made of available electronic equipment and other technical aids as well as such investigative techniques as surveillance, undercover work, etc."[5] Caplin expected the racketeers to be held to the same legal standards as any errant taxpayer, but once these Teamsters officials, mobbed-up businessmen, and

Mafia members were named as targets, they would be given high priority. Not everyone in the department agreed with the tactic. Ramsey Clark (who would be named attorney general several years later by President Johnson) was a committed Kennedy admirer, but he would later admit, "I disagree with the view that it's okay to select organized-crime cases as long as you apply tax criteria....You're using tax law to justify judgments about people on other grounds. Lawyers believe you can make a net-worth case against anybody with substantial income."[6]

Making a tax case could indeed be cut-and-dried and an efficient use of the organized crime division's resources. For instance, if Hoffa took money and didn't pay income taxes on it, he'd be in trouble. The Justice Department didn't have to prove his intent when taking a bribe; it simply had to prove that he accepted the money. With a net-worth analysis, agent-accountants first used his federal tax return to measure his wealth at the beginning of a year. Then they'd see what income he declared the following year. If his actual cash flow turned out to be larger than the amount he paid federal taxes on, a criminal tax-evasion case could be made.

Key to Kennedy's mission would be the person who headed the Justice Department's Tax Division. Kennedy, with Byron White's approval, selected Louis Oberdorfer, who had gone through Yale Law School with White. Oberdorfer, at forty-one, was a smart, experienced litigator. Not long after he settled into the job, he learned a discouraging truth about his staff. "The Tax Division was a patsy in a knock-down-drag-out litigation," he would recall. "The men here were so over-worked and spread so thin that they could be forced to compromise on terms unfavorable to the government."[7]

Justice Department tax lawyers had to handle an over-whelming sixty to seventy cases a year. Usually, they left the division after two years. Morale was poor, attributable in part to a widely publicized scandal in the 1950s involving the division's head, T. Lamar Caudle, who was sent to prison for taking money to fix tax delinquency cases and for cheating on his own taxes.

Bobby Kennedy knew something about rallying the troops. Early on, he organized a series of bull sessions with lawyers from different sections from across the Justice Department—tax, organized crime, antitrust, criminal, and so on. Intermittently, almost always near the end of the workday, they met in his giant office and were served beer and pretzels. Bobby would go around the room, asking questions of each lawyer about his work. When he met with the tax lawyers, Oberdorfer recalled, "From bow to stern, every one of them told him how badly overworked they were, how hard it was to meet their deadlines, and that they had to do less professional work than they were capable of doing and wanted to do because of the enormous overextension." Afterward, Kennedy took Oberdorfer aside and said, "Find out how many more men you need, and let's get them."

Before long, Oberdorfer added dozens of new tax lawyers. "This is one of those historic moments when the tide changes," Oberdorfer would later say. "You can change the whole complexion of this place. You have the president's brother as the attorney general, and he understands your problem. You know it had been a problem here for ten or twenty years." Eventually the number of lawyers in the tax division rose from 146 to 226. "It just made all the difference in the world," Oberdorfer would later say. His lawyers no longer were forced into a position "of sitting back and letting plaintiffs sue us and beat our brains out."

RFK also assembled the team that became known as the Get Hoffa squad, also called the Hoffa squad. He staffed it with key investigators from the Senate Rackets Committee, such as Walter Sheridan and Carmine Bellino. The Hoffa squad was part of the Organized Crime and Racketeering Section, but its mission was personal — finish the job on Hoffa that had been started in the Senate. But whom to put in charge? Bobby had relied on Bellino as investigator in chief in the Senate; the gifted forensic accountant had worked staggering hours to meet deadlines and build cases. Of all the Senate staffers, Bellino was the one Kennedy singled out in *The Enemy Within* for special praise, saying he "probably more than any other staff member was responsible for the over-all success of our work."[8]

The other choice was Walter Sheridan, whose "appearance hides a core of toughness," in Bobby's words. Born on the same day, the two men had become close; Sheridan brought his family to Hickory Hill for staff parties, swimming, and touch football games.

Early in his career as a Senate investigator, Sheridan became a believer in the Bellino method: painstakingly create a bedrock for complicated business investigations with elaborate chronologies. He included precise times and telephone numbers harvested from individual long-distance slips created by operators for each toll call, as well as all dates from ledgers, invoices, and financial statements. But Sheridan had strengths in other equally important areas. He was remarkable in his ability to anticipate a target's counterattacks and take either take evasive action or lay a snare. He felt he was better suited than Bellino was to run the team.

"I think his only fault is lack of imagination," Sheridan once said of the accounting wizard. "He went at things from a figures standpoint and did it probably better than anybody else can or has done.... He did what he was supposed to do very well. I think if he was supposed to run the whole investigation, or been in that role, which he almost was at times, then I think we would have missed a lot of the things we got because he just wouldn't have reached out to them. That's strictly an imagination thing.... Bob trusted him implicitly. I trusted him implicitly. And I think at the beginning, Bob intended to lean on Carmine's experience as an investigator. But I think as other people came in, he realized that there was more to it than Carmine's bag."[9]

Bellino's method to nab Hoffa was by "accounting sheets," while Sheridan's way was "in the alley." As one Hoffa squad member put it: "If they fix a jury or bribe a judge or intimidate a witness you can lose in the alley what you win in the courtroom."[10]

Sheridan got the top job. His new title was special assistant to the attorney general. The appointment struck many of the department lawyers as odd because it was headed by a nonlawyer: Sheridan had one year of law school. But he did have deep experience as an investigator, and after three years on the Rackets Committee, he also had an encyclopedic knowledge of Teamsters shenanigans. Bellino joined the team, too.

Sheridan worked out of an unmarked office. Charles Z. Smith, who joined the team in 1961, was a Seattle prosecutor who brought a successful larceny case against Dave Beck in 1958. He said he and his fellow squad members were supposed to keep it quiet that they had a unit exclusively targeting Hoffa.[11] Informants Sheridan had cultivated at Teamsters headquarters told him that Hoffa had at least two sources inside the Justice Department. As a result, Sheridan and other Hoffa squad members were close-mouthed and secretive, which struck other lawyers as unnecessarily cloak-and-dagger.

But Sheridan's very real concerns were detailed in an April 1961 memo to the head of the Criminal Division, in which he outlined how the Justice Department should go after racketeers. "The second point of attack should be directed at the so-called legitimate people both in the business world and in government service without whose cooperation these people could not operate. This would include employees of Federal investigative and regulatory agencies who are being paid off, Congressmen and Senators who are collaborating, bank officials and businessmen who through fear or corruption are allowing these people to make inroads into legitimate enterprise."[12]

It was a telling confirmation of the Hoffa squad's approach that, in the first week after Kennedy took the helm at the Justice Department, Bellino visited the offices of the Internal Revenue Service, one of his favorite haunts from his Rackets Committee days. There he requested the income tax returns of dozens of targets. Besides his assignment to the Hoffa squad, Bellino enjoyed the title of special assistant to the president, which he relied upon to get around any restrictions for looking at federal tax returns. He camped for days in a small, secluded government office, studying hundreds of pages of IRS returns, documents that — except for psychiatric case notes or an honest diary — are the most potentially revealing documents about a person's private activities to be found. Five years earlier, in an exploratory phase leading up to the McClellan hearings, he and Robert Kennedy kicked off their preliminary probe into Hoffa by reviewing seven years of the labor leader's federal tax returns. Now with enhanced power, the Get Hoffa squad kicked off fresh tax investigations into its target.

Another measure of Bobby's drive to get Hoffa was revealed in his unorthodox choice to run the Justice Department's huge criminal division: Herbert J. "Jack" Miller Jr., a Republican and partner at a fifteen-lawyer firm that represented prominent Republican clients. Miller had no significant experience in criminal law or as an administrator, but he did know quite a bit about Hoffa and the Teamsters. He served in 1959 and part of 1960 as the head of a three-person board of monitors that had been set up by a federal judge to clean up the Teamsters. Through this assignment, he became friends with Walter Sheridan, who shared investigative records with him that had been collected by committee investigators. Working closely with Kennedy, Miller and another monitor tried to use the board to remove Hoffa from office. After forty appeals-court challenges, they failed.

When Bobby called to offer him the job, Miller recalled, he warned the attorney general: "Well, I'm a Republican, and I'm a Republican precinct chairman, and the firm I'm with was started by Colonel Robert R. McCormick of the *Chicago Tribune*, and I represent clients that are the antithesis of what I think the Kennedy administration is going to be all about."

"I don't give a damn about any of that," he recalled RFK saying. "Are you sure you can do the job?"

He said he most certainly could. "In retrospect, it's just unbelievable that he would in effect take that chance with me, because he didn't know me that well," Miller said. But if Bobby was hoping to bring case after case against Hoffa and the Teamsters, he needed a criminal chief with deep knowledge of Hoffa's practices — one who was disgusted by what he saw. Miller — fondly described by one federal prosecutor as someone who "would not hesitate to indict a man for spitting on the sidewalk if he thought that was the best he could get" — took the job. "I dropped my practice," he would later say, "and ended up at the Department of Justice as acting assistant attorney general of the Criminal Division."[13]

As the nation's top lawyer, Bobby Kennedy was dogged in his pursuit of Hoffa but didn't yet appreciate that conduct he could get away with as a Senate investigator was inappropriate as attorney general. Bobby would later come to regret it, but on a Saturday morning in early March 1961, after a little more than one month in office, he telephoned a writer he trusted at *Life* magazine, Hank Suydam, and asked to see him right away at the Justice Department.

Suydam, the magazine's Washington bureau chief, knew that whatever Kennedy had in mind must be important if the attorney general had called him on a weekend, and he hurried over to RFK's office at the department's fifth-floor headquarters on Pennsylvania Avenue, eight blocks from the White House.[14]

Once Suydam arrived, Kennedy shut the door for privacy and revealed what the urgency was all about. He had a "high official" of the Teamsters waiting in a nearby room. He was an honest, idealistic labor leader who had been secretly informing the Rackets Committee about the union for the past two years, Bobby said. The official was so disgusted with Hoffa that he was at the point of making a public break. Would *Life* magazine be interested in telling his story?

After Suydam said yes, Kennedy brought forth a short, slight, fifty-eight-year-old man with flowing white hair and a gray mustache, Sam Baron. He had worked out of Teamsters headquarters since 1953, when Harold Gibbons hired him to organize and manage the union's important warehouse division. Sheridan had cultivated Baron and turned him into an effective spy within the top Teamsters leadership.

Bobby insisted to Suydam that he should tell no one other than his direct supervisor, whom Bobby knew and trusted, about Baron. Otherwise, if word leaked out, Baron's life would be in danger. Suydam thought Bobby was being overly dramatic, but he agreed to keep Baron's story a secret. The three of them sneaked out through the private elevator and took a car by a roundabout way to Baron's home in Virginia.

Baron was just the sort of labor official Kennedy admired and Hoffa despised. An ex-Socialist, Baron had reported on the Spanish Civil War for labor newspapers (it was during this stint that he befriended writer Ernest Hemingway), and he had fought against crooked union leaders as a garment workers' union official. Starting in the 1930s, Baron had become worried about Communists and racketeers in the US labor movement and, like many who saw unionism as a sacred calling, broke with Socialism in the 1930s. The liberal Gibbons considered Baron to be a kindred spirit. Hoffa knew of Baron's reputation as an idealist and scourge of racketeers — at their first meeting, Baron recalled Hoffa saying, "Don't think you're going to stop the boys from making a fast buck, because you're not."

Hoffa tolerated Baron because Gibbons relied on him. As field organizer for the warehouse division, Baron performed important work, recruiting workers at Sears, Roebuck and Montgomery Ward, and was well liked by the rank and file. But, as he would tell RFK and Sheridan, Baron had come to see Hoffa as evil. He was certainly not the working-class hero portrayed by Eddie Cheyfitz. Nor was he a unionist who played rough but still was deserving of sympathy because he lived in a modest home, didn't smoke or drink, and delivered for the rank and file. In fact, Hoffa was "the most dangerous man in America," Baron told the writer, echoing the words of Bobby and Jack Kennedy. Baron recounted the story of Hoffa's unsympathetic reaction to the acid attack on Victor Riesel, who was blinded in the late-night assault. In trying to plant Baron's story with the country's leading national magazine, RFK was deploying a tactic he found effective while working for the McClellan committee — attacking Hoffa with negative publicity. The difference in 1961 was that Kennedy was attorney general, his office was prosecuting Hoffa in federal court in Florida, and it was highly improper to try to use the press to tar someone under indictment by his department. Baron continued to talk to *Life* but decided, for the time being, not to break with Hoffa by public denunciation.

Bobby's aggressive use of negative publicity irritated top supervising attorneys, men like Byron White and Robert Morgenthau, the US attorney in Manhattan. "When he became attorney general he did not have a solid legal background and training," Morgenthau would later say. "He didn't fully understand how to conduct an investigation where you try somebody not in the newspapers but in court." Fortunately, he had surrounded himself with top lawyers, welcomed their criticism, and would become a more skilled litigator. "One of the things that I thought exceptional about Bob was his capacity to learn and to grow," Morgenthau later recalled.[15]

Despite the Justice Department's vast resources, its brilliant lawyers, the Internal Revenue Service's suffocating power, and RFK's unrelenting focus, Hoffa and his union were not only surviving the Kennedys but also thriving. They suffered a loss in reputation after being noisily expelled from the AFL-CIO in 1957. But since then, the Teamsters enjoyed a gain in membership; its ranks jumped from 1.2 million members to 1.7 million by 1961. Unshackled from the federation, the Teamsters no longer had to worry about being careful not to organize workers who might belong to the jurisdiction of an

AFL-CIO member union. Then, in the space of a week in early July of 1961, two events unfolded that further buoyed Hoffa's spirits: the Sun Valley charges against him were tossed out by a federal judge because the grand jury panel hadn't included women and nonvoters, and Jimmy Hoffa was overwhelmingly reelected Teamsters president at a highly publicized, smoothly run convention in Miami Beach.

To avoid a repeat of the relatively slipshod election operation in 1957, Hoffa hadn't wanted to leave anything to chance at this convention. Determined to prevent another challenge over election rules, he followed delegate selection and voting regulations to the letter. He spared little expense to whip the convention into a campaign spectacle; most of the 2,200 Teamsters delegates were decked with Hoffa buttons and Hoffa hats. An airplane lazily circled above the Miami Beach strip, towing a giant banner that read RE-ELECT HOFFA. Among the throngs of noisy supporters were his daughter, Barbara, his son, Jim, and his wife, Josephine, who led a pro-Hoffa conga line with the wives of other delegates through the lobby of the plush Deauville hotel.

Nevertheless, Hoffa still struck some as unnecessarily paranoid about federal forces. When he spoke to a group of ninety Michigan Conference delegates at the Americana Hotel, for example, he warned about female agents and spies working for the Kennedy administration: "These women are mingling with delegates in hotel lobbies, dining rooms, and bars, trying to pick them up and get them into situations where they can be forced to divulge things that are the union's private business. Don't get hooked by these Justice Department hookers."[16] In addition, he warned, 150 FBI agents were mingling among the thousands of delegates and family members spread out across the convention hotels in Miami Beach: "We know who most of them are and where they hang out and are staying." Two days later, in a speech to a group of delegates, Hoffa showed them what he described as a bugging device and warned them to be wary. It had been found on a television in the union's temporary offices at the Carillon hotel, where Hoffa and his wife had the penthouse suite.[17]

Despite his concerns, the five days of proceedings unfolded smoothly and gave Hoffa one victory after another, building to a rousing climax—his election by near-unanimous consent. And Hoffa ended up with more than just another term: he was given new powers and an even tighter grip on his presidency. The delegates approved a change in the union's constitution that gave free legal service to Teamsters officers facing charges of improprieties if the executive board believed the charges to be politically motivated or brought "in an attempt to embarrass or destroy the union." This incredible perk would be worth hundreds of thousands of dollars to Hoffa, who previously had been personally responsible for such costs. In addition, delegates raised his salary from $50,000 to $75,000, making him by far the highest-paid union president in the land. Dues went from forty cents to one dollar a month per member, bumping annual revenues from $8 million to $20 million. Incredibly, the delegates even removed a clause that prohibited racketeers from holding membership in the Teamsters. "Now the Kennedys ought to know the time and effort they've put in trying to destroy the Teamsters have completely failed," Hoffa crowed at one point. "It was a waste of time."[18]

Jimmy Hoffa was in effect permanent president of the biggest, baddest, most powerful labor union in American history. In his acceptance speech, Hoffa was expansive and unusually sentimental, taking a moment to brag about his children: "I pay tribute to my son and daughter. While the headlines in the TV were at their worst, they continued on with their education, living each day as a new day, their heads high, satisfied that their old man was doing what he thought was right. My daughter finished college. She is teaching English, history, and French — the first single generation of either a Hoffa or a Poszywak...to have had an opportunity to complete college." As for his son, Jim, a football star, he went on: "I am happy to say that my son was named an all-star for the entire state of Michigan while the trouble was at its height — on his own glory, not on his old man's. And I'm happy to say that he is now in college [and,] much to my surprise, he is going to be a lawyer." When Hoffa concluded, the crowd leaped to its feet and roared approval as he and his family beamed.

Hoffa's reelection was no surprise to Kennedy. Asked about the result later that day in Los Angeles, RFK replied, "I don't think there is any evidence that Hoffa's reelection was rigged. However, I haven't changed my mind about Hoffa, and I don't think his ostensible popularity with the union — actually, only a small group of Teamsters back him — has hurt the government case against Hoffa."[19] Some of Kennedy's associates from the Rackets Committee expected a great speech-making crusade against Hoffa, but Bobby followed advice to stand down. "I am attorney general now, and I have a responsibility that transcends any personal rivalry," he said. "I'm not going to have a vendetta against anyone."[20]

He had reason to be happy. In the weeks before Hoffa's triumph, the general counsel for the Teamsters, Edward Bennett Williams, quietly visited RFK at the Justice Department and unloaded about his demanding client. Williams had been determined for years to get back in the good graces of Bobby and Jack Kennedy. He began by telling friends and colleagues of the Kennedys that he was disgusted with Hoffa, hoping word would travel back. Even so, Williams had loved the cash flow and security that came with representing the giant labor union.

Now, however, he crossed the line of professional conduct to unburden himself about his troublesome clients. "Ed Williams told me that he was the most disliked individual at the Teamsters other than myself," RFK recalled in a memo he dictated on August 1. "He said he had broken with them and would no longer have anything to do with them. He said he understood the hierarchy was made up of gangsters and crooks and probably the only one who could save them at all was Harold Gibbons. He said [Gibbons] was relatively honest. He said he didn't think Hoffa was stealing money anymore but that he had lost all judgment and you just couldn't deal with him.... [Williams] said that he was just waiting for the proper moment to resign. Subsequently, he said he would go down to the convention in Miami and resign."[21]

At the July convention, Williams would sing a far different tune. After Hoffa introduced him, Williams told the assembled Teamsters leaders, "I am very proud to be introduced as one of your counsel, because for any lawyer to serve this great union professionally would be a post of honor."[22] Without naming names, Williams next attacked the tactics of the McClellan committee. "It seemed to me more that a vendetta was being waged rather than a legislative inquiry being conducted."[23]

RFK never would trust Williams, though he was happy to accept tips and intelligence from him. On the evening of August 1, Kennedy called Courtney Evans, the Justice Department's FBI liaison, and told him that a Hoffa lawyer from Detroit, James Haggerty, was coming to Washington to meet with a lawyer in the criminal division at the Justice Department. It is unclear how RFK knew this, but given the timing of the phone call—coming at the same time as RFK's memo about Williams's unburdening—it's possible that Williams shared the intelligence about Haggerty as a way to earn back

Kennedy's trust. Williams, already playing both sides, would at one point become one of Sheridan's best sources.[24]

Haggerty had no legitimate business with the department at the moment, RFK told Evans. Instead he suspected that Haggerty was meeting with a pro-Hoffa mole inside the Justice Department, someone whom he and the Get Hoffa squad had heard rumors about but weren't able to identify. Kennedy told Evans he wanted the FBI to spy on Hoffa's lawyer to see if it could learn the identity of Hoffa's secret source at the Justice Department, and he requested microphone surveillance of Haggerty's room at the Carlton hotel. The FBI installed the hidden microphone, but, as Evans later informed RFK, nothing much useful was learned.[25]

By the end of its first year, the Hoffa squad had revved up a national campaign against Hoffa and his Teamsters allies, but it hadn't always gone smoothly. RFK's handpicked chief of the Organized Crime and Racketeering Section was Ed Silberling. He believed he had a deal with RFK to run the section under certain terms: he was to have hiring authority, carte blanche about which targets to pursue, even if they were Kennedy Democrats, and a direct reporting line to Bobby.

Eager to make his mark, Silberling quickly ran into problems with the Hoffa squad. The salaries for Sheridan, Bellino, and lawyers such as Charles Z. Smith came out of the organized crime section budget and, in theory, those men reported to Silberling. But in practice, Sheridan reported directly to his good friend the attorney general or to criminal chief Miller, infuriating Silberling. It became an unworkable arrangement for him. "Part of my budget was a cover-up for the Hoffa unit—it burned my ass," Silberling would later say. "I had to justify my budget requests by work produced, but half of the jobs were Hoffa Squad jobs. They used up a lot of the top grades, which interfered with my hiring and besides, I didn't have control over them."[26] Sheridan was never in his office when Silberling or his allies sought him out—and, inconveniently, Sheridan's close colleagues would profess not to know where he was. But if he was needed for an important meeting or crisis, somehow Sheridan would always show up within fifteen minutes. "It was perverted," Silberling would later say.[27]

At first, Silberling had RFK's full backing and hired forty new prosecutors to go after mob guys and their enablers. But he rubbed Oberdorfer, the Justice Department's tax-division head, the wrong way. Oberdorfer called him a "hot rock," explaining that he and the lawyers he hired "were not fair-minded and really were killers, prosecutors using the tax prosecution as an instrument of vengeance and punishment without regard, and not as an aid to the enforcement of revenue law."[28]

Despite the friction, Hoffa squad prosecutors had two dozen separate grand jury investigations into Hoffa and the Teamsters going in Chicago, Miami, Nashville, Los Angeles, and elsewhere by the end of 1961. They chased new leads as well as expanded two promising lines of inquiry that had been developed by the McClellan committee: the Test Fleet case in Nashville and the Central States Pension Fund, based in Chicago. If somebody touched the Teamsters, it seemed as if that person's taxes ended up being investigated. The financial dragnet swept up Jay, Jack, Donald, and A. N. Pritzker of Chicago, whose Hyatt Hotels borrowed $2 million from the Teamsters' Central States Pension Fund for a San Francisco hotel and $4 million for one in Chicago; it caught up Clint Murchison Jr., the millionaire Dallas oilman and founder of the Dallas Cowboys, who also borrowed millions from the Teamsters fund; and it snagged Bernard Spindel, the troubled but brilliant snoop who used his eavesdropping and counter-espionage skills to Hoffa's benefit.

Soon IRS criminal tax investigations targeted Hoffa and those closest to him: his wife, Josephine; his business and union associate Rolland McMaster; the Local 299 official (and future Teamsters president) Frank Fitzsimmons; Fitzsimmons's son; and others.

Most troubling is that investigations were opened into three lawyers who did work for Hoffa: Jacques Schiffer of New York, William Bufalino of Detroit, and Morris Shenker of Saint Louis.[29] Specifically, the Get Hoffa squad targeted Hoffa's attorneys with IRS investigations, which could be seen as crossing a line into harassment and interfering with his right to counsel. Stirring up tax troubles could easily damage a legal career and reputation, or at a minimum it could cause a lawyer to have second thoughts about representing a controversial client like Hoffa.

RFK didn't care. "From the moment he was named attorney general, Bobby was determined to prosecute Jimmy Hoffa," Nicholas Katzenbach would later write. "He was convinced from his work on the McClellan Committee that Hoffa was evil, corrupt, and capable of corrupting our political institutions. The personal animosity between Hoffa and Kennedy made good press copy, and neither was interested in covering it up. More than any other aspect of his tenure, it was the 'Get Hoffa' squad under Walter Sheridan that caused criticism and led to descriptions of Bobby as 'ruthless.'" If that meant going after Hoffa's lawyers, so be it.

"In candor," Katzenbach went on, "I think a number of us felt uncomfortable with Bobby's fixation on putting Hoffa in jail."[30] But more important for the days ahead, two people had no problem with the inquisition, and their last names were Kennedy.

CHAPTER 13

A Brazen Girl

DESPITE ALL THE GRAND JURY investigations into sticky-fingered Teamsters and underworld racketeers, attorney general Kennedy and his war on organized crime still ran into a largely unmovable obstacle in J. Edgar Hoover.

At sixty-six, Hoover presented a sharp contrast to the wiry, tousle-headed youth of his nominal boss. He was blocky and soft but streamlined in his look, with well-tailored, expensive navy blue suits, starched white shirts, and neckties suitable for funerals. His large head, with its slicked-back hair, appeared to be planted directly on his shoulders with no apparent neck, only jowls that sagged below a flat-faced scowl.

Hoover's personal habits struck Kennedy and his colleagues as odd. When the nation's new US attorneys came to the Justice Department in 1961 for orientation and a tour, they were told several times throughout the day by the FBI that maybe they'd get a chance to actually meet the director. Robert Morgenthau, the new US attorney for the southern district of New York, recalled their strange encounter that day with the famous lawman. "We also were told, in his outer office, 'Don't shake Mr. Hoover's hand. Let him shake yours. And don't speak unless he speaks to you.' We were ushered into this huge office and shook his hand and were ushered out into the corridor and that was it. Not even a word of greeting! In the corridor, the agent asked us if we had any questions. One of the US attorneys said, 'Yeah — where can we go for five minutes to laugh?' That got a big laugh, and I guess the story started to make the rounds, because later in the day they told us not to tell that story."[1]

Hoover's eccentricity was enabled by his terrified staff. They spent hours, for instance, briefing new agents about to graduate from the FBI Academy on how to greet Hoover during the graduation ritual. They were told they had to wear dark suits with a folded handkerchief in the breast pocket. Those with crew cuts were instructed to let their hair grow out because the director considered short hair a sign of immaturity. Before greeting the great man, the agents had to line up by height, in descending order. Trainers at the FBI Academy insisted that graduates bring extra handkerchiefs with them so that they could dry their palms just before entering the director's office. Hoover considered sweaty palms to be a sign of weak character, and several new agents had been fired after shaking hands with moist palms.[2]

Bobby was determined to force the FBI to change course and go after Hoffa and the mob. Hoover, on the other hand, was obsessed with hunting down domestic Communists and willing to divert only enough resources to keep the president and his brother happy.

At first, RFK attempted to flatter Hoover's inflated sense of self. "I used to keep his ego up," he would later say. "I'd arrange for him to go over every two or three months to have lunch alone with the president. I made a fuss over him."[3] In the acknowledgments section of *The Enemy Within*, he gave Hoover "special thanks" for "his advice and assistance."

Bobby was using the tactics of his father, who had cultivated Hoover for decades with what may now seem to be crude blandishments, but Joe Kennedy obviously understood the man. If you ever decide to run for president, old Joe had written to Hoover in the early 1950s, the country will be fortunate, and you'll have my full support. At another point, the Kennedy patriarch offered him $100,000 a year to serve as director of security for Kennedy's far-flung business interests. Hoover returned the flattery, then tucked away the correspondence in his Official and Confidential files.

During the Kennedy administration, the public generally still thought highly of the FBI and viewed Hoover as a Cold War hero who worked tirelessly to keep the country safe from the Red menace. Bobby knew otherwise. Hoover spent a lot of time during the workday visiting racetracks and betting on the ponies. Frank Costello, the New York crime boss, occasionally had lunch with Hoover and talked to him on the phone, passing along hot tips on which races were fixed. Hoover made sure to use FBI supervisors across the country to place his bets in time. Invariably, he cashed in.*

As attorney general, as a way to build esprit de corps, Bobby visited Justice Department field offices across the country to meet with prosecutors and FBI agents and talk to them about their work. Hoover hated these unstructured free-for-alls and did what he could to clamp down. Still, Kennedy learned firsthand that out in the field not everything matched the rosy picture painted by the adept public relations practitioners back at

---

* "You have no idea how much those ten-dollar bets cost me," Costello once told prosecutor Bill Hundley.

FBI headquarters. In particular, the Bureau's Detroit office—important in any plan to get Hoffa—had problems. It was plagued by poor morale, likely had a security leak that fed the city's mobsters, and was run by timid managers. It certainly couldn't provide what the attorney general wanted—a crack team in a key city to help the Justice Department nail Hoffa.

In January of 1962, a former agent assigned to the Detroit office, Jack Levine, exposed the problems in a thirty-eight-page report to Criminal Division chief Jack Miller—a scathing critique that eventually found its way to President Kennedy's office. Levine told of "a conscientious agent" from the Detroit office who, while attending an in-service training program in Washington, DC, had told headquarters that supervisors in Detroit "were engaged in falsifying Bureau time sheets and locator cards." His charge was true but reckless: Hoover used overtime stats to persuade Congress to beef up his budget, so agents were pressured to pad their hours. Not long after this unburdening, the head of the FBI's Detroit office was demoted and transferred, as were several other supervisors. "The conscientious agent," Levine sadly reported, "was fired."

But there was far worse. Margaret Vitale, a free-spirited file clerk, "was a frequent companion of three prominent racketeers" operating in Detroit, Levine wrote. Many of her coworkers knew about this risky situation but did nothing. At the time, she had a "serious romance" going with a midlevel rackets guy, she told Levine, and before that she had dated twelve FBI agents in the office, many of whom were married. Those dates were Margaret Vitale's secret weapon. When asked, she told Levine that she had never shared any confidential FBI information with her hoodlum pals. Even so, Vitale warned Levine, she had made it clear that if anyone in the Detroit office informed on her she "would reveal the embarrassing aspects of her affairs with the agents."[4]

Hoover himself knew much more about organized crime than he let on. After the busted Apalachin mob conclave in 1957, Hoover found himself and his agency embarrassed when committee counsel Kennedy asked the FBI for files on the sixty-three men with Italian names who had been arrested that day in New York's southern tier. His rivals at the Bureau of Narcotics had files on all sixty-three, RFK noted in his book in 1960.

By then, however, Hoover secretly had his agents trespassing and breaking into mob hangouts and the homes of Mafia members to plant hidden microphones. In 1959, Chicago FBI agent Bill Roemer concealed a microphone in a second-floor tailoring shop on Michigan Avenue near downtown that was frequented many mornings by Chicago crime boss Sam "Momo" Giancana and other Outfit leaders, such as Tony Accardo, Paul Ricca, and Murray Humphreys. "Worth a thousand agents," Roemer would later say of this single microphone. It went undetected for five years as it taught the FBI about the Mafia's ruling commission, identified elected officials who had taken bribes, coughed up reasons for various mob murders, and even revealed what Momo and his pals said about Bobby and Jack Kennedy.

As word of this remarkable, rich resource spread among the heads of the FBI's fifty-four field offices, they, too, requested their own installations. By March of 1961, the FBI had placed hidden microphones in sixty-seven different locations across the country.[5]

Hoover didn't necessarily use microphone surveillance, or MISUR, to make criminal cases. The intelligence had been obtained illegally, making it useless in court. Instead, when he learned juicy, embarrassing information about political figures, he used underlings to pass the dirt along, typically in a deceptively worded memo. The tone was one of Hoover being helpful — "I have received information I feel would be of interest to you" — and the source was never attributed to a wiretap or bug but rather to a "highly delicate source available to the Bureau." He was letting the elected official or cabinet undersecretary know that the FBI had the goods on him. It went without saying that Hoover would expect support at appropriations time or when he sought legislation protecting the FBI.

"He's sending me stuff on my family and friends and even me, too," Bobby Kennedy, Hoover's boss, would later explain. "Just so I'll know they're into all this information."[6]

On February 27, 1962, with identical memos to RFK and to presidential aide Kenny O'Donnell, J. Edgar Hoover inoculated himself against being forced to retire before he was ready. It had come to the Bureau's attention that the young Judith Campbell had telephoned the president's secretary, Evelyn Lincoln, several times at the White House. Hoover expressed his concern because Mrs. Campbell was an associate of Sam Giancana, "a prominent Chicago underworld figure."[7]

In fact, beautiful, brown-haired Judith Campbell, a self-described "freelance artist," had been sleeping with both the president and a leading crime boss. It was now quite clear to the Kennedys: Hoover had information that, if he chose to leak it, could destroy the presidency.

The news about the president and Judith Campbell was almost certainly known to Hoffa, too. Months earlier, Fred Otash told an FBI agent that he knew Campbell was "shacking up with John Kennedy in the East."[8] Hoffa also was keeping an eye on Marilyn Monroe, the country's reigning movie sex goddess, who was telling friends in Hollywood that she was sleeping with the president. "I think I made his back feel better," she said. Hoffa wanted his wiretappers to find a way to bug Monroe's apartment in hopes of recording her and JFK having sex. Spindel would later claim to have such recordings, but they never surfaced.*

Monroe also developed a relationship with Bobby Kennedy. They met at a February 1, 1962, dinner in his honor at the Santa Monica beach home of his sister Pat and her husband, actor Peter Lawford. Marilyn had too much to drink, and RFK decided to drive her home. His press aide, Ed Guthman, accompanied them to her apartment. The two men helped her inside and into bed, then left.[9] Soon, she was calling RFK so often at the Justice Department that his sister, Guthman, and members of the Hoffa squad teased him about his new girlfriend.

On May 19, ten days before his birthday, President Kennedy celebrated the occasion early at a fund-raising extravaganza for the Democratic National Committee in New York at Madison Square Garden. Fifteen thousand people bought tickets priced from three dollars to $1,000 and were entertained by some of the biggest stars of Hollywood and Broadway—Harry Belafonte, Ella Fitzgerald, Henry Fonda, Jack Benny, Maria Callas, Jimmy Durante. The highlight was an appearance by Marilyn Monroe, who was stitched into a skin-tight flesh-colored dress that glittered with rhinestones. In a breathy, seductive, little-girl voice, she sang, "Happy birthday, Mr. President. Happy birthday to you."

Lou Harris, the pollster, who was paid with some of the

---

* Otash said Monroe, with whom he'd been acquainted for years, once asked him about setting up recording equipment so she could tape her phone calls in her apartment. He said he turned down the job.

money raised that evening, helped out with the event. He also attended the private party afterward with Monroe, other entertainers, the Kennedys, and their friends. "The one that she went after after that was Bobby," Harris would recall. "Oh, she and Bobby just carried on."

At one point, Harris said, "she literally pinned him against the wall, and she had him trapped, you know. Ethel got so disgusted. When she got him home, she said, 'That's the most disgusting thing I've ever seen.'

"Marilyn didn't care. She was very brazen, a brazen girl.... She really went after him. And when Marilyn went after you, it was a sight to see."[10]

In the spring of 1962, Bobby Kennedy had his own pursuit going, quietly pushing for a new law that he hoped could be used to snare Hoffa. The bill called for penalizing labor officials and employers who pleaded the fifth when questioned about possible violations of labor-management laws. It still bothered RFK that during the rackets hearings, Hoffa had given misleading answers, feigned ignorance, or flat-out lied and still dodged perjury charges. He knew he wouldn't be contradicted by his associates because they all "took five" when asked about Hoffa. But while the president of the AFL-CIO, George Meany, and other labor leaders supported the Kennedy administration, the idea that labor officials could be forced to give up their Fifth Amendment rights infuriated them.

Andrew Biemiller was the AFL-CIO's legislative director, which meant his job was to keep an eye on the raft of proposed laws that touched on labor interests. He particularly hated Kennedy's Fifth Amendment bill because its introduction had caught him by surprise. "He snuck a little bill through the Senate taking away Fifth Amendment rights in certain

kinds of labor cases from both employers and union leaders,"
Biemiller, a former congressman from Wisconsin, later would
say. "And when that bill hit the House, we had a fit. Frankly,
I was caught short, I admit. I don't know how it happened.
There was no debate, no anything—it just passed [the Senate]....
It was done so quietly....It was a very clever, in that sense,
maneuver."[11]

With George Meany's blessing and the backing of other
unions, Biemiller set about killing the bill in the House. That
summer, as he worked with friendly lawmakers, his son was
part of a group of Harvard students who met with attorney
general Kennedy in his office.

"My son, like me, never knows when to keep his mouth
shut at times," Biemiller recalled, "and so he sounds off and
said, 'I hear you're in trouble with the labor movement over
this Fifth Amendment bill.' All of a sudden, it dawns on
Bobby that he's my son. He says, 'You go back and tell your
father I need that bill and I want it. You carry that message
to him.' So he brought the message back."

Biemiller shared the story with Meany, who became "mad
as hell." "My God, trying to use a kid to influence us," Biemiller recalled his boss saying.

Biemiller and friendly lawmakers tied up the bill, but the
attorney general wouldn't give up on it. He insisted on meeting with Meany to make a personal plea. Recalled Biemiller,
"Bob starts off saying, 'Man, President Meany, I admire you.
You're the only guy in the country, practically, that's been
willing to take Hoffa on in any kind of a fight. You've showed
your courage.'" Then Kennedy showed his cards. "Now I need
this bill. I want to get Hoffa. I want to put him in jail."

Meany replied, "Look, Bobby, I'm telling you this. I hate
Hoffa just as much, if not more, than you do. But I'm not
giving up the Fifth Amendment right for labor leaders just to

get Hoffa. You'd better find some other method."[12] The unionists succeeded in killing the Fifth Amendment bill.

Bobby Kennedy was disappointed. Friendly union leaders weren't being helpful, nor was his own FBI director. But soon RFK and his team would come up with other ways to trip up Hoffa.

CHAPTER 14

Planting a Snitch

JIMMY HOFFA CERTAINLY EXPLODED IN rage on occasion, but to some it seemed strategic: a thunderclap to knock his opponent off balance in a bargaining session or to squelch back talk at a union meeting. He'd recover quickly, smile, and say, Hey, if I can't yell at my friends, who can I yell at? His joke was that if he yelled at his enemies — they were legion — it would mean he'd never have time to run the Teamsters.

Still, pressure from the Kennedy Justice Department was getting to Hoffa, and by 1962, they were all talking about it — Harold Gibbons at Teamsters headquarters, lobbyist Sid Zagri on Capitol Hill, trucking execs as they prepared for master freight contract bargaining with Hoffa — *Jimmy's losing his grip.*

At the Midwest freight contract talks at Chicago's LaSalle Hotel during this time, he crossed a line. For half an hour, he screamed at industry representatives, red-faced with fury, hurling disgusting vulgarities. He smashed chairs, "quivered and shook like a man out of his mind," and screamed some more, a broken record of profanities and threats.[1] When it was over, he appeared to be ashamed. Even so, apology was never his style.

Hoffa had set an ambitious goal for himself: he needed certain contract terms in this important regional master freight agreement so that within a couple of years he could stitch together the union's regional trucking agreements into a single national master freight contract with a common expiration date — a single agreement covering all the country's long-haul trucking. It was an audacious plan, one that could help stabilize the fragmented, inefficient trucking industry. It also would give the Teamsters much more leverage as they tried to pry better wages from big companies by having all their contracts expire on the same day, putting pressure on the trucking industry as a whole. Kennedy and Senator McClellan warned repeatedly that a national agreement would concentrate too much power in the hands of a man they believed to be corrupt, explaining that Hoffa could use the agreement to bring the nation's economy to a halt by fiat. In theory, perhaps. But transportation economists and Hoffa himself dismissed RFK's fear-mongering about a national trucking strike as not only unrealistic — trains, boats, planes, and nonunion drivers would be pressed into service during a nationwide strike — but also likely to turn public sentiment against the Teamsters.

On May 17, 1962, Hoffa appeared calm as he summoned Sam Baron, the warehouse division's field organizer, to his office to discuss a contract Hoffa was negotiating with a large furniture company. The slight, fifty-nine-year-old man with a heart condition had been secretly filling in Walter Sheridan about events and machinations inside Teamsters headquarters for a couple of years, and he had also talked to the FBI and, through Bobby's intercession, *Life* magazine.[2] Hoffa disliked

Baron (and he knew the feeling was mutual), but he kept him around not only because Baron, a liberal trade unionist, was good at his job but also because Harold Gibbons, who shared his political views and had hired him, was his good friend and protector.

As Baron told him about a problem with the furniture company, Hoffa became increasingly upset. "We really can't discuss this now," Baron said at one point, in response to Hoffa's questions. "Why don't you let me prepare a written report on what has been happening?" Baron wanted to avoid an argument in front of the other Teamsters officials in the room — Gibbons, Zagri, and others.

"You and your fucking written reports," Hoffa replied, according to Baron's account. Before Baron could slip out of the room, Hoffa sprang from behind his big desk, blocked Baron's way, and snarled: "Why don't you admit you don't know what you're doing?"[3]

"But Jimmy, I do know what I'm doing," Baron replied.

"No one talks to me that way," Hoffa shouted, and then punched him in the eye, dropping him to the carpet.[4] When Baron regained his feet, Hoffa slugged him in the face and shoved him over a chair. Looking up in disgust, Baron said, "You bum — you would use your muscle." The others in the room, including his friend Gibbons, did nothing to stop it. Later that day, after discussing the incident with his wife, Baron decided "enough is enough" and visited the US attorney for the District of Columbia and swore out a complaint.

That evening, Hoffa was arrested on assault charges, fingerprinted, and released. On his way home from the police precinct, he joked with reporters and seemed unconcerned. But it was all an act. Hoffa and his lawyers knew he was in peril. A little-noticed provision of the Landrum-Griffin Act of 1959, the reform law sparked by the rackets hearings, subjected union officials to removal if they were found to have used violence to interfere with the rights of a union member. This case of simple assault, like Achilles' heel, had the potential to bring him down. He stood to lose far more than his famous temper.

The next day brought news of added legal troubles for the Teamsters boss, troubles that may have had something to do with Hoffa's blowup with Baron. Federal prosecutors in Nashville charged Hoffa with conspiring to take payoffs from Commercial Carriers, a big Michigan car-hauling company, in exchange for labor peace. Technically, he and the company were charged with violating the anticollusion provision of the Taft-Hartley Act, which forbade a union officer from carrying on private business with a company that employed his members. The indictment, the first one brought by the Hoffa squad, seemed like a stretch. The two charges were misdemeanors, and the alleged misconduct dated back to 1947, when the Flint, Michigan, company ended a punishing wildcat strike — one without the blessing of the union — by its Teamsters drivers with Hoffa's help. Hoffa told the strikers their actions were illegal and that "they'd be sued for every cent they had."[5]

For Commercial Carriers, settling the strike quickly and on favorable terms came at a price. One of the company's principal owners, Bert Beveridge, explained to an associate what had to happen: "It will apparently be necessary for us to lease equipment from someone Hoffa would designate in order to settle the strike."[6]

That someone would turn out to be Josephine Poszywak and Alice Johnson, whose names were on incorporation papers filed in Nashville for a newly registered truck-leasing company that became known as Test Fleet. The two women were in fact Mrs. Jimmy Hoffa and Mrs. Bert Brennan, going by their maiden names. There was little doubt that Hoffa had personally benefited from the deal.

In a letter to the Rackets Committee, Hoffa's lawyer admitted as such when he listed the businesses in which Hoffa held an interest. On the list were a Columbus, Ohio, racetrack, a contract with a heavyweight boxer, an oil-drilling venture, a girls' camp in Wisconsin — and Test Fleet. "Shares in Test Fleet were held by Mrs. Hoffa," the lawyer, George Fitzgerald, wrote in February of 1957. "The above are all of the businesses in which Mr. Hoffa has had an interest since 1950. The only profitable enterprise has been the Test Fleet or Hobren Corporation."[7] The Get Hoffa squad and the FBI spent more than a year going beyond the work of special prosecutor MacKinnon in 1960, but Test Fleet still was not a strong case. Bert Brennan had died in 1961. Some records were missing. And Kennedy's top administrators were split over whether to indict Hoffa at all. Assistant attorney general Ramsey Clark, who had represented trucking companies in private practice, thought Hoffa's conduct, though questionable, fell within standard practice in the industry. "I was against prosecution," Clark would later say. Deputy attorney general Nick Katzenbach and Criminal Division head Jack Miller supported indictment. They also proposed charging Josephine Hoffa as part of the conspiracy, but there Bobby drew a line. "Even though it would have made our case easier, he refused to charge Mrs. Hoffa," Katzenbach would say. "He said, 'She's not really responsible — she just did what her husband told her to do.' And even though it would have made our introduction of evidence easier, he wouldn't name her as a defendant."[8]

If convicted of the misdemeanor, Hoffa still would be able to keep his union presidency. But if the Get Hoffa squad's effort ended in acquittal, Hoffa and his public relations team would trumpet this result as further proof that the Kennedys, by bringing such a flimsy case to court, had a vendetta against the Teamsters boss. And there was little doubt the press would echo that theme. "A definitive and final failure by a Kennedy to bag a Hoffa would be as mortifying a show of impotence as a public cuckolding," a reporter with *The Nation* wrote at the time, "and Robert Kennedy's virility is something he wants the world to be sure about."[9]

Hoffa and the union weren't afraid of using the public to push their side of the story. Throughout 1962, Jimmy and Jo Hoffa traveled the country, holding rallies in Teamsters strongholds—Sacramento, Hartford, Pittsburgh, Philadelphia—as well as in Chattanooga and Johnson City, Tennessee, the state where Hoffa was set for trial that fall. In all, the Hoffas put on twenty-one rallies across the country that year. The events, billed as "Jo Hoffa dinners," were designed to soften Hoffa's image and play a key role in the Teamsters' continuing political outreach—getting union members and their families registered to vote, which presumably would boost the union's clout on Capitol Hill and counterbalance the administration's hostility to Hoffa.

These carefully choreographed events seemed like coronations: the Hoffas were becoming the Teamsters' royal couple. A Philadelphia dinner that spring was typical: several hundred Teamsters and their wives greeted Jimmy and Jo at the airport, which "was paralyzed by the mammoth welcome, described by one bystander as 'big enough for the President.'" Smiling and waving, the couple joined a motorcade of dozens of cars and zoomed downtown under police escort. At a hotel ballroom, Jo shook hands, watched a ladies' fashion show during lunch, then stood to speak.

Unlike her husband, she wasn't a natural in the role as public advocate for the Teamsters cause. Well dressed, sometimes wearing a mink jacket and pearls, her blond hair carefully coiffed, she typically received a clamorous ovation when introduced. She stood and stiffly delivered the same two-minute speech each time. "Only because my children are grown now can I abandon my lifelong role of housewife and mother and be free to aid Jimmy," she would explain. "I have had to sit in silence on the receiving end of the slurs of McClellan and the Kennedys. I am glad to have this opportunity to help through DRIVE."[10] She urged the wives of the Teamsters to not only speak out but also register to vote, join the DRIVE Ladies' Auxiliary, and "support the gains your husbands have won on the picket lines."

Her appearances were effective. "Hoffa's scheme of bringing his wife into the act has proved a great hit, especially with the wives, who feel that she is truly one of them," wrote Hoffa biographers Ralph and Estelle James, who spent months observing the Teamsters operation at the time.[11] The union's semimonthly newsletter, *DRIVE Reporter*, gave its own gloss: "Our President and First Lady...have devoted many long hours in strenuous travel and speaking engagements....Together they symbolize Mr. and Mrs. Teamster USA."[12]

Accompanying Jo as a handler was her old friend Sylvia Pagano Paris, a free-spirited woman whose taste in men ran to mob figures and who had dated Hoffa in the 1930s before he married Jo. Paris worked at Local 299 in Detroit starting in 1940 and served as a union organizer during World War II. When Jo had recurring problems from undulant fever, caused by drinking unpasteurized milk, Sylvia Paris moved into the Hoffas' modest Robson Street home and helped care for her and the two young Hoffa children, Barbara and Jim.[13] Also living at the Hoffa home was Chuckie O'Brien, Sylvia's son by her late first husband, a minor Kansas City Mafia character who had anglicized his Italian name. In the days before antibiotics, most people recovered from undulant fever in weeks to months; for some, the disease lingered, coming and going — undulating — intermittently, causing fatigue, depression, anxiety, and muscle or skeletal pain. With Jimmy gone much of the time, Jo not only had Sylvia's companionship but also had someone to chauffeur her around. When traveling with the family, Sylvia also tried to follow Jimmy's wishes and make sure Jo didn't have too much to drink.

Despite his legal troubles and the pressures of home life, Hoffa did enjoy a couple of small victories that summer in his sorties with Bobby Kennedy. On June 29, RFK visited Nashville and had lunch with federal district judge William E. Miller, who already had been assigned to preside over the Test Fleet trial. Miller was a conservative Republican appointed by President Eisenhower; at fifty-five, he only spent a maximum of four hours a day in court because of a heart condition. When word leaked out about their lunch, some of Hoffa's lawyers were glad to have this knowledge in case they needed to use it as grounds to appeal a future conviction. The attorney general would later say he and the judge did not discuss Hoffa's case.

At about the same time, the US attorney for the District of Columbia was wrestling over whether to bring the misdemeanor assault case against Hoffa. Six Teamsters who witnessed the attack, Gibbons included, either said that Baron had been drinking and went after Hoffa or simply refused to discuss the incident. To try to break through the obstruction, Baron challenged them to take a polygraph test, which he had done and passed. That positive result, as everyone knew, counted for little, because it couldn't be relied upon in court. With multiple witnesses saying that Baron was inebriated, and with only his lone account of the attack, the federal prosecutor reluctantly announced that he had to drop the charges.

Kennedy understood the reasons but was disappointed that Hoffa — to his mind, clearly guilty — once again had outmaneuvered the Justice Department.

Privately, Teamsters lawyer Edward Bennett Williams, still trying to get in good with the Kennedy camp, told Sheridan that he had given Hoffa's helpers the sarcastic nickname the Improvers. Assault was a misdemeanor, but obstruction of justice — which Kennedy would surely feel had occurred — was a felony, he explained, adding: "They have a facility for improving misdemeanors into felonies." His observation would prove to be prescient.

After dropping the assault case, the US attorney for the District of Columbia, at the Justice Department's urging, tried to build a case against the anti-Baron witnesses for perjury and obstruction of justice, but he had no success. At least RFK could take satisfaction in the *Life* magazine exposé about Hoffa, which he had put in motion the year before when he brought Baron's story to an editor. The story, an "as-told-to" under Baron's byline, ran under the catchy headline I WAS NEAR THE TOP OF JIMMY'S DROP-DEAD LIST.[14]

In late September of 1962, Kennedy's Get Hoffa campaign took a dramatic, unexpected turn when one of Hoffa's trusted union associates, Edward Grady Partin, found himself in a dangerous fix. A hulking, charismatic ex-con with a deep southern drawl, Partin was incarcerated in the East Baton Rouge Parish, Louisiana, jail on kidnapping charges. He had helped a fellow union official in Teamsters Local 5, Sidney Simpson, snatch Simpson's five-month-old son and two-year-old daughter from his estranged wife, who had legal custody, and then hide their children from her.

Partin had controlled Teamsters Local 5 in Baton Rouge

for more than a decade with a free-spending, head-knocking, dictatorial style not unlike Jimmy Hoffa's. When dissidents in Local 5 made trouble over Partin's leadership and would not bow to threats, Partin was said to have forged their names on withdrawal cards and refused to let the newly excommunicated union members take part in a meeting. In June of 1962, the Justice Department charged him with thirteen counts of embezzlement and thirteen counts of falsifying union records.

On top of his troubles in federal and Louisiana courts, Partin was indicted on September 26 by neighboring Alabama authorities, accused of first-degree manslaughter and leaving the scene of an accident. Shortly after midnight on Christmas morning, Partin had crashed into the rear of another car at high speed, sending it pinwheeling off the highway. One passenger, a serviceman from Texas, died, and two others were seriously injured. Partin zoomed off in his new Oldsmobile—until its damaged radiator caused the car to overheat and seize up on the highway about fifty miles from the crash. Alabama state investigators matched broken trim on Partin's car to trim fragments found scattered around the crash scene.[15]

Partin had made bail on the June federal embezzlement charges, but when the bail bond company learned of his kidnapping and manslaughter charges, it revoked his bail. Because of the young ages of the Simpson children, Partin faced aggravated kidnapping counts, which carried a life sentence. In the Baton Rouge jail, Partin "for the first few days acted sort of brave," but when he was unable to make bail on the kidnapping charges "he became more excited and nervous," Simpson, his cell mate at the time, would later say. So Partin came up with a plan. "They want Hoffa more than they want me," Simpson would recall Partin saying.[16]

Partin sent word through a trusted jailer to the district

attorney for Baton Rouge, Sargent Pitcher Jr., that he would be willing to inform on Hoffa in exchange for immunity from his federal charges. But Partin insisted he would talk only if suspicion could be avoided by sneaking him out of his cell in the early hours of the morning, when most prisoners were sleeping and less likely to wonder about his whereabouts. At three in the morning on September 29, he met with Pitcher and his chief investigator, lawyer William Hawk Daniels, and gave them a fantastic story. That summer at a meeting with Hoffa at Teamsters headquarters, Partin recounted, the labor boss was extremely upset. Beckoning Partin to the window in his capacious office, Hoffa fumed, "That son of a bitch Bobby Kennedy—he has to go!" At that time, Hoffa had just been indicted in the Test Fleet case and was facing assault charges. Hoffa asked Partin if he knew where to get his hands on plastic explosives, which he described as powerful and able to explode without leaving a trace. Partin replied that he did not. Then Hoffa pointed to a long-range rifle in his office and said he knew where he could get a silencer for it. Kennedy showed "a lot of guts," Hoffa went on, in driving around by himself in a convertible and swimming alone in his pool.

Partin's accusations, if true, were a matter of national security, far too important for a local district attorney to handle, so Pitcher alerted all the appropriate federal officials: the US attorney for New Orleans, Hoffa Squad special prosecutor Frank Grimsley in Atlanta, and the head of the New Orleans FBI office. The FBI special agent sent a memo to FBI director Hoover saying that Partin would furnish information on Hoffa "for a consideration."

Grimsley asked the FBI to help conduct the first interview of Partin by federal officials, but Hoover's office ordered local FBI agents to boycott the debriefing "in view of the undesirability of having the Bureau made a party to an interview wherein a deal is made." The FBI knew of Partin's shaky background and didn't trust him.

Grimsley picked up on this and told Walter Sheridan that Partin had offered to take a lie detector test to prove he was telling the truth. Sheridan and Criminal Division chief Jack Miller accepted Partin's offer and asked the FBI to arrange a polygraph. In the meantime they recounted Partin's chilling story to Bobby Kennedy. He didn't appear afraid or angry after hearing of Hoffa's supposed threats and went about his business for the day.

As Sheridan left the building that night, he encountered his boss. "What do we do if that fellow passes the test?" RFK asked with a bemused smile.

"I don't know, but I think he might," the investigator replied.

Bobby shrugged and made his way to his car.[17]

Partin had come to the attention of the Rackets Committee a few years earlier. Two members of Local 5 wrote to Senator McClellan in December of 1958 with complaints about Partin's "corrupt practices": "We have been threatened by Mr. Partin if we interfere in his operation of the local." The two Teamsters urged the committee to investigate and said they could "get more information from other sources if the committee should come" to Louisiana. Kennedy wrote back a letter of thanks.[18]

Committee investigators didn't follow up, but if they had, they likely would have learned that Partin had ties to mobbed-up vending-machine companies in Baton Rouge and New Orleans. Records from the New Orleans Metropolitan Crime Commission indicated that in 1959, Partin threatened a work stoppage at the Kaiser Aluminum plant in Gramercy, about an hour west of New Orleans, to pressure the company into using vending machines owned by a company in which he was said to have an interest, Baton Rouge Cigarette Service.[19] Partin was just the sort of racketeer Bobby Kennedy went after during the rackets hearings. RFK pounded Hoffa at the televised hearings for failing to push men like this out of the Teamsters.

On October 3, 1962, RFK's team finally had its chance, and Partin underwent the test. An FBI agent cinched him into the polygraph apparatus, which measured his pulse, respiration, blood pressure, and galvanic skin response, then asked the burly teamster a series of questions about Hoffa's threats against the attorney general. Unfortunately for Partin, he flunked the test. In his report, FBI examiner James Schmidt wrote that Partin's "answers to significant questions showed possible deception."

Because Partin's answers to the easy "control" questions were "erratic," the FBI agent said he could not conclude whether Partin "was telling the truth or lying" about Hoffa's threats against Robert F. Kennedy. But when Partin learned he failed the test, he panicked. He needed to offer something of value to authorities to keep himself out of prison, and he pleaded for a second chance. He hadn't slept in three days, he told the FBI, and was too discombobulated from being in jail. Could he please take the test again, under better circumstances, after he made bail and was released?

One reason Partin was anxious and unable to sleep in jail may have been a drug habit. Partin abused drugs, including heroin, from about 1959 to 1963, his friend Simpson would admit years later. He said Partin often took amphetamines and stayed up for two or three days in a row, acknowledging "that Partin seemed fresh all the time, that he didn't seem to need sleep, that he could go days without sleep, and that he ate very little at times."[20] Simpson said he once retrieved hypodermic needles from Partin's apartment at his friend's request and on occasion noticed purplish track marks on Partin's arms. To cover them up, Partin would wear long-sleeved shirts in the Louisiana heat.[21]

In the Baton Rouge jail, Simpson later recounted, "I asked him why he was doing this to Hoffa." Partin replied, "What difference does it make? I'm thinking about myself. Aren't you thinking about yourself? I don't give a damn about Hoffa." Meanwhile, he and Simpson arranged for the two young missing children to be brought to the courthouse, where they were handed over to authorities, who returned them to their mother. With the kids back with their mother, Partin was eligible for bail and soon was released.

Immediately, Partin and the district attorney's investigator, Daniels, checked into adjacent rooms at a Holiday Inn in Baton Rouge and got busy. Since Partin faced charges in both federal and state courts, he had more than one master to serve if he was going to try to reduce his various charges by cooperating with prosecutors. Over the next four days, he placed or received phone calls constantly, and Daniels ended up recording more than eighty conversations, including at least two between Partin and Hoffa.[22] Partin later bragged to Simpson that Daniels was going to have the kidnapping charges dropped, and the twenty-six federal charges would be dismissed if he "told the story that Daniels and the feds wanted" him to tell.[23]

That first day at the Holiday Inn, October 8, Partin telephoned his primary target at Teamsters headquarters in Washington and told him: "Ah, what I was thinking, Jimmy, after I get this thing straightened out...and everything, if you get an opportunity or something, I would like to get with you and talk with you and talk this thing out." Hoffa replied, "Well, I'll be here all week."

The next day, Partin met with two FBI agents, took another lie detector test, and this time he passed. In conversations that day with agents, he said that in the past he had heard Hoffa say he wanted to kill someone, usually when someone crossed him or upset him enough to provoke his quick temper. However, these threats against Kennedy seemed different. Hoffa actually talked about steps for carrying out the threat. Even so, Partin told the FBI, he wasn't sure if Hoffa was serious about carrying out an assassination plot.

One agent wanted to know why Partin had waited until October to share the news that Hoffa had talked of killing the attorney general in early July. What if Hoffa had acted in the meantime?

Partin replied that over time Hoffa's threats weighed on him more and more. He began to worry for the future of his family. Because he knew so much damaging information about Hoffa, he felt his own life was at risk. And if he were killed, there'd be no one to support his children.

The threats, if true, weren't of much legal use unless Hoffa took some steps to put a plot in place. To prove his bona fides, Partin told the FBI he would be game for revisiting Hoffa while wearing a hidden recorder to see if he could capture the Teamsters boss repeating his plans to seek explosives.[24] Partin even told his handlers that he had a way to deftly bring up Hoffa's earlier request while deflecting suspicion: the theft of explosives from a Louisiana construction site recently had made the local newspapers. He could mention that theft to Jimmy and then ask if he still wanted him to try to obtain some.

But before things got too far along, Partin wanted to make his terms of cooperation clear to the FBI. As Hoover later explained to RFK in a memo, if the government planned to "proceed with prosecution" of Partin for diverting union money, he saw "no point in meeting with Hoffa for the benefit of the government."[25] Hoover's memo was a curious document. Snitches often play an important role in criminal cases, but putting details of any quid pro quo on paper was not standard practice. Also, it posed legal problems for prosecutors if defense lawyers ever could get their hands on such a document. A master manipulator, Hoover may have wanted to protect Hoffa, following the proverb "The enemy of my enemy is my friend." But whatever the explanation, the Hoover memo diminished Partin's value as an informant in the future.

Back in Washington, Sheridan and RFK, along with Jack Miller and others, discussed whether to take up Partin on his offer to secretly record future talks with Hoffa. RFK knew about both Partin's polygraph results because Hoover, again by memo, had made certain to inform him of the unsuccessful test and the later successful test. Bobby eventually said no to having Partin wired, deciding it was too risky. If Partin got caught, his value to the Get Hoffa squad would plummet to zero. Hoffa and his lawyers, no doubt, would use the revelation to postpone the Nashville trial and embarrass the Justice Department. But RFK did want Partin to work as a spy inside the Hoffa camp. To make that happen, prosecutor Grimsley relayed the news to Partin that his federal embezzlement case had been put on hiatus.

After receiving such assurance, Partin telephoned Hoffa on a recorded line. It was October 18, four days before Hoffa's trial was to start. He reached the Teamsters president at a hotel in Newark, New Jersey, and invited himself to see Hoffa in Nashville. "I hate to interrupt you, Jim, but I need to talk to you on...when I can—you, you said you'd be there on the twenty-second in Nashville. What's the best day to come?" Hoffa said he'd arrive there on Sunday the twenty-first.

"Will Sunday or Monday be all right?" Partin wanted to know.

To which Hoffa distractedly replied, "Right."

At this point, Walter Sheridan relayed a controversial new assignment to Partin. There was no burning need to have him get Hoffa to repeat his threats on tape. Given the looming trial, Sheridan and the others wanted Partin to inform them of any attempts by Hoffa or his associates to tamper with the Nashville jurors.

Hoover didn't think Partin should meet with Hoffa in Nashville, wired or otherwise. In a teletype to the head of the Memphis FBI office, the FBI director wrote: "Sheridan aware of possible embarrassment but insists Partin meet with Hoffa. Bureau will not equip Partin with electronic device since AG has stated he does not want Partin so equipped." The FBI decided it would discreetly surveil Partin to see if he actually met with Hoffa and then compare Partin's account of the meeting, relayed through Sheridan, with what the agents actually observed — routine tradecraft to test the veracity of informants.

This encounter between informant and Teamsters president had the potential to either help or hurt the fortunes of both Hoffa and the attorney general. Hoover ordered his field supervisors to keep him informed of every detail about the upcoming meeting. "This cannot be too strongly emphasized," the director said by teletype.

On Sunday, October 21, the day before the Test Fleet trial commenced, Hoffa landed at Nashville's Berry Field in a twin-engine prop plane. He strode through a light mist to the terminal as journalists scurried toward him, notebooks flopped open, cameras rolling. Jimmy repeated lines he had used many times before: "Bob Kennedy is using the FBI as his own personal police force." He is "using the taxpayers' money for his own vendetta." Kennedy is "usurping the powers of his office." Hoffa even dropped the name of the Third Reich's despised leader, saying RFK was "making his own policies and starting out just like Hitler did."

Hoffa had a point about tax dollars. Had the defendant not been Hoffa and the attorney general not been Kennedy, the case wouldn't have been brought. "Never in history had the government devoted so much money, manpower and top level brainpower to a misdemeanor case," journalist Victor Navasky would later write.[26]

After delivering his Kennedy diatribe, Hoffa climbed into a red Thunderbird sedan driven by Ewing King, the tall, chinless, newly elected president of Teamsters Local 327, and headed to the Andrew Jackson Hotel downtown. There, for the next two months, Hoffa used the entire seventh floor as his legal war room and as a remote headquarters from which he ran the union's affairs.

World events soon intruded. The next evening, President Kennedy went on national television at seven o'clock and told an audience of one hundred million Americans that Soviet missiles capable of carrying nuclear warheads were detected in Cuba. He said that he had demanded that the Soviets remove them and that he had ordered a naval blockade to stop any continuing buildup. JFK had nothing reassuring to say to the American public. It was the height of the Cold War, and the United States and the Soviet Union appeared to be sliding toward the unthinkable—a nuclear conflict. Two days earlier, after meeting with advisers in the military, CIA, and State Department, JFK privately told Bobby and top aide Ted Sorensen, "We are very, very close to war." RFK didn't need to be told. He had been playing a crucial role in White House discussions about how to respond to the provocation, then in its sixth day.

Living on nerves and little sleep, Bobby still found time to focus on Hoffa. After the president's sobering address to the nation, RFK called Walter Sheridan at home, his voice weary and tense. When are you going to Nashville?

After jury selection, Sheridan replied. He explained that the two federal prosecutors trying the case, Jim Neal and Charles Shaffer, didn't want him at the courthouse yet. Since he was known as the relentless head of the Get Hoffa squad, the government lawyers were worried that if Hoffa spotted Sheridan, the Teamsters boss might try to provoke an incident that could trigger a mistrial.

After a pause, RFK overruled the trial lawyers and told his friend, "I think you better go down there tonight."

Sheridan arrived in Nashville after midnight. "I went to sleep in the early morning hours," he later explained, "thinking about the very real threat of nuclear war and the possibility that Jimmy Hoffa and I would end up dead together in Nashville, Tennessee."[27] He soon discovered that Neal had been overly cautious. Hoffa didn't recognize Sheridan, even though he had been standing between RFK and Hoffa in perhaps the most well-known news photo of the two men's confrontations at the Senate hearings.

Throughout the thirteen-day missile crisis and the two-month Test Fleet trial, Sheridan and Kennedy would discuss the case almost daily. And in the first week of the trial, it became clear that somebody was trying to meddle with the jury.

One day into jury selection, a woman in the large pool of prospects revealed in open court that the previous evening she had been telephoned by a man who said he was a newspaper reporter and wanted to know what she thought of Jimmy

Hoffa and the Teamsters union. Such conduct was completely improper. The judge asked the dozen or so potential jurors in the courtroom if anyone else had received such a telephone inquiry. Another prospective juror raised his hand and said he had a similar call from a man who identified himself as Mr. Allen from the *Nashville Banner*. Judge William E. Miller had no choice but to dismiss them from jury duty.

As was quickly determined, there was no reporter named Mr. Allen at the *Nashville Banner*, the afternoon daily owned by the conservative Stahlman family. It was certainly news nonetheless: a phony reporter calling prospective jurors in the high-profile trial. Sheridan, Neal, and the Justice Department team worried about news stories revealing this suspicious contact with members of the jury pool. The stories could provide legal grounds for a mistrial, and a delay would play into Hoffa's hand. "Problems have a way of solving themselves," Hoffa liked to say. "If you stall long enough the troubles, or troublemakers, will disappear."[28] Even worse, from Sheridan's point of view, he had barely started working with his new spy inside Hoffa's retinue. That effort would be thrown off by a new trial and difficult to restart.

The editor of the *Nashville Tennessean*, John Seigenthaler, one of Bobby's closest friends, didn't want to do anything that would hurt the Justice Department's case against Hoffa. But the *Banner* publisher, James Stahlman, was furious and felt compelled to act. He began pulling together a front-page editorial defending his paper's integrity and offering a $5,000 reward for information about the fraudulent Mr. Allen.

Walter Sheridan and the team were alarmed to learn of Stahlman's plan and pressed the attorney general into service even though he was at the White House, deeply involved in Cuban Missile Crisis talks. It took until that afternoon before Stahlman was connected with RFK, who wanted him to hold off on publishing a story about the suspicious phone calls. Kennedy pleaded with him to soft-pedal the issue. "The one thing that Mr. Hoffa is interested in is to obtain a mistrial, to get this put off, to get it killed in some fashion," RFK told him. He had watched Hoffa play the delay game, to his benefit, for the past five years.

Stahlman, a segregationist, was not a fan of the Kennedys or their Justice Department. Just a month earlier, the department had helped James Meredith try to enroll as the first black student at the University of Mississippi, which resulted in riots and brought thousands of army troops to the campus to restore order. With Stahlman's secretary on a phone extension taking shorthand of the conversation, Stahlman told Bobby that the *Banner* had no choice but to defend itself and publish a story about the suspicious calls. "What we have put in the paper is going to do your case no injury," Stahlman, not a lawyer, informed the nation's top lawman. The editorial was a flamer, offering the $5,000 to anyone who "successfully produced for trial the contemptible liar and phony guilty of these false telephone calls."

RFK was crestfallen. "This is what they wanted," he told Stahlman. "As long as they can get someone to take public steps, they can get delays, and it doesn't bother them a bit."

But Stahlman said his paper was under false attack. "What has happened has made it necessary for me to defend the reputation of my newspaper, which has existed for eighty-six years," Stahlman lectured Kennedy, "and I don't intend to have it sacrificed for Jimmy Hoffa, the federal government, or anybody else."[29]

Only three jurors were selected the first day of voir dire. Then early the next morning, one of them, James Tippens, a gray-haired insurance broker, came to court early and visited Judge Miller in chambers and told him that he probably shouldn't serve on the jury. Tippens revealed that his neighbor, Lawrence "Red" Medlin, an operator of a sandwich store, had offered him $10,000 in hundred-dollar bills—$5,000 right then and $5,000 later—if he voted to acquit Hoffa. Tippens later gave a full account of Medlin's offer: "He said, 'We've got a chance to make some big money.' And I became suspicious, and I said, 'Now, if it has anything to do with the Hoffa case, Red, I'm not supposed to talk about it.' And he said, 'Well, there is a lot of money involved. There is ten thousand dollars. And nobody will know where it came from.' And I said, 'Well, I'm not interested at all.' And I said, 'I'm not at all interested in it, and I'm not supposed to talk about it.' He said, 'It will only take one vote, and it may not take that.' I said, 'Well, I don't care anything about that, either; if it was a million dollars, it wouldn't make any difference.' And then we proceeded to talk about something else."[30]

Astonished, the judge dismissed Tippens from the jury, then told the FBI to interview the man. Then Miller called in the lawyers for both sides for a private talk. While he wasn't accusing anyone of misconduct, the judge said, he was on high alert for tampering, and this better not happen again.

It took four days to select a jury, with Hoffa directing the defense's moves. On the final day, he huddled twice with his four-man legal team and indicated two prospective alternate jurors that he wanted bounced with peremptory challenges. The final panel had seven women and five men, with four alternates, if needed.

The government's opening statement fell to a young Justice Department lawyer named Charles N. "Charlie" Shaffer

Jr., only five years out of Fordham University School of Law but already a smart, aggressive trial attorney who had handled some major trials for the US attorney for the southern district of New York. Before being added to the Get Hoffa squad, Shaffer had been interviewed by Sheridan and, later, Robert Kennedy, and he believed in their mission. "Some people say Kennedy was out to get Hoffa. Well, let me tell you they are one hundred percent right. When I was hired I knew I wasn't going to prosecute draft dodgers."[31]

Jimmy Hoffa, Shaffer told the jurors, had not "put up a nickel" for Test Fleet, yet "substantial" dividends from Commercial Carriers "wound up in Hoffa's pocket in the name of his associates in the deal." Those dividends, he would show, paid for the Hoffas' 1950 income taxes, stock in a coal company, and a hunting lodge in Michigan's Upper Peninsula. Throughout it all, Commercial Carriers paid one of its own managers to oversee the Test Fleet operation, handle insurance, keep its books, pay license fees, and maintain the equipment—all without cost to Hoffa. It all pointed to a payoff to Hoffa for labor peace.

Wisely, Hoffa sought the best local counsel he could get and landed Z. T. "Tommy" Osborn Jr., a tall, handsome, honey-toned advocate who had gone to law school at night and, like Hoffa, had started out poor. The son of a traveling preacher, Tommy Osborn possessed such a combination of smarts and unpretentious charm that courthouse regulars said he "could talk a vine out of climbing a wall." Earlier that year, Osborn won the *Baker v. Carr* case, the landmark decision by the US Supreme Court supporting a one-man, one-vote standard for political redistricting.

Tall, wearing horn-rimmed glasses and a confident smile, Osborn countered Shaffer's thrusts point by point and painted Hoffa as a victim of government overreach. Commercial Carriers often bought tractor-trailers and leased them to drivers, he said. Further, there was nothing secret about this routine setup. It had been revealed in "disclosure after disclosure" in filings with the federal Interstate Commerce Commission and the Internal Revenue Service.

As for Mr. Hoffa's role, he had been questioned at length about Test Fleet before two different congressional committees, once in 1953 and again in 1957, Osborn went on. Jimmy Hoffa testified "frankly and voluntarily, and under the cross-examination of Mr. Robert F. Kennedy—"

Neal cut him off: "Objection!"

The only difference between 1953 and now, Osborn continued, is that Robert Kennedy was named attorney general. Further, in bringing this case so long after the fact, the federal government, through "delay and lack of diligence," put Hoffa at a disadvantage. Three helpful witnesses were now dead and many records long discarded.

With Judge Miller holding court for only half a day, Hoffa had time to head to his temporary home and manage both his defense team and some of the union's business as well. His hotel suite typically was crowded with his support team, including his foster son, Chuckie O'Brien, and his four trial lawyers—Tommy Osborn, James Haggerty, William Bufalino, and Daniel Maher. For most of the two-month trial, Ed Partin hung around Hoffa's suite or the hotel lobby or sat in the courtroom. In the mornings, he often arrived outside Hoffa's hotel suite with the day's newspapers. He moved furniture around to accommodate meetings, brought in ashtrays, and collated and stapled copies of paperwork. He was there when witnesses were interviewed. He watched witnesses go over statements that were compiled from earlier interviews. He heard defense lawyers disagree over tactics. He joined Hoffa and his lawyers for dinner and often asked him how he

thought the trial was going. Nearly every day he was in Nashville, Partin found a way to telephone Sheridan or sneak away
to meet him. The two men had agreed on a subterfuge—
Partin used the name Andy Anderson when calling and leaving messages. Sheridan's code name was John Black.

Hours after Partin first arrived in Nashville, he found
what he had been sent to find, he would later tell his handlers. In Hoffa's suite, he met Local 327 president Ewing King,
who volunteered that a meeting had been "set up on the jury
that night," Partin told Sheridan. In short order, Partin said,
Hoffa told him "they were going to get to one juror or try to
get to a few scattered jurors and take their chances." A day
later, Partin told Sheridan, Hoffa told him he might need him
at some point "to pass something for him," hitting his rear
pants pocket as if checking for his wallet. Partin was leaving
to return to Baton Rouge for a day or two—he would travel
back and forth several times during the trial—and told Hoffa
he'd be happy to help.

Partin's information, if true, was priceless to Sheridan
and the Hoffa squad. They had an informant inside what
they believed to be a criminal conspiracy—attempted jury
tampering—that could be investigated by the FBI and the
Justice Department as it unfolded. They now had two inter-
twined missions: convict Hoffa inside the public courtroom
and secretly craft a jury-tampering case against him outside
the courtroom.

In placing a spy alongside a criminal defendant and his
lawyers in the midst of a trial, Kennedy's lawyers knew they
had to walk a constitutional tightrope. One huge concern:
they were not supposed to accept or act on information Partin
might provide about Hoffa's legal strategy or witness testimony. Otherwise, the government risked violating his fair
trial rights under the Sixth Amendment. And there were other

delicate issues. When he and Partin talked, Sheridan took notes on hotel-room stationery or pieces of paper, careful not to take down too much, keeping the notes cryptic. He did so because the Jencks Act said that nearly complete or verbatim notes of a witness were discoverable, meaning that Hoffa would be entitled to copies of any extensive notes if his lawyers demanded them. Sheridan crafted his reports, then threw out any notes he used.

Partin wasn't as careful. He "has been boasting in and around Baton Rouge" that he won't be convicted on any federal charges or "any other charges brought against him by local authorities," Hoover alerted Sheridan in a memo.[32] Partin was claiming that his clout came from "his close friend" senator Russell Long. Hoover was putting Sheridan and the Hoffa squad on notice that Partin, their insider, was boastful and loose-lipped, a serious flaw in an informant.

It was important for Sheridan, as handler, to know that Partin was free with his talk, but from Sheridan's point of view, it would be better if this information weren't captured in official reports. As the proxy for the attorney general, Hoover's nominal boss, Sheridan was able to do something about it. Four days later, Hoover wrote to the special agent in charge of the New Orleans office, telling him that Sheridan "did not desire any further coverage of Partin of any nature" and to submit "a closing report."[33]

It was a testament to Sheridan's clout with Bobby Kennedy — and to the attorney general's ability to force Hoover to assist the Get Hoffa squad — that Sheridan could essentially give FBI agents assignments and their supervisors would sign off on them. In Nashville, Sheridan asked FBI agents Bill Sheets and Ed Steele to check out the tips he was getting from the lawless Partin. "The Bureau didn't want anything to do with Partin — they were afraid of him," Sheridan would later explain. "They tried to be cautious. The Bureau's inclination was to leave him alone because he might be a double agent. So I had all the contacts with him. The Bureau didn't 'refuse' to work with him, but the reality of the situation was that if I didn't they weren't going to do it."[34]

Sheridan also had FBI agents put round-the-clock surveillance on Teamsters official Ewing King after Partin passed along a promising lead: King told him he was trying to influence a woman on the jury through her husband, a longtime highway patrolman. Using Teamsters' political heft, King would promise him a promotion. Partin didn't have a name, but when Sheridan and Neal checked juror questionnaires, they saw that juror 10, Betty Paschal, was married to a patrolman. "There was no way Partin could have known that on his own," the investigator would later say.[35]

On a Saturday evening, agent Steele, supervising the stakeout team, heard King's code name mentioned over the two-way radio from the surveillance car: "Topcat is moving." King drove his red Thunderbird to a restaurant parking lot, waited, and was met by a business agent for Local 327 in a blue Chevrolet. They swapped cars, and King headed to Woodbury, about fifty miles southeast of downtown Nashville. Shortly after one in the morning, agents saw what amounted to gold: the blue Chevy parked in the driveway outside the Paschal home and a uniformed patrolman standing next to the car, talking to King through the rolled-down driver's-side window.

Inside the courtroom, the government's conspiracy case dragged on, each financial record and witness account painstakingly presented. Syndicated columnist Drew Pearson visited the courtroom and was not impressed. "The lawyers were lethargic, jurors looked puzzled, spectators and newsmen seemed bored."

But of the twenty-nine government witnesses that Neal and Shaffer put on the stand over two months, none stung Hoffa as much as the appearance on November 28 of his longtime lawyer and friend George Fitzgerald. Of the dozens of lawyers who had worked for Hoffa over the years, Fitzgerald knew him the longest and the best, having represented him almost continuously since 1935. Of all the lawyers, he likely knew the most about Hoffa's cash-and-carry business deals. For the previous few years, Sheridan had softly cultivated the aging, silver-haired lawyer, trying to pry him away from his most important and lucrative clients, Hoffa and the Detroit-area Teamsters locals. It was unrealistic to expect a lawyer to reveal client confidences; it was unethical, and anyone who did so would become a pariah in his field. But Sheridan had softened Fitzgerald enough so that he would discuss his own conduct without pleading the fifth or concocting a story.

Properly subpoenaed and under oath, Fitzgerald was asked to explain why he had cashed a $15,000 Test Fleet dividend check payable to and endorsed by Mrs. Hoffa in her maiden name. Because Hoffa asked him to, he replied. He transferred that amount to Jimmy Hoffa by writing him a $15,000 personal check, the lawyer said.

Hoffa was visibly shaken. Fitzgerald's testimony not only undercut Hoffa's defense but also made him look sneaky, untrustworthy. Soon thereafter, in a hallway outside the courtroom, Hoffa yelled at him. "You're all through," Hoffa said. "Turn in your books and records. You better start thinking about the seventy-five-thousand-dollar loan." (Hoffa had approved a loan for Fitzgerald from the Teamsters' Central

States Pension Fund.) Fitzgerald soon left Nashville for Detroit, where he disconnected his home telephone and hid out.

Exactly one week later, Hoffa was subjected to another significant scare. The jury was on a break when a skinny man in a tan trench coat slipped into the courtroom. He pushed his way past the waist-high, swinging wooden gate that separated the public seating from the trial tables, the jury box, and the judge's bench. Then he reached under his coat and brought out a handgun that resembled a Beretta. It had a long barrel that "just went on and on and on," prosecutor Neal would later say. The man, Warren Swanson, twenty-eight years old, was a former mental patient who said he had a vision that told him to do it. "It sounds crazy," he would later say, "but I just got a message from a higher power."

He leveled the barrel at Neal, then swung it at Hoffa and fired point-blank. In rapid order there were three popping sounds.

Swanson had been living in a Cincinnati hotel room months earlier with nothing to do but read a Gideons' Bible, which he did obsessively. Out his window he spotted a sign for an upcoming Teamsters convention. A voice took over his head, repeatedly saying Hoffa's name and telling Swanson to kill him, he said. Swanson ordered the gun through the mail after reading a magazine ad for a high-powered gas pellet gun — "Drives pellets through four-inch blocks of wood!"

At the sound of gunfire, Hoffa threw his arms in front of his head, then rushed Swanson and punched him in the face, knocking him to the floor. Chuckie O'Brien, thinking Swanson may have killed the "old man" — his foster father — kicked Swanson's head, sending blood flying, then held him down until the marshals handcuffed the assailant. "My man Chuckie O'Brien held that fellow down," Hoffa proudly recounted. "I raised that kid."

The night before Swanson visited the courthouse, he loaded cylinders of compressed carbon dioxide into the air gun. His intent, he later admitted, was to assassinate Hoffa. But his cheap weapon lost some compression overnight. The lead pellets merely raised some welts on Hoffa's arm and torso. "He's just some jerk with a gun," Hoffa would later tell reporters. "No question that this guy is a psycho. He needs medical attention." Swanson soon would be sent to the medical center at a federal prison in Missouri.

When order finally was restored in the courtroom, the judge said, "Will somebody clean up all that blood?" Next, Judge Miller suspended the trial and had the jurors, unaware of the attack, put up in hotel rooms with marshals overseeing them in an effort to shield them from the upcoming media stories about the sensational attempt on Hoffa's life.

With the jury out and sequestered, Sheridan and Neal figured it was a good time to tell the judge about the attempt to influence juror Betty Paschal. Neal explained the evidence in a motion, the judge read it, then he cleared the courtroom except for the defendants and lawyers for each side. For extra precaution, he had the marshals tape newspaper over the small windows in the courtroom doors. In the hallway, reporters jostled for a view, as one reporter wrote, like kids taking turns to watch a baseball game through a knothole.

The prosecution said Hoffa's men had tried to bribe the patrolman husband of a juror. The defense, furious and a little scared, angrily objected to accusations. But the motion worked — Judge Miller dismissed Betty Paschal. She would later tell reporters she had no idea why she was bounced from the jury.

The next morning, Hoffa asked the judge to postpone the trial. His wife was supposed to come to Nashville to testify on his behalf, but now she was too terrified. He was afraid for his life and was under such "shock, stress, and strain" from the attack that he couldn't effectively assist his lawyers in his defense. Judge Miller pointed out that from his perch he had had "a ringside seat" to the incident. He called Hoffa's request "utterly groundless if not fantastic," and ruled that the trial, which was nearing its end, would carry on.

In mid-December, Hoffa took the witness stand in the crowded courtroom. Rather than shocked and strained, he appeared relaxed and confident. He had always prided himself on his ability to handle questions, make his case, and not get flustered. Questioned by his lawyer, Hoffa said he and his late friend Brennan at first were going to put the company in their names, then decided it would be a "good thing" for their wives to have independent incomes in case anything should happen to Hoffa or Brennan. After that, he had nothing to do with Test Fleet. It was true that he had used some of the dividends given to him by his wife, but he viewed the money as loans and he always repaid her. He flatly denied the testimony of his fired lawyer, Fitzgerald, about swapping a $15,000 dividend check in Jo Hoffa's name for one Fitzgerald made out to Hoffa. Rather, Fitzgerald needed a short-term loan, so Hoffa gave him his wife's $15,000 dividend. The lawyer wrote them a $15,000 check, which Hoffa said he held for three weeks, until Fitzgerald had funds to cover it.

"Hoffa was, as usual, an impressive, though testy, witness," Sheridan had to admit.[36]

Soon enough, James Neal gave the closing argument, speaking for over two hours. He had to prove that the ownership by the two women was a sham. You have seen painted, stroke by stroke for weeks, a "portrait of the payoff," he said.

On Hoffa's side, Osborn hammered at the weak points in the government's case: it hadn't shown one dime going to Hoffa.

Further, Hoffa's own lawyer told him the setup that put the shares in his wife's maiden name was completely legal.

On Sunday, December 23, the jurors filed into the courtroom for the last time. After seventeen hours of deliberations spread over three days, they were deadlocked, seven to five, for Hoffa's acquittal. When the judge asked who thought they were hopelessly deadlocked, all twelve raised their hands. "If the members of the jury cannot agree, they cannot agree, and that is it," Miller said, clearly disappointed.

Judge Miller's mood was as dark as his robes. In open court, he accused Hoffa's associates of trying to tamper with the jury. He said, "Illegal and improper attempts were being made by close labor union associates of the defendant to contact and influence certain members of the jury." He explained that Teamsters Ewing King and another Hoffa associate, switching cars to throw pursuers off their tracks, had contacted the husband of juror Betty Paschal, whom he dismissed after a secret hearing. There also were attempts to influence another juror, Gratin Fields, which explained why Mr. Fields was dismissed after hearing weeks of testimony. These continued attempts, Miller told the jury, were why he had them sequestered for the past three weeks. Just before he did so, while they were on a break, the judge told them, a deranged man with a pellet gun had invaded the courtroom and fired shots at Hoffa. He turned to the prosecutors and said he was ordering the US attorney in Nashville to empanel a special grand jury and investigate these "shameful" tampering attempts. It was clear that Hoffa's legal troubles were far from over even though he had just escaped a conviction.

Although it's hard to be certain, the jurors may have deliberated without interference. That they did not convict Hoffa, hardly a sympathetic figure in Nashville, revealed the case to be as weak as some senior Justice Department lawyers had believed. At the same time, Hoffa likely had a winning case before his associates "improved" a misdemeanor into a felony—jury tampering. His legal troubles were to linger, no matter the Test Fleet result.

After the hung jury was announced, Hoffa was to head to one of two planes waiting to take him, his son, Jim, his lawyers, and the rest of his entourage back to Detroit. But before leaving the federal building, he called the reporters together and before a bank of microphones announced that he was "naturally disappointed" in the verdict. With yet another failed prosecution, he said, it should be clear to all that Kennedy was personally conducting "a vendetta" against him. Then he wished "the jury, the reporters, and everybody connected with the trial a merry Christmas" and headed to the airport.

On the private flight to Detroit, Hoffa relaxed with his minions, playing a few hands of gin rummy, then took a nap. Before dozing off, he warned them, "Bobby, small and dangerous as he is, is liable to try anything. What does it cost him? Not a nickel. The taxpayer picks up the tab."[37] Several hours later in Detroit, Hoffa was asked about the attorney general, and this time his holiday spirit was much weaker. "That spoiled brat…that crumb-bum." Then, almost affectionately, Hoffa said, "Someday I'm gonna break both his arms."

CHAPTER 15

Trouble at Home

IT WAS EARLY 1963 WHEN the attorney general called special prosecutor Bill Hundley into his cavernous office and surprised him with an offer. He had decided to shake up the organized crime section and wanted Hundley to take his old job back and run it once again.

Hundley was caught off guard. Kennedy had obviously gotten over the terrible clashes the two of them had during the rackets hearings, when Hundley, chief organized crime prosecutor in the Eisenhower Justice Department, brushed aside the half-baked criminal referrals that the McClellan committee's chief counsel sent his way. Hundley took this development as a sign of growth in a man he once derided as a callow young lawyer. Meanwhile, Hundley had impressed RFK with his professionalism and easy, down-to-earth manner, which appealed to everybody from jurors to FBI agents.

There's a problem, Hundley told Kennedy at their meeting. He didn't want his old job back. He was forty, had three kids under the age of three, and needed the fatter paycheck that could come with a thriving private practice. He was looking to leave the Justice Department.

"Bill, take it for a year, and I'll take care of you," Bobby promised. As was his nature, he persisted, and Hundley agreed.

This meant Kennedy was pushing out section chief Ed Silberling, whom RFK found to be petulant and a poor leader. Silberling "had had some important successes," RFK was to say. "And he turned out to be not very satisfactory—difficult to get along with and finally I removed him."[1]

Silberling would blame his demotion on his aggressive investigations into corrupt politicians, who, he believed, were necessary partners if organized crime were to succeed. "Unfortunately, we found substantial corruption in Democratic strongholds with people who had supported JFK strongly," Silberling was to say. "And I was not reluctant to go ahead and prosecute, which caused problems with members of the Democratic National Committee coming to Bobby."[2] Perhaps Silberling's most sensitive prosecution involved the portly mayor of Gary, Indiana, George Chacharis, accused of taking payoffs from construction companies in return for city contracts.[3] "I was ordered to pull my man out of the grand jury and have him stopped," Silberling would later say. He thought Bobby was protecting Chacharis, who helped carry Indiana in the 1960 presidential campaign for the Kennedys and was in line to be US ambassador to Greece. Ever aggressive and ingenious, Silberling hatched a work-around. "I had my man give information to the IRS and so instead of [Chacharis] being prosecuted for extortion...he was prosecuted for failure to pay taxes on the bribes he received."[4] After the grand jury brought charges against him for evading $227,000 in taxes on the bribes, the mayor pleaded guilty.[5] No matter. Brash, impolitic Silberling was out.*

---

* Despite his ruthless reputation, Kennedy found it hard to fire people he had recruited, and he made calls to other agencies to see if a suitable position for Silberling could be found. Silberling would return to New York, where, a year later, he ran for Congress, with Bobby even campaigning for him.

Kennedy's choice of Hundley to jump back in as organized crime chief surprised just about everyone — particularly
Sheridan, head of the Get Hoffa squad, who didn't fully trust
Hundley and his less-than-fanatic pursuit of the Teamsters
boss. "Kennedy and I were never on the same page when it
came to Hoffa," Hundley would later say. "When I came back
as head of Organized Crime, he set up a group within my
section we called the Terrible Twenty. They were out to get
Hoffa. Technically, they were to report to me, but he still
didn't trust me with Hoffa. Don't get me wrong. I wasn't for
Hoffa. However, I didn't like twenty attorneys targeting him."
He eventually came up with a theory to explain RFK's obses-
sion with the Teamsters president. "Robert Kennedy had a
great capacity for love, but he also had an equally great capacity for hate," Hundley explained. Much of Kennedy's hate for
Hoffa, he believed, stemmed from Hoffa's outwitting RFK
time and again. "With him, it was a game he had to win,"
Hundley was to say. "Whether it was touch football or a prosecution, he had the Kennedy win-at-any-cost attitude."[6]

With changes in leadership, a reinvigorated Get Hoffa
squad — Neal, Shaffer, and Sheridan — brought witness after
witness before a Nashville grand jury in early 1963, carefully
building a jury-tampering case against Hoffa and his associates. Edward Grady Partin was the linchpin of the case, but
bringing him before the secret proceedings to lay out Hoffa's
misdeeds posed great risk. What if Hoffa somehow had a
mole inside the grand jury? He had accomplished that feat
before — notably, in Detroit in the 1950s, having small Minifon recorders hidden in the pockets of half a dozen Teamsters
business agents called to testify in an investigation into his
Local 299. If word leaked out that Partin was a turncoat, who
knew how Hoffa might retaliate?

However, Partin was the sole witness to much of what he

said were Hoffa's attempts to fix the Test Fleet trial. As a result, Partin's account was essential for the grand jurors to consider if they were to return an indictment against the Teamsters boss. This put the Get Hoffa squad in a quandary: if Partin told all to the grand jury, the government risked exposing him to Hoffa long before any trial; but without Partin, RFK had no case. "If we don't take him in, aren't you obstructing justice?" Shaffer asked his colleagues as they mulled over what to do. At headquarters, Bobby's top brass weighed in with different ways to overcome this dilemma. "Every genius had a solution," Shaffer said, until he came up with a solution himself. "I told Sheridan to put him in the grand jury and have him take the Fifth Amendment."[7] As it turned out, one of Hoffa's lawyers gave Partin the same advice, which he followed.

Weeks later, in the spring of 1963, RFK called his top advisers together into his vast, walnut-paneled office to help him decide what to do next with Hoffa. A Chicago grand jury being run by prosecutor Charles Z. Smith and other Hoffa squad lawyers was building a promising conspiracy and fraud case against Hoffa and several of his business associates. They were accused of giving or getting kickbacks to facilitate loans from the Teamsters' Central States Pension Fund. Should the Nashville jury-tampering case take a backseat?

One thing Kennedy's team all agreed on: if Hoffa were to be indicted, the case against him "had to be something strong and heinous," Sheridan said. The jury-fixing case "was both. But there were problems with it. The witness against Hoffa, Ed Partin, was the only one who could really tie him into the conspiracy."[8] Other top Justice Department officials worried that the case could be weakened by the argument that Partin "had been planted in the Hoffa camp," Sheridan recalled. Ramsey Clark opposed bringing charges because of a possible

Sixth Amendment violation—Hoffa's right to effective counsel. It could be argued that Partin, government informant and
hanger-on with Hoffa's legal team, had interfered with the
union leader's defense by being able to tell the government
what tactics Hoffa's lawyers were considering. Archibald Cox,
who as solicitor general handled Justice Department cases
before the US Supreme Court, strongly disagreed. He said
he'd be happy to defend that case against any Sixth Amendment appeals before the Supreme Court, if it came to that.[9]

Hundley opposed the jury-fixing case for reasons more
practical than legal. He didn't believe the case could be won
because it came down to Partin's word against Hoffa's. "I didn't
like the case because I didn't believe the principal witness,"
Hundley would later say. "They gave him a polygraph in jail
and he flunked, and then they let him out and he passed."[10]

But with Sheridan, Neal, Shaffer, Miller, Katzenbach, and
others favoring indicting Hoffa for jury tampering, RFK eventually joined them.

In early May of 1963, Sheridan confirmed with Partin that
he would testify in open court against Hoffa for jury tampering. On May 8, Partin wore a hidden microphone and met in
Nashville with Ewing King, the head of the Teamsters local
who, along with Hoffa and others, was a target of the jury-
tampering investigation. Partin was tasked again with trying to
improve the case again Hoffa and King, asking questions and
hoping King would incriminate himself on tape. King did not.

A few days later, Hoffa and three others, including mobbed-
up Chicago insurance man Allen Dorfman, were charged with
jury tampering and conspiracy. Partin was putting himself in
jeopardy, but by indicting Hoffa, so was the Kennedy team.
If Partin took a powder and decided not to testify, RFK would
have to dismiss the case—a reversal certain to be exploited
by Hoffa as further proof of a Kennedy vendetta.

Partin, with a decade of negotiating contracts under his belt, knew he had leverage and had already put it to use. His kidnapping charges in Baton Rouge had been dropped; his federal embezzlement case was postponed indefinitely, and eventually it would be dropped, too. But Partin wanted something more. Walter Sheridan had grown fond of his roguish double agent; he appreciated the risks he had taken and believed the government should do whatever it could legitimately do to help him. It was illegal to pay a witness who testified in federal court, but Sheridan came up with a plan that modestly rewarded Partin. Although he had been continuously employed by Local 5 for more than a decade, he was $1,200 behind in support payments for his five children. Sheridan secured approval from his superiors to send four monthly payments of $300 each to Partin's estranged wife. They originated as checks made out to Hoffa squad prosecutor Frank Grimsley of Atlanta and were drawn from the Justice Department's confidential informant account. He cashed the checks, bought corresponding money orders, and sent them to Mrs. Partin.

They all had to be careful. If this subterfuge were uncovered by Hoffa's team, it could damage the government's already less-than-sturdy criminal case.

The hard work of Hoffa squad prosecutor Charles Z. Smith and a large team of Justice Department lawyers, accountants, and FBI agents came to fruition that June. Smith and others on the Hoffa squad had been running federal grand jury investigations in Los Angeles, Chicago, Miami, and twenty-six other cities for the past two years, attempting to untangle the financial machinations behind some of the more pungent Hoffa-approved loans from the Teamsters' rapidly growing

Central States Pension Fund. By the early 1960s, the fund served as a keystone for Hoffa's powerful hold over the International Brotherhood of Teamsters. In a formula unique in the labor movement, Hoffa had dropped the retirement age for eligible Teamsters in the huge Central Conference to sixty and promised each retiree two hundred dollars a month, the highest retirement payout for union pensions in the country.[11] Hoffa boasted about this benefit constantly, and it helped him maintain support among the rank and file.

Scrutiny of the pension agreement's fine print revealed how, with only average employer contributions, Hoffa accomplished this feat: after five years, payouts dropped by more than half, when Social Security benefits kicked in at age sixty-five. There were almost no allowances for disability benefits or vested pensions for those leaving the industry before retirement age. Hoffa cannily reaped the greatest propaganda value from the widest swath of Teamsters by lowering retirement age and "boosting" pension payments.

With more than $200 million in the fund to invest, Hoffa and his union were powerful financiers. Distrustful of the stock market, dismissive of Wall Street bankers, Hoffa continued investing the pension fund in real estate deals, many quite risky and characterized by sweetheart terms. In 1959, for example, he pushed through a $1 million loan to Sunrise Hospital, outside Las Vegas, a venture owned in large part by his old Detroit associate Moe Dalitz, the Purple Gang mobster who had moved into the Nevada casino business in the late 1940s. With Sunrise and other ventures — and with Hoffa's help — Dalitz continued to remake himself as a wealthy and, for Las Vegas, respectable business magnate. Hoffa made no secret about the union's goal with the loans: "to reward friends and make new ones."

By 1963, the Justice Department's dragnet had evidence

that certain Hoffa friends, lawyers, and business partners often served as middlemen on the loans and took hefty finder's fees, some of them funneled back to Hoffa or to trusted aides such as Allen Dorfman. On June 4, a twenty-eight-count indictment was handed down in Chicago, charging Hoffa and seven others with fraudulently obtaining $20 million in loans and diverting more than $1 million for their own uses.

Now Hoffa would have to defend himself in yet another city by putting together a legal team, learning the intricacies of a complex case, and assembling enough cash to pay for it all.

The FBI continued to expand its campaign to bug the social clubs, smoke shops, and back offices where mobsters let their guard down. An inspired target in Detroit was the home of Sylvia Paris, the longtime close friend of the Hoffas and mother of Jimmy's aide and foster son, Chuckie O'Brien. By the early 1960s, she had become the mistress of Detroit Mafia leader Tony Jack, a.k.a. Anthony Giacalone. Michigan authorities and the FBI had had files on her for years, and they had grown significantly thicker in July of 1959.

One summer evening in upscale Bloomfield Hills, a Detroit suburb, one of Paris's neighbors wrote down the license plate number of a suspicious car parked nearby. Shortly thereafter, the car took off, and Paris's home burst into flames and was completely destroyed. She lived there with her son, Chuckie O'Brien, his wife and two small children, but they were out of town at the time. When police learned of the suspicious car, they traced it back to a Teamsters driver, an ex-cop who knew Hoffa and who had recently been arrested for setting fire to his tractor-trailer. Police and fire officials came to believe that Paris had her home torched to collect insurance money. After getting the proceeds of her policy, she found a new $40,000 home nearby.[12]

By the spring of 1963, the FBI was monitoring Paris from morning to night, with three different agents listening in shifts. Often a fourth lurked discreetly in the neighborhood, advising his colleagues when he spotted someone new arriving at her home and, if possible, identifying him or her by sight so that the intercepted audio could be labeled more easily.[13] Paris had regular guests from the Detroit underworld, particularly Anthony Giacalone and his friend Anthony "Nino" Cimini. With her two children gone and her husband always away, Josephine Hoffa often joined them. As the FBI electronic surveillance would reveal, Jo had an affair with Nino, a secret that her husband later learned about.

Still, Jimmy Hoffa continued to trust Sylvia Paris. In April of 1963, Hoffa, accompanied by Chuckie O'Brien, stopped at the home, obviously unaware the FBI had it under electronic surveillance. Hoffa burned some papers there, apparently in a fireplace or in the small basement incinerator. What the papers were about or whether the FBI passed this information to the Hoffa squad remains unknown.

Hoffa faced other challenges, both professional and personal, besides turning up on the FBI's secret electronic surveillance. He ran the Teamsters with such an abusive hand that some key staffers, for revenge or because of guilty consciences, went behind his back to fill in Sheridan on the drama. Staggered by the burden of two complex criminal cases in two different cities, Hoffa let himself get out of shape. He was disgusted with himself, which put him in an even fouler mood. Hoffa went on a crash diet for two weeks, limiting himself to four ounces of steak and tea at every meal, trying to lose twelve pounds. He wasn't home much and relied on others such as Sylvia and Chuckie to help with his family. Josephine was depressed and drinking heavily, worried that Jimmy might end up in prison or worse. In June, lawyer Ed Williams talked to Sylvia Paris on the telephone and asked her to tell Josephine "not to worry" about her husband's legal troubles. Williams said he was on top of things and was sending two of his associates to Detroit to do some legwork to help out.[14] Williams and his firm, at Hoffa's urging, also had taken on Paris's lover, Anthony "Tony Jack" Giacalone, as a client after he was charged with bribing a Detroit police officer.

But Jo Hoffa did worry. When her husband had to hurry to Chicago unexpectedly, she took this as bad news and worried about his safety. This set off Sylvia, who later recounted her conversation with Jo to Tony Jack. "Oh, boy, I shut her up," Sylvia told him, then recounted the conversation. "You stop that fucking noise right now; stop that fucking noise right now! Your husband never did do time. What little [time] Tony did he'll never forget for the rest of his life. Every day he thinks about it.... You stop that right now about your husband."[15]

By July, Jo had gotten worse, and she needed to be treated for her drinking. Sylvia was overheard on the FBI's hidden microphone trying to get her friend to pull herself together: "Are you listening to me? Because I love you, Josephine. I don't want anything to happen to you. You are all I've got. I haven't got anybody. Sure, I mean, I got my mother, but I mean, same time, she can take care of herself and everything. That's all I got. I've got nobody else."[16]

On July 30, Sylvia talked to a doctor about Jo, telling him she couldn't be with her friend Mrs. Hoffa at all times to make certain she stayed safe. "It sounds bad, Doctor. If she's going to take all them tranquilizers, and then she's going to drink with them, what can I do for her?"

Two weeks later, Josephine was visiting at Sylvia's home when she collapsed. Ending up in Grace Hospital, she was sedated and apparently strapped to her bed. At her home, Jo had been caring for her own mother, who was nearly blind, so Sylvia brought Jo's mother to her home. But more than a week later, Josephine was still in the hospital. Hoffa was upset with his mother-in-law, believing it was her demands that were affecting his wife's health. He'd put Jo's mother in a county home, Hoffa told Sylvia. He wasn't going to let her kill Josephine.[17] His wife was released from the hospital soon thereafter.

In the face of the Hoffa family's personal dramas, Paris increasingly began to feel put upon by Jo Hoffa and resent that she had to remind Jimmy to pay her for the work she did for the family. Teamsters business agents—like her son, Chuckie—who served as gofers for the Hoffas made a good salary, she was heard to complain, so why didn't she get paid? Her grievances and Tony Jack's greed perhaps inspired a plot by him and his brother, William "Billy Jack" Giacalone, to make a big score at Hoffa's expense.

In the fall of 1963, Billy and Tony were overheard discussing ways to break into Hoffa's safe at his luxury apartment in Washington, DC. They figured that Hoffa had as much as $500,000 in cash secreted inside. "Sylvia says it's got to be in that closet," Tony told his brother, sharing inside information from his girlfriend. "That's what I'm thinking, too. That's the only way I can figure him having some big safe."

Their conversation was picked up by an FBI microphone hidden in the Giacalones' business office. The brothers said they would fly to Washington under assumed names when Jimmy was away. They discussed the alarm system and methods to crack the safe. To hide their tracks, they would stage their burglary so it could be blamed on Jo and her drinking.

Tony Jack had a set of keys to the apartment, likely obtained through Sylvia. Billy Jack would take Jo "out cabareting" while his brother managed to crack the safe. "Knock her out. Leave the bottle in the bed with her. That's better yet."

Because it would look like an inside job, the Hoffas might suspect Sylvia had something to do with it, the mobsters knew, but that didn't concern them. They'd be safe, Tony Jack said, because his girlfriend was tough and wouldn't crack under pressure. They could kill her and "she wouldn't open her mouth," Tony said with pride.

Billy Jack was amused just thinking about it. "They'll go out of their fucking minds if something like this ever happens," he said.

Robert Kennedy had his own challenges that fall. For the previous few months, he believed he was dragging down his brother politically, particularly over the Justice Department's enforcement of civil rights. Along with others, he had pushed Congress to pass the president's civil rights bill, anathema in large parts of the South. It contributed to the president's approval rating dropping from 76 percent early that year to 59 percent by the fall — not terrible but sinking steadily. Bobby felt his civil rights role "was such a burden to carry in the 1964 election" that he wanted to resign immediately as attorney general and turn to the campaign, but Jack insisted he wait. To resign now, he told his younger brother, would make it appear as if the Kennedys were running out on civil rights, which wasn't the case.

On November 20, 1963, RFK and his alter ego, Walter Sheridan, both turned thirty-eight, and RFK's staff organized a joint party in his spacious Justice Department office. Bobby, who often wore his emotions like a flag, appeared to his aides to be depressed and disconcertingly glum. The party seemed like an exercise in strained gaiety, full of uncomfortable people. At one point, sensing he was putting a damper on the festivities, Bobby climbed onto his desk, drawing everybody's attention. Ramsey Clark knew what was going to happen next. "As was so characteristic of him, sometimes when he really, personally felt the most depressed, you might say, he would balance that with capricious things, almost silly things," Clark would later explain.

From his perch, with everyone looking his way expectantly, Bobby gave an impromptu speech. With a blend of sarcasm and a touch of self-pity, he noted how wonderful it was that he had become such an accomplished man at age thirty-eight. He had turned into such a valuable asset to his brother that the president's reelection next year was all but a certainty. And, Bobby said, he owed his success to his promotion of such wildly popular causes as expanding civil rights for blacks and going after the head of the nation's biggest, most powerful labor union.

Everyone got the attempted humor, but it didn't salvage the event. As the party broke up, Ramsey Clark and another aide, John Douglas, headed to the elevator and talked about their boss's sour mood. "I guess Bob won't be here by Christmas," Douglas said.[18]

That same night, the White House held its long-standing annual reception for the judiciary. Usually, federal judges, top Justice Department administrators, and influential lawmakers were invited guests. But once in office, Bobby expanded the gala to include clerks, telephone operators, investigators, and other worker bees in the Justice Department. Many had been in government for decades but had never been inside the White House or personally met a president. That night, the color guard played "Hail to the Chief" as the president and First Lady arrived at the East Room, where about seven hundred guests, including Supreme Court justices and their wives, were mingling.

After the First Couple slipped out of the reception, Bobby joined them upstairs in their private quarters. Jackie told Bobby she was looking forward to the president's trip to Texas, her first campaign visit with him since the 1960 election. Glad to have her willing to hit the campaign trail with him, Jack said he was looking forward to the Texas trip, too.

On Friday, November 22, RFK began the second day of a Justice Department conference with federal prosecutors who had come from across the country to talk about their campaign against organized crime and labor racketeering. Hoffa was on the agenda, as was Louisiana crime boss Carlos Marcello. At noon, Kennedy took a lunch break and drove out to his home in McLean, Virginia, with Robert Morgenthau, the attorney general in Manhattan, and his criminal chief, Silvio Mollo.

Just as they were finishing lunch, FBI director Hoover called Kennedy with the news the president had been shot in Dallas. "I asked him or got into whether it was serious," RFK would later say, "and I think he said, 'It's serious....I'll call you back when I find out more.' "[19]

Bobby went inside and tried to reach Kenny O'Donnell, who was traveling with the president. Before long, family and friends called or arrived at Hickory Hill, wanting to support each other at this terrible moment. Bobby, ever his brother's protector, called White House national security adviser McGeorge Bundy and told him to move the president's confidential White House files across the street to the national security staff offices at the Old Executive Office Building and keep them under guard. He also ordered a Secret Service agent on the White House detail to dismantle the secret taping system that JFK had the agency surreptitiously install in the Oval Office and the Cabinet Room. Bobby was the only cabinet member who knew of its existence.

At half past two, Hoover called again and informed RFK, "The president's dead." Bobby was struck by the FBI director's lack of emotion. "He was not a very warm or sympathetic figure," he would recall.

When Ed Guthman, the Justice Department spokesman, arrived, Kennedy asked how he was doing.

"I've seen better days," he replied.

"Don't be so gloomy," RFK said. "I don't need that now."

Soon, they were pacing the lawn, Bobby pouring out feelings that surprised his close colleague. "There's so much bitterness," RFK told him. "I thought they'd get one of us, but Jack, after all he'd been through, never worried about it." Guthman was struck that Kennedy used the word "they" to describe who had murdered his brother. Then Bobby said — perhaps thinking of Partin's account of Hoffa's threat to kill him — "I thought it would be me." In those first hours, he, Guthman, and their friends at Hickory Hill were asking the same questions almost everybody across the country wanted to know: Who killed President Kennedy, and why?

Jimmy Hoffa was in a Miami restaurant when he learned that Kennedy had been shot and killed. He was said to have stood up, climbed on a chair, and cheered. He called one of his lawyers, Frank Ragano in Tampa, Florida, who was about to leave his office to give a lecture at a legal seminar at the Hillsborough County Courthouse. Ragano was famous locally for representing Florida crime boss Santo Trafficante Jr., who had lost his lucrative Havana casinos after Fidel Castro took power in December of 1959 and later shut them down.

"Have you heard the good news?" Hoffa asked his lawyer. "They killed the son of a bitch. This means Bobby is out as attorney general. Lyndon will get rid of him."

Back in Washington, Teamsters vice president Harold Gibbons heard the news at a late lunch at Duke Zeibert's and hurried back to Teamsters headquarters. He and top Hoffa aide Larry Steinberg had the flags on the building brought to half-mast and composed a letter of condolence to the president's widow. Gibbons, generally in charge in Hoffa's absence, said the headquarters staff could take the rest of the day off. Then he called Hoffa in Miami and told him what he had done. Hoffa screamed at him, "Why the hell did you do that for him? Who the hell was he?"[20] Gibbons told him it was the right thing to do, but Hoffa continued his rant. When Hoffa got his secretary on the phone and heard her crying, he demanded to know why. Gibbons, Steinberg, and others thought his conduct was appalling, but Hoffa didn't care. "I'm no damn phony," he said.

Gibbons had had enough. His power as Hoffa's possible successor; the good life, with a lavish expense account; the opportunity to push for social programs that represented the best ideals of trade unionism—all these perquisites weren't enough to offset this latest ugly degradation. "Listen, when you get back here, you can get yourself a new boy," Gibbons was to say. Within days, he, his secretary, Steinberg, and Dick Kavner, a Saint Louis organizer who had joined the International staff, resigned en masse.

It did not take long before the smothering sorrow from Jack's death would deaden Robert Kennedy. But in those first hours after the horrible news from Dallas, Bobby was full of furious energy, a man in charge. That afternoon, before he left to meet Air Force One, which touched down at 6:00 p.m., carrying the body of his brother and President Lyndon Johnson, he began calling trusted associates in the Kennedy network, loyalists working in agencies across government. One of the first he talked to was Sheridan. Did he think that Hoffa might be somehow involved in his brother's death? he asked his top investigator. Sheridan's answer was a not unsurprising yes. If Partin was to be believed, one of their most dangerous enemies had threatened to kill Robert Kennedy with a long-range rifle as he rode in a convertible. What if Hoffa had turned his rage at RFK to the older, more powerful brother? Bobby asked Sheridan if he would fly to Dallas and make some private inquiries.

By then Lee Harvey Oswald was under arrest for killing a Dallas police officer and suspected of killing President Kennedy. In addition to Hoffa's potential involvement, RFK also worried that the Outfit, Chicago's crime family, may have sent a hit man after his brother. He called Julius Draznin, a savvy, well-sourced National Labor Relations Board expert in Chicago who knew all about the Outfit—boss Tony Accardo, Sam Giancana, and their Vegas underboss Johnny Roselli, a murderous crew of dedicated Kennedy haters. Draznin would spend the rest of 1963 working his sources in law enforcement and the labor rackets, chasing leads, and sharing intelligence.

John McCone, director of the CIA and a neighbor, arrived at Bobby's house in midafternoon. He was a devout Catholic and the CIA outsider whom the Kennedys had put in place when they fired Allen Dulles after the agency's colossal 1961 failure at the Bay of Pigs. Kennedy took McCone outside and asked him if the CIA had anything to do with the assassination of his brother. The question shouldn't have shocked McCone. Kennedy knew that the CIA embraced political murder as an acceptable tactic, and the White House didn't fully control or trust the CIA; the agency had tried several times to assassinate Castro, even after he and his brother told the agency to limit itself to overthrowing Castro by sabotage, espionage, funneling weapons to anti-Castro loyalists, and creating insurrection from within. RFK later explained McCone's answer to Sheridan. "You know at the time I asked McCone... if they had killed my brother, and I asked him in a way that he couldn't lie to me, and they hadn't."[21]

On Sunday, November 24, Dallas strip club operator Jack Ruby walked down a ramp into the garage under the Dallas police headquarters, where reporters and TV cameras were covering the transfer of Oswald to the county jail. Ruby had a .38-caliber Cobra revolver in his right coat pocket. He had been crying for a couple of days, upset about the assassination, and closed his Carousel Club to pay respects to the Kennedy family. When he spotted Lee Oswald being led toward a waiting car, handcuffed to a tall Dallas homicide detective in a white Stetson, Ruby rushed up and shot Oswald in the stomach on live national television.

At that very moment in Washington, DC, Robert Kennedy and Jacqueline Kennedy were kneeling before the casket of the slain president. It was a sunny afternoon as a crowd of three hundred thousand people lined the two-mile funeral-procession route from the White House to the Capitol. Those in the crowd with transistor radios spread the startling news from Dallas.

At this point, amid the confusion and lack of knowledge, the Secret Service, Hoover and his FBI, the CIA, and others assumed there was a link between Ruby and Oswald. Uncertainty and fear fed the notion of conspiracy. Secret Service agent Forrest Sorrels of the Dallas office, who had been questioning Oswald off and on for two days, took a call from Secret Service head Jerry Behn in Washington.[22] "It's a plot," Behn told him. "Of course," Sorrels responded.[23] General Maxwell Taylor, head of the Joint Chiefs of Staff, would say, "There would be the feeling that the killing of Oswald by Ruby had been done to suppress something."[24] Later that day, Sheridan passed along an unconfirmed tip to the FBI that Ruby, a few weeks earlier, may have received money from Hoffa's business associate Allen Dorfman in Chicago. This rumor was another lead to check out, another piece of information that swirled about in the days after the assassination, confusing the search for the truth and turning suspicions toward Hoffa and the Teamsters.

Investigators turned to Ruby's long-distance telephone records, always a first step in a quick background investigation. Sheridan recognized the names of many and was concerned. In the weeks before the assassination, Ruby had placed numerous calls to a rogues' gallery of characters associated with Hoffa and crime boss Carlos Marcello of New Orleans. On November 7 and 8, Ruby talked to Barney Baker, the occasional Teamsters business agent who, with his enormous girth and self-deprecating charm, enforced picket lines and handled shakedowns, displaying a fierce, honor-among-thieves loyalty to Hoffa. After reaching Baker on November 8, Ruby telephoned Dusty Miller, head of the Southern Conference of Teamsters, at the Eden Roc hotel in Miami and spoke for four minutes. A week or so earlier, he talked on the phone to Irwin Weiner, a Chicago bondsman well known as a front man for the Chicago Outfit who also was a business partner of Allen Dorfman and wrote millions of dollars' worth of bonds for the Teamsters union. Perhaps the most troubling call was to a phone number listed as the business office of Nofio J. Pecora, a lieutenant of Carlos Marcello, the Mafia boss in Louisiana. Pecora's office was tucked in a trailer park he owned.

For the Thanksgiving holiday, RFK and his family didn't join the Kennedy clan at the traditional gathering in Hyannis Port on Cape Cod but stayed instead in McLean. They invited about twenty friends to a brunch, including Walter and Nancy Sheridan, reporters Mary McGrory and Joseph Kraft, and other friends and Justice Department colleagues. Sheridan was struck by the effort Bobby and Ethel made to make everyone feel at ease when they had every reason to mourn. He felt uncomfortable being there. "You didn't want to bother; you didn't want to intrude," Walter would recall. They put up "a great front."

"Everybody was trying, I guess, to be reasonably gay and cheer him up, but as usual, it was he who wouldn't let anything be other than gay. But you could tell, looking at him, of the strain."[25]

Bobby asked him if he knew anything about Hoffa's reaction to the assassination. He knew that Sheridan kept track of Hoffa's whereabouts and activities almost by the hour. Sheridan didn't want to tell RFK about Hoffa's disgusting display in Miami, "but he made me tell him," Sheridan later said. He said that Hoffa got the news while in a Miami restaurant, and "he got up on the table and cheered."

Soon word was leaked to the press, likely by Sheridan, that Gibbons, Steinberg, and others had clashed with Hoffa over how to respond to the death of the president. The defections clearly embarrassed Hoffa, and in early December he told reporters that Gibbons and the others were at their desks now and "will be at their desks January first." Hoffa's savage reaction to JFK's death set off a storm of complaints, and even he had to backtrack. The union's *DRIVE Reporter* newsletter dated December 15 displayed the front-page headline TEAM- STERS MOURN PRESIDENT'S DEATH above a portrait photo of JFK, and condolences were expressed in Hoffa's voice: "We in the Teamsters extend our sincere sympathies to his entire family." The change of heart may have been linked to an effort to soften up the Justice Department. Later in December, through intermediaries, Hoffa made an offer to RFK and Justice offi- cials: he would step down as Teamsters president, maybe even leave the union, if the Justice Department dropped all the charges against him. The hush-hush offer was turned down.

When news of the failed negotiations leaked out, Hoffa was furious. He called the reporter responsible, Ed Woods, Wash- ington correspondent for the *St. Louis Post-Dispatch*, and yelled at him. Hoffa denied making such an offer and said Woods bought himself "a nice lawsuit," then shouted, "You are delib- erately trying to screw up my trial."[26] Hoffa faced his jury- tampering trial in a few weeks in neighboring Tennessee, and if any potential jurors read the story in the widely circulated *Post-Dispatch*, they might have the impression that in agreeing to step down Hoffa was guilty of at least something.

After a flurry of orders and executive actions in the week after his brother's assassination, Bobby Kennedy sank into despair and inactivity. He stayed away from the Justice Department office for weeks. Bobby's first work-related phone call noted in the Justice Department phone log after Dallas was on Janu- ary 9. He was inconsolable. Friends said he looked smaller and clearly was depressed. He took to wearing one of Jack's old bomber jackets and smoking the small dark cigars his brother favored. At night he drove around Virginia by himself in the family convertible — top down, no matter the weather — as if inviting attack or offering himself up in exchange for Jack. At a football game around Christmas, he played with unusual ferocity, even for him — angry, unconcerned about injuring himself or others. He didn't endear himself to his fellow players at first, but no one blamed him or said anything to him, then several others on the field decided to match his mood. "Bobby was absolutely relentless," Pierre Salinger would later say. "He attacked the man with the ball like a tiger, slamming, bruising, crushing, and so did everyone else. One guy broke a leg, and you couldn't count the bloodied noses and contusions....Everybody was trying to get the hate and the anger out of their systems."[27]

In late December, President Johnson appointed an independent commission to investigate the Kennedy assassination under the guidance of US Supreme Court chief justice Earl Warren. There were already theories about who was responsible for killing the president, and although most accepted Lee Harvey Oswald as the gunman, questions abounded about whether others might have been involved — the Soviets, Castro, right-wing extremists, Mafia assassins.

RFK and Walter Sheridan suspected that Hoffa might be behind the assassination but had nothing to go on beyond the similarities to Partin's story about Hoffa's assassination plot. In the year after Partin first told his story to the Justice Department, he added new details that confirmed suspicions: Hoffa suggested that the gunman shoot Bobby when he was riding in a convertible in the South, where the slaying might be blamed on a right-wing extremist upset with the Kennedy civil rights push.

RFK wanted someone on the Warren commission to keep watch during the massive investigation, to look out for documents or any leads—whether from the FBI or any other source—that hinted at Hoffa's or the Teamsters' involvement in his brother's murder. Sheridan was the Teamsters expert, but he was busy running a unit of twenty Get Hoffa lawyers and was too widely known as a Teamsters antagonist. The better choice was Charlie Shaffer, the aggressive prosecutor on the Hoffa squad who had worked the Test Fleet case and was working on the jury-tampering trial as well.

"A lot was said between me and Sheridan about the fact that the attorney general wanted somebody on the Warren commission to keep tabs on what was coming in the door, whether Hoffa was involved," Shaffer was to say. "I was probably the only one who could do it. I did meet with the attorney general, and he asked me to do it."

Shaffer showed up at the Warren commission's rented offices on the fourth floor of the new VFW Memorial Building, a block from the Supreme Court, and reported to his colleague Howard Willens, deputy criminal chief, who was assigned to be one of three supervising lawyers on the commission. Only decades later did Shaffer reveal to Willens that RFK had secretly told him to report back to him if he heard anything at the Warren commission linking Hoffa to the president's murder.

Shaffer did arouse some suspicion, since he came and went at the unusual hours required if he was to keep up with some of his Justice Department cases. This practice soon caught the attention of J. Lee Rankin, the general counsel for the Warren commission, the top executive below chief justice Earl Warren and the commission members themselves.

"Just what do you do around here?" Rankin asked Shaffer. "I see you come in at two in the afternoon and you're gone at four. Today you come in at eleven."[28]

"I work on my own time. That's the way I am."

"This won't do."

"Let me tell you something," Shaffer replied, handing him a card printed with the number of the attorney general's private line. "You call this number if you've got any complaints."

Rankin did call the attorney general, who apparently vouched for Shaffer. When Shaffer returned to the office after being away a couple of days for a case he was trying in Florida, he recalled that "Rankin stood up and gave me a salute, in a joking way."[29]

At the second meeting of the commission staff, on January 24, 1964, Rankin said that all requests for information from the FBI or any other government agency "should go through Mr. Willens and Mr. Shaffer."[30] This development made it easier for the Hoffa squad lawyer to keep an eye on anything that might be tied to the Teamsters.

Shaffer found several intriguing threads that tied Hoffa associates to Jack Ruby and listed them in an early March 1964 memo. "On the day before the assassination of our late president, Jack Ruby was seen in and about the Dallas Cabana, a hotel built by Teamster funds....Within 10 days of the assassination Ruby was in telephone communication with Barney Baker, a Teamster friend of James R. Hoffa who recently served a prison sentence." Frank Chavez, the brutish, violent secretary-treasurer of Teamsters Local 901 in Puerto Rico, an accused murderer, was a friend of Ruby's. Chavez, too, had contact with Oswald's killer several times from 1961 to 1963.

It was against this backdrop that Clarence Smelley, from Birmingham, Alabama, called the commission, ended up in contact with Shaffer, and insisted that he had information connecting Hoffa to the Kennedy assassination. He claimed to have a tape recording of a meeting he had with Hoffa and Oswald in Hoffa's office in Washington in September of 1961. Smelley also said he had new information about Hoffa's attempts to fix the jury in Nashville.

It almost seemed too good to be true. Still, Smelley was subpoenaed to a federal grand jury in Nashville and told to bring his tapes. When Smelley didn't respond to the subpoena, Judge Miller ordered him arrested and told agents they could search the man's residence for the audiotapes. Shaffer hustled to Nashville to deal with Smelley. There he learned that Smelley had no audio tapes of Hoffa and Oswald but did possess a history of mental illness.

Over the weeks, Shaffer reported what little existed directly tying Hoffa to the crimes in Dallas. He talked not to the distant, understandably depressed RFK but to his stand-in on assassination information, Walter Sheridan. Kennedy, at least officially, provided even less back to the Warren commission. After a spurt of energy in the days after the assassination, he seemed uninterested in the trail that led to his brother's killer, even if it took him right to Hoffa as a coconspirator. He never told the commission about his fears that Hoffa, the mob, Castro, or Cuban exiles were possibly responsible for the president's death in Dallas. Part of Bobby's torpor, his friends believed, was more than survivor's guilt; it was fear that his ruthless pursuit of men like Hoffa and Carlos Marcello possibly brought violence to the Kennedy family.

CHAPTER 16

Get to the Jury

BOBBY KENNEDY WAS NOT JUST another lawyer, as Hoffa crudely quipped in the days after the JFK assassination. RFK had certainly plummeted far from his position as the second-most-powerful man in Washington, but the momentum of a vast Justice Department and the tenacious Get Hoffa squad was not easily deflected. Hoffa was beset by other problems as well in early January of 1964. Key aides such as Gibbons and others were in a behind-the-scenes revolt and, as a result, were not on hand during the most important negotiation of his career—his long-sought, ambitious plan to forge a national master freight contract for the Teamsters drivers. Hoffa had set a strike deadline of midnight on January 15 for the country's six nationwide trucking companies. Then he had to be prepared only a week later for his jury-tampering trial in federal court in Tennessee. He was well aware of the high stakes this full week would bear: success with the truckers would give him remarkable power, but a conviction would end his reign as Teamsters president and could put him in prison for twenty years.

302

He may not have had some of his longtime team members around him, but when faced with a crush of decisions, Hoffa rarely sought the opinions of others or consulted files or notes. Those methods were the crutches of "file-cabinet minds" — of people who hadn't trained themselves to think and organize their thoughts but instead would "scribble information on a piece of paper and file it away."[1] He liked to hold up a pencil and lecture his staff: "This here sharp-pointed instrument is one of the most dangerous in the world. It is a crutch that people lean on instead of using their brains. It has wrecked more men than anything I know of." Instead, Hoffa would sit quietly by himself, elbows on his desk, cupping his hands over his nose, his forefingers pointing to his forehead. He told himself to discard emotion and think rationally, one step at a time, about each decision he had to make. He insisted the mental exercise worked and urged his son, Jim, a law student, to adopt it.[2]

Hoffa's proposed national master freight contract sought uniform wages and, more important, a common expiration date that would give the Teamsters president the power — for the first time — to essentially call a nationwide trucking strike. Over the years, trucking company owners typically found Hoffa to be a firm but reasonable bargainer. But with this round of talks, they were worried. Hoffa was demanding an increase of wages and benefits that added 10 percent to the roughly three-dollar-an-hour wage for long-haul truckers, a package costing $600 million. Some executives at the big trucking firms speculated that Hoffa, given all his personal and political pressures, might take out his frustration on them. They feared he'd use the national contract negotiations to convince his enemies, as well as the four hundred thousand over-the-road and local Teamsters drivers, that he was still in complete command of the nation's biggest, toughest union.

Days into contract talks behind closed doors at Chicago's Edgewater Beach Hotel, Hoffa signaled to bargainers on both sides that he didn't intend to push as far as he could. He ended up delivering about $300 to $400 million in increased wages and benefits — "a great contract!" he crowed — and members voted to approve it. Although Hoffa didn't achieve uniform wages for all Teamsters drivers across the nation, as he had sought, he did end up with a common expiration date, March 31, 1967, for all Teamsters locals under the national contract, a significant advance for union members in the decentralized, cutthroat trucking industry. The contract was "a personal triumph," one that would "tighten Mr. Hoffa's grip on the union and...increase his power in dealing with the industry," as the *New York Times* explained in an editorial. In all, it was a historic accomplishment, one that vaulted Hoffa into the ranks of great labor leaders.

One of his archenemies, antiunion senator John McClellan of Arkansas, called Hoffa's triumph a threat to national security. The union "is now powerful enough by itself to put a stranglehold on our nation's economy," McClellan wrote for the mass-circulation *Reader's Digest*, replaying alarms he first sounded in 1957. "If they called a national strike, you could not get an ambulance to take sick people to the hospital, more hearses to carry the dead. Farmers could not get produce to urban areas; food manufacturers could not send in canned goods. Milk would not be delivered. Market shelves would soon be swept clean. City dwellers would literally face starvation."[3] McClellan's article came packed with a bit of hysteria. The new contract didn't cover milk drivers, produce haulers, ambulance drivers, or many other Teamsters groups. The senator made no mention of rail, airlines, ships, and non-union trucking firms, all free to carry goods without fearing Hoffa's lash.

But negative publicity about the new Teamsters contract came at a tricky time, just before Hoffa's lawyers in Tennessee would try to select an impartial jury. In fact, anti-Teamsters publicity had flooded Nashville's newspapers and television stations over the past two months. John Seigenthaler, RFK's friend and former special assistant and the editor of the *Nashville Tennessean,* pounded Hoffa and the Teamsters in the newspaper day after day with tough, critical coverage. Many of the stories detailed the twists of a Hoffa-related scandal that had sickened Seigenthaler and shocked Nashville's legal community: in early November of 1963, lawyer Tommy Osborn, the gifted appellate advocate, had been caught — on a hidden tape recorder worn by a snitch — talking up a scheme to buy the vote of a prospective juror in Hoffa's upcoming jury-tampering trial. The informant, a Nashville policeman named Robert Vick, worked off duty as an occasional private eye for Osborn's law firm, mostly to check the backgrounds of prospective jurors.

Osborn, who had clawed his way up from dirt-poor roots, had a deep affinity for the underdog, and by 1963 that included Hoffa. Osborn believed that the Teamsters president was the target of an unfair RFK crusade. With all its heft and resources, the Justice Department could crush almost anyone in its path, Osborn believed, even someone as powerful and wealthy as Hoffa. Only the year before, Osborn had been persuaded by Hoffa to represent him in the Test Fleet case, a decision he made against the advice of his Nashville friend John Jay Hooker Jr., a young lawyer who knew the Kennedys through Democratic politics. Hooker would later say that he had warned Osborn to stay away from Hoffa. "Hoffa will feel he is being persecuted instead of prosecuted," Hooker told Osborn. "He will decide the only way out is to fix the jury."[4] Osborn brushed off the advice.

It took the Test Fleet trial to convince Osborn that Hoffa had been the victim of unbridled Justice Department power. It seemed to Osborn that prosecutor Jim Neal and his colleagues anticipated many of the defense's moves. Surely the Get Hoffa squad had benefited from what Osborn believed were the illegal fruits of wiretaps and bugs. In time, Osborn would learn that there had indeed been a bug inside Hoffa's defense team — a walking, talking human microphone named Ed Partin.

For all his legal savvy, Osborn didn't detect the fact that Vick, his occasional private investigator, had also become a government informant. By the summer of 1963, Vick was promising Sheridan that he'd keep an eye out for jury tampering or any illegal activities tied to Hoffa's upcoming trial. Sheridan thus had another informant inside Hoffa's legal camp.

In early November of 1963, as part of his preparation for the jury-tampering trial, Osborn showed Vick a list of the scores of people in the upcoming federal jury pool. After some study, Vick told Osborn that one of the men on the list was his cousin. The lawyer jumped up and said, "Why didn't you say so!" and dragged him from his office to an alley for a secure conversation, Vick would later say. Osborn proposed paying the prospective juror $5,000 right then and $5,000 later if he made it onto the jury and hung the case. Osborn was so convinced that Hoffa was up against unfair prosecutors who used dirty tricks that he rationalized his wrongdoing.

It astonished Sheridan, Neal, and Get Hoffa squad members to learn from Vick that Osborn was actually trying to fix the jury in a jury-tampering case. They were puzzled that the lawyer didn't realize the Justice Department would be on high alert for such misconduct. Sheridan believed his slippery informant, but Neal, who considered Osborn a friend and respected him, hoped it wasn't true. The FBI taped a small recorder on

Vick's back and sent him to try to get Osborn's treachery on tape. On November 11, Vick revisited Osborn in his office and told a lie—that he had talked to his cousin and found him "susceptible to money for hanging this jury." Osborn didn't suspect a setup.[5]

> **Osborn:** Your next contact with him would be to tell him if he wants that deal, he's got it.
> **Vick:** Okay.
> **Osborn:** The only thing it depends upon is him being accepted on the jury. If the government challenges him there will be no deal.
> **Vick:** All right. If he is seated.
> **Osborn:** If he's seated.
> **Vick:** He can expect five thousand then and...
> **Osborn:** Immediately.
> **Vick:** Immediately, and then five thousand when it's hung. Is that right?
> **Osborn:** All the way, now!
> **Vick:** Oh, he's got to stay all the way?
> **Osborn:** All the way...

The lawyer, perhaps an amateur in such dark arts, didn't become suspicious when Vick began leading him:

> **Vick:** Now, I'm going to play it just like you told me previously, to reassure him and keep him from getting panicky. You know, I have reason to believe that he won't be alone—you know?
> **Osborn:** Tell him there will be at least two others with him....We'll keep it a secret. The way we keep it safe is that nobody knows about it but you and me—where could they ever go?

The next day Sheridan played the tape for Bobby Kennedy and Jack Miller at the Justice Department. A day later, back in Nashville, Sheridan and FBI agents Bill Sheets and Ed Steele provided a transcript and played the tape to the two federal judges sitting in Nashville, William E. Miller and Frank Gray Jr. At first they could not believe what they heard. When they called in Osborn and played the recording, he admitted that yes, that was his voice. They took away his license to practice in federal court, and Osborn soon was charged with trying to bribe a juror.

Jim Neal was heartbroken to see Osborn destroyed. He blamed Hoffa, whose magnetism, money, and underdog persona captivated the risk-taking defense lawyer.

Then came a small victory for Hoffa: his lawyers convinced the federal court that their client could not get a fair trial in Nashville after the *Tennessean* and the *Banner* flooded the town with stories about the Tommy Osborn scandal. So Hoffa's jury-tampering case was reassigned to federal district judge Frank W. Wilson, a 1961 JFK appointee, and assigned to federal court in Chattanooga, in southeast Tennessee.

On January 17, Hoffa, his son, Jim, daughter, Barbara, and a few lawyers landed by private plane at the Chattanooga airport and stepped onto the tarmac before a crowd of more than one hundred cheering supporters. Some waved banners saying WE'LL ALWAYS BE FOR JO AND JIMMY HOFFA and THANKS FOR THE CONTRACT, JIMMY. The Hoffas were swept into a waiting Cadillac limo, and local police escorted a forty-car caravan of Teamsters into Chattanooga's downtown.

Five other defendants, each with his own lawyer, were being tried along with Hoffa on jury-tampering charges stemming from the Test Fleet case. Cecil Branstetter represented Larry Campbell, a black business agent in Teamsters Local 299 accused of trying to arrange a juror's bribe from a Louisville pay phone. Thomas Parks, Campbell's uncle, who worked in a Nashville funeral home, was charged with trying to corrupt juror Gratin Fields through payments to his family. Parks's lawyer, Jacques Schiffer of New York, had previously represented Hoffa and associates of New York mobster Johnny Dio. Tennessee lawyer Dave Alexander represented Nicholas Tweel, a West Virginia cigarette vendor who ended up in Nashville by chance during the Test Fleet trial to confer about a pension-fund loan with Allen Dorfman, the suave, mob-connected Chicago insurance man. Dorfman, represented by Harvey Silets, and Tweel both were charged with telephoning prospective jurors. Ewing King, the recently defeated president of Teamsters Local 327 in Nashville, was charged with trying to influence a woman on the jury by securing a promotion for her husband, the highway patrolman. King was represented by local lawyer Harold Brown.

With oversize confidence and a heavy hand, Hoffa ordered his lawyers around, directing his own defense. His tactics may have been astute more often than not, but this practice offended brilliant practitioners such as Ed Williams. As a result, Hoffa could hire good lawyers but not those of Williams's caliber. Hoffa's Chattanooga team included James E. Haggerty, former head of the State Bar of Michigan, who had fought for Hoffa and the union for years. White-haired, balding, a dedicated smoker, Haggerty suffered a bleeding ulcer in the middle of a Teamsters court fight in 1960 that put him in a Detroit hospital for a while. He was effective, not showy, and had won Hoffa's trust. Harry Berke, with thirty years of legal experience in Chattanooga, served as Hoffa's local counsel, a counterbalance to good old Tennessee boys Neal and John Jay Hooker Sr., the two lead prosecutors.

Neal had been Hoffa's tough, unflappable antagonist at the Test Fleet trial. "The most vicious prosecutor who ever handled a criminal case for the Justice Department," Hoffa described him. A short, cocky, broad-chested ex-marine, Neal took Hoffa's description as a badge of honor. John Jay Hooker Sr. was a towering, flamboyant, silver-tongued lawyer who fancied three-piece suits with a fresh flower in his lapel; a chain holding a Phi Beta Kappa key was draped across his expansive gut. Bobby Kennedy, at Seigenthaler's urging, persuaded Hooker to leave his Nashville private practice temporarily and serve as a special prosecutor with Neal. Hooker was known for his old-school courtroom theatrics. His leading role pushed Hoffa squad prosecutor Charlie Shaffer from the trial table to supporting player. Rounding them out were Justice Department lawyers Jim Durkin and Nat Lewis, whom Hoffa dubbed Instant Law for the young lawyer's remarkable recall of court decisions and incredible speed at fashioning tidy, tight legal pleadings.

Everyone was lawyered up and ready to go, and once the trial commenced, Hoffa gave his much-hated nemesis a rare gift without realizing it.

After playing a commanding role in the hours and days after his brother's assassination — securing the secret White House tapes, arranging the late president's funeral, trying to figure out who might be behind the assassination — Bobby Kennedy had sunk into a dark hole. He was listless, depressed, unable to sleep, uninterested in work. Around this time, his friend John Seigenthaler arrived in Washington, hoping to see RFK, and called his secretary, Angie Novello. She said to come right over — he's getting a haircut.

Seigenthaler found Kennedy in his dark-paneled Justice Department office with the blinds drawn, a barber clipping his hair. RFK was seemingly immune to Seigenthaler's greeting. "Nothing, no words—it was probably two minutes, but seemed like twenty," the Nashville editor would later say.

Clip, clip, clip. "How do I look?" RFK finally asked.

"You look like hell," Seigenthaler replied.

"I can't sleep."[6]

Lean to start with, RFK had lost so much weight that in his custom-made suits he looked as if he had shrunk. He was in a "haze of pain," Seigenthaler would later say. "I just had the feeling it was physically painful, almost as if he were on the rack or that he had a toothache or that he had a heart attack."[7]

Then Hoffa, paradoxically, helped pull Bobby away from paralyzing grief. Once the jury-tampering trial started, Walter Sheridan began calling RFK almost daily. Staying involved in the Hoffa trial kept "him going because everything else seemed to be falling apart," Ethel would later say. Sheridan understood this dynamic and didn't wait for RFK to ask him for updates. Rather, he filled him in on each new development, knowing "it meant a lot to him."[8]

At this point, Sheridan struggled with an important decision, one that the success of the prosecution likely hinged upon: How aggressive should the Justice Department be in trying to protect this new jury against tampering? Sheridan had no doubt that Hoffa or his associates would try it again; it seemed to be standard procedure. On the Rackets Committee, RFK, Sheridan, and the investigators had pursued leads about jury tampering at three different Hoffa criminal trials— his bribery acquittal and the wiretapping trial (which resulted in a hung jury), both in 1957, and his wiretapping acquittal in 1958. In the 1960s, if Partin was to be believed, there were repeated, grandiose attempts to fix the Test Fleet jury. And only two months earlier, Hoffa's lawyer Osborn supposedly wanted to bribe a prospective juror in the current case. "We assumed that there would be efforts to tamper with the jury in Chattanooga, even though this was a jury tampering trial," Sheridan would later explain. "Based on our past experience, we realistically had no choice but to make that assumption."[9]

So Sheridan and his squad put together a jury-protection plan that, as time would tell, did not always work as desired.

Judge Wilson allowed the clerk of courts to withhold from all parties the first names, addresses, and occupations of the prospective jurors until January 20, the first day of trial. Prosecutors Neal and Hooker believed that once the jury was finalized they could persuade the judge to sequester its members at a nearby hotel, with US marshals serving as security. In this scenario, the twelve jurors and four alternates would face a serious risk of tampering only during the week or so of jury selection. Based on what they had learned during the Test Fleet trial, Sheridan and the Hoffa squad knew that potential fixers fell into two groups: Hoffa associates who had little reason to attend the trial but did so anyway and local Teamsters officials who might know people on the jury list.

At Sheridan's and Kennedy's request, the FBI agreed to assign two dozen FBI agents to blanket the trial during its first week or so. Sheridan had the agents put three men under surveillance — Teamsters Local 515 president William Test; his predecessor, George Hicks; and Hoffa's occasional driver and bodyguard Chuckie O'Brien, who traveled with him nearly everywhere. Other agents, perched in offices with a view from above of the courthouse's two entrances, photographed people coming in and out, hoping to spot patterns and anyone acting suspiciously.

Prosecutors sharply warned the FBI agents not to spy on Hoffa or any other defendants or their lawyers, explaining that it might trespass on their fair-trial rights. But this prohibition proved to be practically impossible, as Hoffa often walked to and from the courthouse to his nearby hotel with Chuckie O'Brien as well as his lawyers. It didn't take long before the Hoffa entourage felt the shadowy presence of clean-cut men in nondescript cars who seemed to be every-where. One day, outside the courthouse, George Hicks, the beefy ex-president of the Chattanooga local, complained to a reporter for the *Wall Street Journal:* "Some car's been following me wherever I go. Here it comes now." Hicks shouted to the riders in the bland auto: "Just goin' to the post office for some stamps. You can wait for me." The license number of the car turned out to have been "taken off the records," a tip-off that the car belonged to the FBI.[10]

Despite the tails, Hoffa kept to his schedule. Early in the mornings, Hoffa left the aging Hotel Patten and spent time at the nearby YMCA lifting weights, hoping to drop some pounds and ease his stress. Knowing how to make an entrance upon his return to the courthouse, Hoffa strode in and boomed out to reporters that Kennedy's fifth try to put him in jail "just isn't going to happen." Inside the small, dark-wood-paneled courtroom, he directed his rage at Neal and Hooker, hoping his hateful stares might throw them off their game.

Still, the smothering presence of government agents both inside and outside the hotel persuaded Hoffa and his law-yers to bring in temperamental problem solver Bernard Spin-del, the wireman, for counterespionage. The weekend after the jury was seated, Spindel loaded several hundred pounds of electronics gear onto a commercial flight from New York to Nashville, then made his way to Chattanooga by rental car. Somehow the FBI learned that Spindel was coming to Hoffa's aid.

As he left the Nashville airport, two FBI cars tag-teamed him on the two-hour drive to the Hotel Patten. Spindel checked in and tried to figure out what the Kennedy team was up to.

Sheridan, Neal, and more than a dozen others had hoped to keep Partin's cooperation a secret from Hoffa and his henchmen until the moment Partin stepped into the witness box. In contrast to many state courts, federal courts did not require the defense and prosecution to exchange witness lists before a trial. Surprise attack by a last-minute witness could be a useful tactic.

Keeping Partin under wraps denied Hoffa's lawyers time to dig up dirt on his background and also deprived Hoffa associates of any opportunity to pressure Partin into rethinking his turncoat ways by threatening him or his family. Being extra cautious, Sheridan had secured a rental cabin on Lookout Mountain, south of Chattanooga on the Georgia border, and stashed Partin there with a couple of US marshals as bodyguards.

On February 4, just after the lunch recess, Sheridan used the back stairs and lookouts waved all-clear hand signals to sneak Partin into the witness room that led into Judge Wilson's third-floor courtroom. When Hooker called him as the next witness, Hoffa looked up, stunned momentarily, then exclaimed, "My God, it's Partin!"

It took several minutes before the defense lawyers understood where Hooker was leading Partin. In a soft-spoken drawl, the big Baton Rouge teamster began describing what he had heard and whom he had met during his time inside Hoffa's entourage at the Test Fleet trial. Shortly after meeting Nicholas Tweel for the first time in a hotel lobby, Partin said, his new acquaintance confessed that he had come to Nashville at Dorfman's request to "help him set up a method to get to the jury—"

At the word "jury," Schiffer sprang up and demanded a mistrial. The other defense lawyers also jumped up to object, except for Haggerty, who calmly asked the judge if the jury could be excused so he could argue a motion. Hoffa's chief defense lawyer needed to find a way to keep Partin off the stand.

"It is obvious he is in the employ of the US government," Haggerty said of Partin after the jurors left. "It is obvious he was planted for the purpose of undercover work." Mr. Hoffa's fair-trial rights had been violated as a result. "Partin had discussions with me, with all the lawyers," Haggerty told the judge. "He was always hanging around; I never knew for what reason....He was at the hotel and Mr. Hoffa's suite where lawyers conferred at night."

Neal and Sheridan had expected this argument and prepared for it ever since Partin showed up at Hoffa's Nashville's hotel room in October of 1962. The government didn't plant Partin into the defense camp; rather, Hoffa had invited Partin to Nashville, Neal told the judge. Partin even sat guard outside Hoffa's room at the labor leader's request. As for interfering with Hoffa's constitutional right to effective counsel, Neal argued, government lawyers had instructed this witness to look out only for illegal activities such as jury fixing. Partin was told not to pass along strategy or details about Hoffa's legal defense.

But one after another, the Hoffa lawyers who had taken part in the Test Fleet case told Judge Wilson that Partin almost certainly had relayed their advice and trial tactics to Neal and his colleagues. Bill Bufalino indignantly recalled a time when five or six defense lawyers sat around a table in Hoffa's Nashville hotel suite, discussing trial strategy one evening, as Partin lounged nearby, mindlessly shuffling a deck of cards. Bufalino said he had outlined for the group how he was going to question a truck driver on the stand the next day.

But when it came time to question that witness, Bufalino told Judge Wilson, the moment he told the trucker, "I bring you back to 1953," Neal objected, saying, "Your Honor, they are getting into a different area." Bufalino, taken aback, said he asked Neal, "How do you know where I am going, what I am going to ask?"

Neal then had asked to argue a point outside the hearing of the Nashville jurors. After they left the courtroom, Bufalino, who towered over Neal, asked again, "How do you know what I'm going to ask? All I said was '1953.'"

"I am psychic," Neal replied.

"That's on the record," Bufalino told Judge Wilson, and Neal had no rebuttal. The impression was left that Partin had passed defense strategy to Sheridan and Neal in Nashville.

Also during the Nashville trial, Bufalino testified, Partin put himself in the role of agent provocateur. "I have some recollection that Partin said something about a particular juror, I don't know which one, that he was in the army with one, and he was starting to suggest that maybe he should get in touch with that fellow. . . . I said, 'Look, I want to have absolutely nothing at all to do with any such discussion. Lay off that. We have a cinch case. This case is absolutely nothing. And then so far as I am concerned I suggest you just forget about anything like that.'"

Judge Wilson had several questions to weigh before deciding if Partin could tell his full story to the jury. Among them were whether Partin had inserted himself into Hoffa's legal team and whether he was promised anything by the Justice Department in exchange for his cooperation.

Answers to both questions could be found in government records, but they were not made available to Hoffa's lawyers at the time. Partin's recorded phone calls with Hoffa on the eve of the Test Fleet trial showed that Partin, already a government spy, had invited himself to see Hoffa — not the other way around. FBI reports from October of 1962, which came to public light decades later, revealed that Partin wouldn't cooperate with Bobby Kennedy's staffers unless they dropped the twenty-six fraud and forgery counts connected to his running of Teamsters Local 5.

Hoffa's lawyers were entitled to these records. The US Supreme Court's landmark *Brady v. Maryland* decision in May of 1963 placed prosecutors under an obligation to disclose exculpatory evidence. With these records in hand, Hoffa's lawyers could have impeached key parts of Partin's account. Instead, when Jacques Schiffer cross-examined Partin about whether he had been promised favorable treatment by the Justice Department — by this point his union embezzlement case had been repeatedly postponed and was essentially moribund — Partin could say at this point without fear of getting caught: "I was never promised anything, and I never asked for anything."

(When the Justice Department moved to dismiss the twenty-six-count indictment against Partin four years later, federal judge E. Gordon West in New Orleans called it "a payoff for testimony in the Hoffa case." The Justice Department insisted it had made no deal with Partin, whose legal troubles in Louisiana continued throughout the 1960s. West, a Democrat appointed by President Kennedy, didn't believe it. "It is making a mockery of justice," West said of the dismissal of charges. "Are the interests of justice to be served by granting of lifetime immunity to this defendant because of the wishes of some previous Attorney General?"[11])

In the defense room on one of the breaks in testimony, Hoffa went into a rage, hurled a chair into the wall, and lashed out at his lawyers. Because of Partin's testimony, Hoffa was afraid he was going to get convicted. "I have seen some great coups in my time," a Hoffa lawyer admitted privately to Sheridan in the hallway, "but that was the greatest coup I have ever seen."[12]

The next morning, February 5, Judge Wilson overruled motions by defense lawyers and allowed Partin to testify. Failing to silence Partin in court, Hoffa's team now had to find a way to destroy him on the stand.

Neal took Partin through his carefully prepared story. Hoffa had called him into his hotel suite and "told me to stick around for a few days because he might want me to call a few people," Partin told the court. "He said they were going to get to one juror or get to scattered jurors and take their chances."

As jury selection continued and as he packed to return to Baton Rouge, Partin testified, Hoffa "told me that when I came back he might want me to pass something for him, and he put his hand behind his back and hit the back pocket." When he returned to Nashville three days later, Partin said he asked Hoffa privately if he needed him to do anything. Hoffa, without naming prospective Test Fleet juror James Tippens, replied angrily that "the dirty bastard went in and told the judge we offered him ten thousand dollars, and we are going to have to lay low for a few days." Later, Partin said, he told Hoffa the trial didn't look to be going well, and Hoffa replied: "Don't worry about it too much because I have the male colored juror in my hip pocket. One of my colored business agents, Campbell, came in and took care of it."

After Partin testified, someone blasted a shotgun one evening into the Baton Rouge house where Partin's father was staying as well as into the home of a Local 5 union officer loyal to Partin. It looked as if Hoffa or someone loyal to him was trying to intimidate Partin and his supporters. No one was at home during either attack. After the gun blasts, prosecutor Charlie Shaffer in Chattanooga was "ready to move heaven and earth" to get to the bottom of the violence, but Partin nudged him in the ribs and waved him off. He had arranged for the show of violence in Baton Rouge, knowing it would hurt Hoffa's reputation while making Partin seem more heroic. "That was pure Partin," Shaffer would later say. "It was a shocking revelation about Partin and his ingenuity."[13] Even so, Shaffer kept Partin's actions a secret. In court, Neal referred to the attacks as "terrorism," proof that Partin deserved extra protection.

Hoffa's lawyers hadn't prepared for Ed Partin. They needed to learn what Hoffa might have said to him during the weeks of the Test Fleet trial or at any other time. Depending on what they learned, they might be able to anticipate the thrusts from Hooker and Neal and possibly counterattack, but they were still convinced the government might be listening in. "We had been trying to get a conference with Mr. Hoffa," Harry Berke, Hoffa's local lawyer, would later testify, "but we were afraid to discuss the matter of defense and the evidence and so forth in either Mr. Haggerty's room or Mr. Hoffa's room....So I suggested that we go — that we just go out maybe and get a drink, a Coca-Cola, somewhere, and sit down and discuss the next day's proceedings."[14]

Berke had his son and law partner, Marvin, bring his car around, and Hoffa, Berke, and another lawyer walked to the car. At this point, teams of agents watching the courthouse sprang into action. "They are proceeding to the vehicle now, quite an entourage, will copy," one agent said by radio transmission. Then a supervising agent warned him to stay away from tailing Hoffa. "I don't think you want to go near this vehicle due to its contents [Hoffa]. Ah, they are ready to pull out in front now, and I think the package you are interested in is...uh, it looks like he is heading over [to] the Avis rent-a-car place." The "package" was Bernard Spindel, the man Sheridan and Neal had assigned them to watch.

At his father's direction, Marvin Berke drove to an urban renewal site not far from downtown, a desolate stretch where buildings had been demolished and there was little cover for the FBI tail car. As Berke slowed down, so did the tail car. The two cars played cat and mouse, going around corners, speeding up, slowing down, until Hoffa and the other passengers decided to return downtown. Spindel, with his electronics gear, had been monitoring the FBI radio calls, which were transmitted on the FM band before it was widely used commercially. Agents referred to Hoffa as "Big Boy" and to Chuckie O'Brien as "the ex-boxer."

"As you probably know, the vehicle, uh, the Big Boy, just got back to the hotel, evidently he parked the car," one agent radioed. "There are a few fellows that are going in the same direction, [including] Mr. Big and, uh, his necessary assistant, so I don't think you want to be anywhere around that lot right now."

On February 7, Schiffer handed the judge a sealed envelope that he said contained proof that the defendants and their lawyers were being followed. Inside were typed transcripts of the FBI radio communications intercepted by Spindel. The FBI was trying to track Spindel, and instead he tracked them. Neal was furious and decided to bring Spindel to court to explain how he made the transcripts, hoping to show that the electronics expert had violated section 605 of the Communications Act of 1934, which made it a crime to divulge radio or telephone communications without permission.

Later that day, Elmer Disspayne, a deputy US marshal, headed to the Hotel Patten's ninth floor to subpoena Spindel, with Sheridan tagging along because he knew what Spindel looked like — hulking, rumpled, brown hair with a bald spot. But it turned out to be a trap, Sheridan would later admit. A few minutes behind Disspayne, Hoffa rode the elevator up with photographers and television camera operators in tow, ready for a little showmanship of his own. On the Teamsters-occupied ninth floor, Hoffa confronted Disspayne, accusing him of infiltrating their legal sanctuary, stealing their files, and sabotaging the defense effort. Hoffa threw down his overcoat and briefcase, squared his stance, and yelled that the two of them should "have it out" right then. The marshal pushed by to make an exit, but television news stories and photos ran across the country and embarrassed the government.

By then, the mood at the courthouse was ugly. "A grimness and hatefulness had settled in and it would remain that way for the rest of the trial," Sheridan would later say. "Hoffa was in a rage."[15] He had directed his obscenities at Neal but expanded them to include Sheridan, who tried to stay out of Hoffa's way. It wasn't always possible. After one break, when Hoffa walked in his direction, Sheridan ducked into the reception area of the US attorney's office. Hoffa and his group followed him in.

"I understand you got cancer, Sheridan, is that right?" Hoffa asked.

"No, that's not right."

"How long does it take to work?" he sneered, then stalked off.

At that point, Hoffa would have been happy with a mistrial or grounds for a new trial. One way to accomplish this was to provoke the judge, a prosecutor, or one of the marshals into an outburst. The ugliness infected everybody and perhaps clouded judgments, making Hoffa's chances better than usual at getting someone going. Al Butler, supervising marshal, was standing at the courtroom door when Hoffa and his entourage returned from lunch. Butler was spelling his men, who were tired of being harassed. Hoffa said, "Oh, look: they've sent the boss."

Much taller than the stubby Hoffa, Butler turned his head left and right, chin up, as if scanning the horizon. "Is someone talking to me?" he asked, and then made a big show of looking down at Hoffa. "Oh, there you are, down there." Hoffa turned purple with rage, Butler would later say. "I expected to get hit. I didn't think he could control himself. You might get a mistrial, but you'd get assault on a federal officer."[16]

Hoffa prided himself on his power to persuade. He had relied on it to organize workers, bargain for benefits, and over the years convince juries he was telling the truth. On February 25, 1964, it came down to his word against Partin's. Looking over the jury the previous few weeks, he wasn't pleased with what he saw—only one black person, one union member, and a high number of people with college degrees among the eight men and four women. Each evening, teams of US marshals escorted them to a nearby hotel or restaurant and chaperoned them until bedtime. The federal agents clipped articles from newspapers and magazines before letting jurors read the day's news. They listened nearby when jurors made phone calls, which were limited to immediate family only. Would the jurors resent the government or the Teamsters for the limitations placed on them? They appeared to get along with each other and seemed, at least to some of Hoffa's lawyers, eager to serve as jurors. Courthouse wisdom held that people who seemed eager to serve on a jury favored the prosecution.

Hoffa wore a dark blue suit, white shirt, and black shoes. At fifty-one, he still had a full head of hair, black with some gray at the temples. He carried only reading glasses and a slim manila folder containing telephone records. Prompted by Berke's questions, he told the jury about his tough upbring-ing, his rise through the union, his dedication to his family. At Berke's request, Hoffa's two young-adult children, Jim and Barbara, sitting in the front, stood up so the jury could see them.

One by one, he denied each of Partin's accusations while occasionally glancing at the jurors. "I flatly deny it." "It's an abso-lute fabrication." "I positively did not make that statement."

He tried hard to destroy Partin. He testified that back in Nashville in 1962 he and lawyer William Bufalino went over the troubled situation in Partin's Baton Rouge local and dis-cussed all the various criminal charges he faced. "I just couldn't envision what this man was talking about," Hoffa told the jury. "And finally I asked him whether or not he was physically ill or whether he should have some type of treat-ment, because he was nervous, upset, almost incoherent, talk-ing about the twenty-six counts that he had."

Hoffa testified, "He pleaded for another chance. He blew up. He stormed out of the room, and that is the way we left it."

Hoffa was as well prepared as he could be when Hooker rose to cross-examine him. Meanwhile, Neal pulled a stunt that may have pushed Hoffa off his game. Neal rolled in a metal cart, the kind used as a stand for a slide projector or a tape machine, and parked it next to his trial table. Neal wanted Hoffa to wonder whether the government possessed tape recordings that it intended to play during cross-examination.

Time and again, prosecutors had said there were no wiretaps or microphone surveillances of Hoffa. But Hoffa knew that Partin, as an undercover informant, could have been wearing a hidden microphone during the Test Fleet trial and could have legally captured their conversations. It would be nearly impossible for Hoffa to recall everything he and Partin had talked about eighteen months earlier, during the crush of the Nashville trial. So when Hooker asked Hoffa if he knew that the husband of a juror was a highway patrolman, he was evasive, unable to give a firm answer, worried, perhaps, about being contradicted. Asked whether Ewing King told him he had been followed by FBI agents after his late-night back-country visit to patrolman Paschal, Hoffa again had to avoid being pinned down, worried that he might be contradicted by recordings. He said he didn't recall. "He may have said that."

Yes, he may have talked on the phone with Dorfman about the jury, but so what? "I talk about this jury every single night with my attorneys at the hotel," Hoffa said, looking to the jury. "It would be ridiculous if I didn't. My life depends on this verdict."

It was Hooker's turn to try to provoke the witness, and Hoffa told him at one point to stop shouting at him. "I can't hear you when you holler at me."

"Mr. Hoffa, is there something wrong with your hearing?"

"No. It's just that I'm not used to people shouting at me."

At one point, Hoffa told Hooker to stop interrupting him. "You're not used to being interrupted, are you, Mr. Hoffa?" Hooker boomed back.

It had not been one of Hoffa's strongest court appearances, and he knew it. He had been evasive and testy, and he apologized to the jury, hoping to leave them with a better impression. "Neal was quite pleased with himself that he had put Jimmy in the position of not being able to do his best when Hooker cross-examined him," Seigenthaler would later say. "His cross-examination was really brutal. Jimmy was really suffering."[17]

In his closing argument, Neal said Hoffa and his codefendants took part in "one of the greatest attacks on the jury system ever known in America." When it was the defense's turn, Haggerty described the case as "a foul, filthy plot" conceived by a convicted felon and violent kidnapper, "an untrustworthy liar" whose accusations were "conceived in a Louisiana jail cell" as part of a "diabolical plot" by Walter Sheridan to get Hoffa.

Not to be outdone, defense lawyer Schiffer ended his closing argument by flinging a handful of coins across the prosecutors' table and shouting, "I say to the Washington prosecutors, including Mr. Sheridan, take these thirty pieces of silver and share them — you have earned them." His reference was biblical, about Judas Iscariot betraying Christ for thirty pieces of silver. But if Schiffer meant that the traitor was Partin, that made Hoffa a Christ figure, a hard sell to even the most sympathetic jurors.[18]

The day the jury came back with its verdict, Josephine Hoffa was in a Detroit hospital being treated for heart problems. Her two children were in the courthouse with their father, just as they had been seven years earlier at his bribery trial in Washington, DC, when JFK was still a senator, RFK was an inexperienced chief counsel for a Senate committee, and, against all expectations, a jury believed Hoffa and Edward Bennett Williams over FBI photos and an eyewitness.

After five hours of deliberation, the jury found Dorfman and Tweel not guilty. It did find King, Campbell, and Parks each guilty of one count of attempted jury tampering. As for Hoffa, the eight men and four women convicted him on both counts. Hoffa had been resting his thick forearms on the defense table and staring at the backs of the jurors, who stood in a semicircle facing the judge as their foreman announced each verdict separately. When Hoffa heard his name and the word *guilty*, color drained from his face. He leaned back and reached his hand to his daughter, Barbara, and son, Jim, sitting just behind him in the first row of spectators. Barbara began to cry, and her husband, Robert Crancer, put his arm around her. Hoffa "moved his arm up and down several times as though trying to reassure them."[19]

Upon hearing the Hoffa verdict, Walter Sheridan bolted out of the courtroom. In the hallway, the soft-spoken investigator pumped his right fist in the air and with a big smile shouted, "Guilty — two counts!" He found a phone and called RFK out of a high-level meeting. "We made it!" Sheridan said.

"Nice work," Bobby replied.

Hoffa's face stayed impassive until he was surrounded by reporters outside the courtroom. "Of course I'll appeal," he snapped. "What do you think?" The whole thing was "a railroad job," a "farce of American justice,"[20] he said before heading with his family back to the hotel and then to the airport.

When Judge Wilson sentenced Hoffa and the others a week later, he had prepared remarks. "You stand here convicted of seeking to corrupt the administration of justice itself. You stand here convicted of having tampered, really, with the very soul of this nation. You stand here convicted of having struck at the very foundation upon which everything else in this nation depends, the very basis of civilization itself, and that is the administration of justice....Now, if a conviction of such an offense were to go unpunished and this type of conduct and this type of offense permitted to pass without action by the court, it would surely destroy this country more quickly and more surely than any combination of any foreign foes that we could ever possibly have."

With that, Wilson hit Hoffa with eight years in prison and a $10,000 fine. Codefendants Larry Campbell, Thomas Parks, and Ewing King were sentenced to three years. Wilson found lawyer Jacques Schiffer in contempt of court and sentenced him to sixty days in prison.

Hoffa was unbowed. "You can rest assured of one thing," he said on his way out of the courthouse. "The entire membership of the Teamsters union is behind Hoffa in this fight. The wages, working conditions, health, the welfare and the pensions, the things we have got for them. This is what they want, and this is why they are all behind Hoffa in this."

Bobby sent a US Customs plane to Tennessee to bring Sheridan, Neal, and the others back to a party at Bobby and Ethel's home to honor them for the Hoffa conviction. Bill Sheets and Ed Steele, two FBI agents who had worked long hours on the case, were invited to the party but had to decline. Sheridan understood why — "because they would have to explain to J. Edgar Hoover what they were doing at Bob Kennedy's house." RFK handed out a thoughtful memento: leather-bound copies of the verdict to each person who worked on the jury-tampering case.

After seven years of relentless pursuit — after the snarling face-offs on nationally televised Senate hearings, the insults back and forth, the threats of violence against him and his family, the public humiliations after Hoffa escaped criminal charges time and again — it seemed as though Bobby Kennedy would have something to celebrate at a party. Instead he was subdued, sour. "There was nothing to celebrate," Ken O'Donnell would later say. "He had [had] enough tragedy of his own." Kennedy once hated Hoffa, but after the death of his brother, something had changed. He thought Hoffa's eight-year sentence was too long. A journalist friend, Murray Kempton, had a long talk with RFK while the Hoffa trial unfolded in Chattanooga. "Robert Kennedy knew how to hate; he hated on his father's behalf; he grew to hate on his brother's; but these last weeks that he has endured have now left behind a man we recognize as being unskilled at hating on his own," Kempton would write.[21]

He was only thirty-eight, but with deep lines around his eyes and a few gray streaks through his often uncombed brown hair, he looked like an aging enfant terrible. He had an adoring wife, eight healthy children, and a Band of Brothers willing to follow him into battle.

He had dedicated himself to his brother's success and Hoffa's demise. These two missions had defined his adult life and were over — one because of assassin's bullets, the other because of a verdict from a Tennessee jury.

"I'm tired of chasing people," Bobby said wearily. "I want to go on to something else."[22]

EPILOGUE: IN LOVE WITH NIGHT

IN THE MONTHS AFTER HIS brother's murder, Robert Kennedy tried to figure out the "something else" he wanted to do. He had talked about being a high-level government trouble-shooter or ambassador to increasingly troubled South Vietnam, but his closest friends assumed he'd follow the example of his two brothers and the long-held wishes of his father by seeking elective office. Bobby and his brothers had discussed his running for governor of Massachusetts, but since Jack's death and LBJ's elevation to the White House, the Kennedy camp dreamed of his being chosen by Johnson to step into the open seat for vice president in 1964. Bobby displayed few of the skills and even less of the temperament useful for high-level campaigning. He had a pinched, high-register voice, with a Boston-Nantucket accent far thicker than Jack's. Before a crowd, he spoke clumsily from prepared remarks, one leg pumping nervously behind the lectern, hands often trembling. He hated being touched, except by children, and he stiffened around grabby pols such as LBJ, who used backslapping and shoulder hugging as tools of persuasion. He would never have thrown himself into a fence-line crowd of admirers, as his brother had done in Miami only days before his murder.

By most accounts at the time, RFK had been too disabled

by grief to make such an important decision, but he clearly took steps in early 1964 that tipped his hand. He signed up for speech lessons at the von Hesse Studios of Effective Speech and Human Relations, a New York firm run by Elisabeth and Maxeda von Hesse, who had vastly improved First Lady Eleanor Roosevelt's speech making. In January of 1964, RFK not only arranged to hear feedback on speeches he'd already delivered — including renting a theater and hiring a union projectionist to replay films of his past speeches — he also committed to six two-hour sessions of private coaching at the von Hesse studio in Manhattan.

After Hoffa's conviction that spring, RFK still hadn't decided whether to try to bull his way onto the ticket in November of 1964 as LBJ's vice president or to run for the US Senate from New York State, his home for much of his boyhood. Before he could make up his mind, he was rocked by a fresh reminder of the perils of elective office. On a foggy night in June, senator Edward Kennedy found himself traveling in a twin-engine, five-seat Aero Commander, hurrying to introduce the keynote speaker at a Massachusetts Democratic convention. His companions were keynote speaker senator Birch Bayh of Indiana; Bayh's wife, Marvella; a Ted Kennedy aide; and an experienced pilot. The plane took off hours later than planned because Kennedy and Bayh first had to vote on the landmark Civil Rights Act of 1964, delayed that day by filibuster. Looking to land at a small western Massachusetts airport near Springfield, the pilot approached too low in the fog, snagged treetops in an apple orchard near the runway, then crashed. Both the pilot and the aide, sitting in front, were killed. Though injured, Birch and Marvella Bayh were able to walk from the fuel-soaked wreckage. The senator returned to the plane and pulled Teddy to safety. Rushed to a nearby hospital, Kennedy was found to have three crushed vertebrae, two broken ribs, a collapsed lung, and massive internal hemorrhaging. "It was about a week before we knew he was going to live," a surgeon who operated on Teddy over two and a half days at the hospital would later explain.[1]

RFK and Walter Sheridan traveled all night, reaching the hospital about four in the morning. Bobby's older brother Joe and older sister Kathleen both were killed in plane crashes in the 1940s. Now his remaining brother was hanging onto life and possibly paralyzed from the neck down. When Bobby ducked in to see his brother, Teddy exhibited the "Kennedys don't cry" grace under pressure and was able to reprise a favorite family gibe about Bobby. From the narcotic haze of his hospital bed, Ted Kennedy looked up at his older brother and asked: "Is it true that you are ruthless?"[2]

Bobby and Sheridan later took a walk in the warm summer dark. After stretching out on the grass outside the hospital, RFK told his friend, "Someone up there doesn't like us." He wondered aloud whether he should try for vice president — LBJ would have to be pressured to take him — or run for the Senate. Sheridan wanted him to try for vice president.

The next morning, reporters and photographers flooded the hospital, some even making it into Ted Kennedy's hospital room, until Bobby kicked them out. Your family has had so much heartache and hardship, a reporter said to Bobby. Do the Kennedys intend to retire from politics?

That was a question RFK had been wrestling with since Dallas. "The Kennedys," Bobby sternly said, "intend to stay in public life."

Only six weeks after his Chattanooga conviction, Hoffa again faced off against the Kennedy Justice Department, this time in Chicago, facing prosecutors Charles Z. Smith and Bill Bittman, who were trying the Central States Pension Fund fraud case.

This trial attracted less news coverage than other Hoffa trials. The public stakes were far less dramatic now that RFK's seven-year losing streak against Hoffa had finally been broken.

Along with seven codefendants, Hoffa spent thirteen weeks in federal court over the spring and summer of 1964. Each had been charged with twenty counts of fraud and one count of conspiracy to skim pension-fund assets for personal gain. Presenting the complex financial shenanigans to a jury required reams of paper, scores of witnesses, mind-numbing testimony, and likely the tightest security Chicago had ever seen around a single court case. Jurors in the federal case were sequestered. Each day they were shuttled back and forth from Naval Station Great Lakes, a training center forty-five minutes north of the city. In the mornings, US marshals sneaked them into the courthouse by freight elevator. Two marshals slept on cots each night at the courthouse to guard the boxes of documents and stacks of exhibits and pleadings that prosecutors Smith, Bittman, and others on the Justice Department team were relying on to convict Hoffa. Making regular appearances in the sixth-floor courtroom to show support for their pal Jimmy were mobbed-up Joey Glimco, head of the Teamsters' Chicago taxicab local; Paul "Red" Dorfman and his stepson, Allen; and others. Some observers were astonished that Hoffa's lawyers did not banish these men on the chance that jurors might recognize them and take offense.

In the last weeks of the trial, Smith and Bittman were assigned federal bodyguards after they were jeered at and spit on by Hoffa supporters as they came to and from court. When the eight-man, four-woman jury began deliberating on Friday evening, July 24, 1964, judge Richard Austin barricaded the sixth-floor hallway with two massive wooden benches, closing off his courtroom and its nearby jury room from reporters, camera crews, and Hoffa hangers-on. When news that jurors had reached a verdict flashed out early Sunday afternoon, Austin's courtroom quickly filled up. Hoffa sat as immutable as an engine block, steely-eyed, one elbow on the trial table, chin on his fist, his other arm flexed across the back of his chair.

When the verdicts came back guilty for all seven defendants, Hoffa's son, Jim, a law student, rushed from the courtroom, presumably to break the bad news by telephone to his mother and sister before they heard it on the radio. Moments later, he angrily shoved aside a reporter so that he could reenter the courtroom. His father had charmed and dodged his way around the justice system for seven slick years, only to suffer two felony convictions in four months, a stunning comeuppance. This conviction stung worse than the one for jury tampering. Vast swaths of the 1.7 million Teamsters membership, with help from Hoffa and the union's press office, honestly believed that Robert Kennedy had a vendetta against their president and over the years gave him the benefit of the doubt. But a conviction for skimming cash from retirees' pension funds — in effect, picking the pockets of pensioners — could not be spun in Hoffa's favor.

Hoffa was determined to stay in office and out of prison. He wasn't up for election until 1966, which gave him plenty of time for reputation repair and for scorched-earth legal appeals. Under the Johnson administration, Hoffa expected to face a less tenacious Justice Department, especially if RFK, as expected, stepped down as attorney general.

His counterattack, not surprisingly, focused on Partin. His lawyers asked the Supreme Court to overturn his conviction on Fourth Amendment grounds, arguing that Partin had in effect intruded into Hoffa's constitutionally protected home — his hotel room, where he had lived for nearly three months during the Nashville trial. They also argued that Partin had interfered with Hoffa's right to effective counsel, violating the

Sixth Amendment, by spying on his legal team and sharing defense tactics with the Get Hoffa squad. Out on the street, if Partin was to be believed, Hoffa intermediaries beseeched the Baton Rouge Teamsters official to change his story. He could name his price if he swore that the Justice Department had pressured him to make up a story to get Hoffa. The Hoffa team also papered the appeals court with accounts from prostitutes who said that they had sex with jurors and marshals during the trial, and one woman said the judge, drinking in a bar, told her he was out to get Hoffa. Their stories were denied, and one of the women was later convicted of perjury.

Eventually, a majority of the justices would rule against the convicted Teamsters president. Hoffa was indeed protected in his Nashville hotel room just as if he were in his own home, they reasoned, but he had invited Partin into that temporary home and freely talked about jury tampering. "When Hoffa made incriminating statements to or in the presence of Partin, his invitee, he relied, not on the security of the hotel room, but on his misplaced confidence that Partin would not reveal his wrongdoing," said justice Potter Stewart, writing for the majority. Chief justice Earl Warren, who had been a no-nonsense district attorney in California, vehemently disagreed. "Here the Government reaches into the jailhouse to employ a man who was himself facing indictments far more serious (and later including one for perjury) than the one confronting the man against whom he offered to inform. It employed him not for the purpose of testifying to something that had already happened, but rather for the purpose of infiltration to see if crimes would in the future be committed.... Certainly if a criminal defendant insinuated his informer into the prosecution's camp in this manner he would be guilty of obstructing justice." Warren's blistering dissent was no consolation to Hoffa. It would not keep him from prison's gate.

Robert Kennedy was at a turning point as well. On August 27, 1964, the final day of the Democratic National Convention in Atlantic City, New Jersey, he took the stage to introduce a film about the life of President Kennedy. RFK cast a slight, sad figure, not that of the wiry, relentless pursuer of popular imagination. Yet before he could reach the lectern, the convention hall exploded with a deafening roar from the delegates, who had jumped to their feet and were cheering.

Only five days earlier, he announced he was leaving the Justice Department and running for a seat in the US Senate, representing New York, a long-awaited move, one he needed to make in order to step beyond Jack's candescence. With the president's remains entombed beside the eternal flame in Arlington National Cemetery, his widow in tasteful mourning and isolation and their two children shielded from public view, a deprived citizenry was transferring its needs to Robert Kennedy.

In the hotel ballroom, delegates screamed, others cried, as Bobby let it wash over him. He made moves with his hands as if to say, "Enough," but they refused, pounding their hands and roaring, a raw, brimming expression of loss for the fallen leader. Again, Bobby tried to speak but had to wait until the crowd exhausted itself. The wild acclaim was truly for his brother, he told himself, but it also revealed that the Kennedy mission was still alive and he would carry it out. After twenty-two minutes of ovation, he was able to make himself heard and read a passage from Shakespeare's *Romeo and Juliet* that he said reminded him of his brother:

And, when he shall die,
Take him and cut him out in little stars,
And he will make the face of heaven so fine
That all the world will be in love with night
And pay no worship to the garish sun.

He closed his remarks and walked off backstage and found a fire escape where he sat down and wept.

On September 2, Kennedy stepped down as attorney general. He left behind a Justice Department that was both bigger and more nimble, one so committed to fighting organized crime that Hoover could not undo its progress. Under RFK's generalship, the department brought several hundred indictments against mob-connected businessmen, hoodlums, and racketeers. It washed out the International Brotherhood of Teamsters, bringing 201 indictments against union officials or their associates, resulting in 126 convictions.[3]

Where the attorney general fell short was in failing to bring FBI director Hoover to heel. The unmovable bureaucratic operator kept his power even though he dragged his feet or worked against such Kennedy initiatives such as protecting civil rights and attacking organized crime. Kennedy failed, too, in assisting the Warren commission's investigation of the Kennedy assassination. Although RFK privately believed that Hoffa or the mob or anti-Castro Cubans may have had something to do with his brother's murder, he kept his concerns private, a failure that undercut the commission's goal—to tell the public who killed the president and why. After several commission requests for assistance, RFK, in the summer of 1964, sent the commission a last-minute letter that in its bland tone was more telling in what it didn't say: "I know of no credible evidence to support the allegations that the assassination of President Kennedy was caused by a domestic or foreign conspiracy."

That fall Robert Kennedy floundered as he ran for the Senate. Despite the expensive coaching, his speeches were flat and uninspired, and his feud with Hoffa cast a long shadow over his political future. The liberal wing of the Democratic Party in New York didn't trust him. Many viewed him as "ruthless Bobby"—the aggressive pursuer of Hoffa, the all-too-willing commie hunter for senator Joe McCarthy, the receptive son of anti-Semitic ambassador Joe Kennedy. RFK oversaw a distracted, disorganized campaign, counting on fond feelings for his late brother Jack. To his surprise, RFK fell behind in the polls to silver-haired senator Kenneth Keating, the moderate Republican incumbent. Despite his distaste for LBJ, who had dismissively turned him down as a running mate, Kennedy needed Johnson's help and campaigned jointly in New York with the president, whose popularity at the time far exceeded Bobby's. RFK's fortunes weren't helped in mid-October, when scurrilous campaign literature showed up across the state, saying Kennedy was against blacks and Jews, was pro-Arab at Israel's expense, and was antilabor. At the bottom of the leaflets was the small "union bug," a symbol indicating that the literature had been printed by a union shop. It was smudged, likely deliberately, but the code number could be made out. The attack literature was the work of Merkle Press, printer for several Teamsters publications, including *The International Teamster,* which had a circulation of nearly two million. Kennedy may have given up his power as the top law enforcement official, but Hoffa certainly didn't want him to succeed in a new arena. Despite the dirty tricks, RFK won his Senate seat with 53 percent of the vote, riding LBJ's coattails. Johnson won in a landslide, taking 68 percent.

After exhausting his appeals to the US Supreme Court, Hoffa entered the high-security federal prison in Lewisburg,

Pennsylvania, in March of 1967, still saying he was the victim of a Kennedy vendetta. By then, the public was more aware that the FBI had illegally eavesdropped on mobsters and dissidents. The US Supreme Court, starting in the early 1960s, had broadly expanded constitutional protections for criminal defendants, and in this culture, Kennedy's pursuit of Hoffa was seen by many as unfair, an overreach. To that end, friends and loyal Justice Department colleagues made attempts to soften that perception, saying that Bobby had no urge for Old Testament–style retribution now that Hoffa had been successfully snared.

Perhaps, but some high-level aides in the Kennedy camp have told a different story. David Burke, a key adviser to senator Edward Kennedy in the 1960s, recalled a meeting with a top Teamsters official and the always approachable Teddy. The teamster sought to improve Hoffa's lot in the high-security Lewisburg federal prison. At the time, Robert Kennedy was running for president in the 1968 Democratic primaries and Ramsey Clark was LBJ's attorney general. Burke, who later became president of CBS News, recalled: "The immediate question was, 'Would Robert Kennedy now talk to Ramsey Clark about the possibility of Jimmy Hoffa being transferred from the mattress factory to the farm, so he could get outdoors?' And then eventually, if Robert Kennedy was ever elected, 'What could we expect? And for that we may give some assistance.'

"A day or two later, Robert Kennedy arrived in Indianapolis. I remember he was taking a bath. Edward Kennedy went into the bathroom, and I went in with him, and related to him this conversation. Robert Kennedy said, 'Well, I'll tell you. What you can do is, you go back to your fellow from the Teamsters and you tell him that I will not speak to Ramsey Clark. As far as I'm concerned, Jimmy Hoffa can stay in the mattress factory forever. And if I'm ever elected president of the United States, he has a darn slim chance of ever getting out of jail.' "[4]

Robert Kennedy, of course, was never elected president of the United States. After winning California's Democratic presidential primary on June 5, 1968, he was shot to death in the kitchen of Los Angeles's Ambassador Hotel by an obsessed young Arab nationalist, Sirhan Sirhan, disturbed by RFK's support of Israel. Hoffa learned about the death of his enemy at Lewisburg. "I can't honestly say I felt bad about it," he was to say. "Our vendetta had been too long and too strong."[5]

Hoffa was determined not to let prison break him or his hold on the union. Before he went in, he arranged to have longtime Detroit Teamsters official Frank Fitzsimmons — "a guy I took off a truck and hand-carried all the way from shop steward," by Jimmy's account — serve as acting president. He had known the doughy, plodding Fitz for thirty years and trusted him. When he stepped down as president, Hoffa left a record of bringing superior job benefits to millions of members and much-needed stability to the trucking industry. But his impressive gains were overshadowed by the misdeeds that enabled the Kennedys, the McClellan committee, and others to broadly tar all Teamsters with the crimes of a few.

Fitzsimmons admitted he was a caretaker and said he'd give the office back to Jimmy when he got out of prison. Hoffa was pardoned by President Nixon in 1971, but he was saddled with restrictions that kept him from holding union office until 1980. Soon Hoffa's lawyers were working to have those restrictions removed while Jimmy visited locals around the country, shaking hands and building support for a run for president at the union's 1976 national convention. But by then, Hoffa's onetime protégé Fitzsimmons not only was enjoying the power and perks of high office but also had support from union-connected mob figures who found him more pliable than Hoffa when it came to pension-fund loans and side deals.

On July 30, 1975, James Riddle Hoffa disappeared outside

the Machus Red Fox restaurant in suburban Detroit after being stood up for a meeting scheduled with local Mafia member Anthony "Tony Jack" Giacalone. Authorities spent years investigating, but after decades of effort they concluded that a criminal case could not be brought. The FBI and Hoffa's son and daughter believe the Mafia had their father killed. Still unsolved after forty years, the mystery of the murder is likely proof of its underworld provenance.

Like the Kennedys, Hoffa was murdered while running for elective office. But unlike them, he was not slain in public. Hoffa vanished when no one was looking. His body has never been found. There has been no service. There is no grave site or accounting of who was responsible. "We never had anything," his daughter, Barbara Crancer, a retired judge, was to say. "I'd like to have an ending."[6] In the years since, authorities have pursued credible leads to this most famous unsolved murder, digging up concrete driveways, suburban backyards, a pasture on a Michigan horse farm, and elsewhere, the failed quest now a cruel running joke. Family members have learned to steel themselves at word of the latest credible tip and the rumble of a backhoe. "We don't get our hopes up," Hoffa's daughter says.

Kennedy was buried at Arlington National Cemetery thirty yards from his brother's memorial and its eternal flame. RFK's small gravestone lies flush with the well-tended green lawn and is marked by a simple white cross. Nearby, three marble panels stand etched with two quotations from two enduring speeches by RFK. One includes these hopeful words, which Robert F. Kennedy borrowed from an ancient Greek tragedy and said explained his life's goal: "To tame the savageness of man and make gentle the life of this world."

ACKNOWLEDGMENTS

My gratitude goes out to everyone who helped me with time, guidance, and support over the past decade as I juggled the book's research and writing while working as investigations editor at the *Seattle Times*.

I want to thank the many librarians, archivists, and freelance researchers who took the time to track down essential documents and resources. Among them are Bill Davis, National Archives, Washington, DC; Martha Murphy, National Archives, College Park, Maryland; Kris Bronstad and Morgan Gibson, University of Tennessee, Knoxville; Phil Runkel and Susan Stawicki-Vrobel, Marquette University; James M. Roth, Maryrose Grossman, Laurie Austin, Kora Welsh, and Stephen Plotkin at the John F. Kennedy Presidential Library and Museum; Deborah Rice, Walter P. Reuther Library, Wayne State University; Kevin Bailey, Dwight D. Eisenhower Presidential Library and Museum; Thomas R. French, College of Law, Syracuse University; Harry Miller and Simone Munson, Wisconsin Historical Society; Caronae Howell and Tara Craig, Columbia University; Peter Meyer Filardo, New York University; Abigail Malangone and Craig A. Ellefson, Richard Nixon Presidential Library and Museum; Brigid Shields, Minnesota Historical Society; Kristen Nyitray, Stony Brook University;

ACKNOWLEDGMENTS

Susan Halpert and Lesley Schoenfeld, Harvard University; David Kessler, University of California, Berkeley; Ian Frederick-Rothwell and Claudia Anderson, LBJ Presidential Library; Christopher Walker, George Washington University; Claude B. Zachary, University of Southern California; Jason R. Moore, District of Columbia Public Library; Gregory J. Plunges, National Archives at New York City; and Diane Windham Shaw, Lafayette College.

I thank those who generously agreed to interviews, some of them repeatedly: John Seigenthaler, Edwin Guthman, Charles N. Shaffer, Charles Z. Smith, Barbara Crancer, Nancy Sheridan, Louis Harris, Ron Goldfarb, John A. Terry, Wallace Clemmons, Kevin McEvoy, Michael Riesel, and others. Journalist Dan Moldea, author of the essential *The Hoffa Wars*, provided encouragement and answered questions, for which I am grateful. Friends Deborah Nelson and Tom Brune generously provided a place to stay and morning espressos during research trips to Washington, DC. Others who helped me over the years include William Tabac, Ira Chinoy, Tom Maier, Deborah Coy Kuhlmann, Seymour Hersh, Athan Theoharis, Gus Russo, Lane Williams, Victor Navasky, Willy Stern, Raquel Rutledge, Mark Feldstein, Betty Grdina, Shelley L. Davis, David Burnham, Brad Spencer, Paul Locigno, Naomi Eide, Norm Sinclair, and especially Helen O'Donnell. She went beyond the call of duty to share transcripts of dozens of hours of interviews with her late father, Kenneth O'Donnell, a close friend of both Bobby and Jack Kennedy.

The Fund for Investigative Journalism provided financial support at a key time. My thinking about labor racketeering and other themes explored in *Vendetta* was informed by the work of historians David Witwer and Thaddeus Russell.

Special thanks to the talented professionals at Little, Brown and Company who brought this book to life. Geoff

ACKNOWLEDGMENTS

Shandler, more than a decade ago, read a six-page proposal and saw a book. He, Michael Pietsch, and Reagan Arthur were patient beyond belief as they allowed me to extend deadlines time and again. John Parsley, a great editor, inherited this project last year after Geoff left Little, Brown, treated it as if it were his own, and improved it greatly. Copyeditor Barbara Clark was superb. Thanks also to Mike Noon, Elizabeth Garriga, and Malin von Euler-Hogan. I am fortunate to have as protector, adviser, and friend literary agent *par excellence* Esther Newberg, whose wisdom has guided me so well for more than twenty-five years.

My profound appreciation goes to Joan Fechter, family friend and ace researcher, who has worked with me for more than fifteen years on two books. Thanks also to my understanding editors (and friends) over the years at the *Seattle Times*, Dave Boardman, Kathy Best, and Jim Simon, who gave me the support and leeway that allowed me to be both newspaper editor and author.

My deepest love and thanks goes to my wife, Maureen, who worked with me in the early days of my research for the book, and our two sons. They all too often endured a distracted husband and father who spent weekends and evenings tucked away in an office, behind piles of books and papers. I am excited that my passion for writing has infected Christopher. And especially rewarding for me were research trips to Harvard and the JFK Library in subzero weather with Jameson, who helped to dig up documents that found their way into the book. For all their support, I am a lucky man.

A NOTE ON SOURCES

I was able to draw upon several extraordinary resources for this book. More than fifteen years ago, I secured access to the business archives of the International Brotherhood of Teamsters, a precisely catalogued collection of several million pages of Teamsters records that were microfilmed, indexed, and stored at the union's headquarters in Washington, DC. At the time, I was a journalism professor at the Ohio State University. I used my own funds, and later several small research grants, to copy more than five hundred rolls of microfilm and their voluminous indexes, as well as audio tapes and films, which covered the years 1900 to the late 1980s. Among the categories of records: General Files, Administrative, Governmental Affairs, Research Department, Legal Department, General Executive Board, Personnel, and so on. To my knowledge, I was the first non-Teamster to access these materials. I used only a slim portion of this vast collection for my book, and hope to find a home for this important historical resource at a research library or archives.

The files of Senate investigative committees, typically full of richly detailed memos, financial records, and interview transcripts, are closed for fifty years after the date of creation. As a result, I had to wait until 2007, years into my research for *Vendetta*, before I could begin combing through the earliest documents of the Senate Rackets Committee (1957–1960), which are held at the National Archives in Washington, DC. Three years had to toll before I could complete the job. Again, in many cases, I was the first person to study these investigative files since Robert F. Kennedy and his staff half a century earlier.

Unfortunately, the twenty-eight boxes of the "General Papers of the Chief Counsel," records RFK created as a public servant working for the Senate Rackets Committee, remain closed at the John F. Kennedy Presidential Library. Archivists there tell me they have been waiting for RFK's widow to sign a deed of gift before making them available. I am particularly grateful, however, to Nancy Sheridan, who gave me permission to conduct research at the JFK Library in the personal papers of her late husband, investigator Walter Sheridan, some thirty-one linear feet of records that were otherwise closed.

NOTES

Prologue: Dark Forces

1. Miller Davis, "JFK Roasts GOP, Reds: The Arrival," *Miami News*, November 19, 1963, 1A.
2. Frank Ragano and Selwyn Raab, *Mob Lawyer* (New York: Scribner, 1994), 146.

Chapter 1: The Blinding

1. Jay Maeder, "Dark Places, Victor Riesel, April 1956, Chapter 269," *New York Daily News*, December 15, 2000.
2. Jason Marks, "12 Who Made It Big," History of Baruch College, http://www.baruch.cuny.edu/library/alumni/online_exhibits/digital/2001/history/exhibit/chap_09/who_made_big/made_big.htm.
3. New York Herald Tribune News Service, "Labor Writer Riesel's Eyes Burned by Acid Thrower After Broadcast," *Washington Post*, April 6, 1956, 1.
4. Henry Suydam Jr., Washington Bureau Chief, *Life* magazine, to Edward K. Thompson, editor, *Life* magazine, March 6, 1961; record number 124-10285-10105; file 63-5327-A-NR, section CR, series HQ; John F. Kennedy Assassination Records Collection, National Archives at College Park, College Park, MD.
5. Evan Thomas, *Robert Kennedy: His Life* (New York: Simon and Schuster, 2000), 71.
6. Jonathan Kwitny, *Vicious Circles: The Mafia in the Marketplace* (New York: W. W. Norton, 1979), 268.
7. *Textile Procurement in the Military Services: Hearing Before the Permanent Subcommittee on Investigations of the Committee on Government Operations, United States Senate.* 85th Congress, First Session Pursuant to S. Res. 188, 85th Congress, Part 8, 2447, Part 8, 2447, May 17, 1956

(testimony of John Dioguardi, vice president of the Equitable Research Association).

8. James M. Bambrick, Division of Personnel Administration, National Industrial Conference Board, New York, memo of interview, file 18-5-177, Committee Papers, compiled 1957–1962, Records of the Select Committee on Improper Activities in the Labor or Management Field's Case 18-5 from the 85th through 87th Congresses, Record group 46: Records from the US Senate, National Archives and Records Administration, Washington, DC.

9. The price of Hoffa's power grab was paid by the Puerto Rican and African American workers in minimum-wage jobs in the city's garment shops. Under the sweetheart contracts, they ended up with a few cents above the one-dollar-per-hour minimum wage, no sick leave, a handful of holidays, no vacation pay, and if they complained, they were fired. If the workers joined forces to fight a dishonest employer, the employer "simply picks up his cheap machines from Brooklyn, and with the help of the Dio-Hoffa-O'Rourke axis, moves to the Bronx, where he finds another friendly union to dominate and intimidates a new crop of unskilled and unlettered workers," John McNiff, executive secretary of the Association of Catholic Trade Unionists, testified: Collusion "has made it virtually impossible for an unskilled Puerto Rican worker, supporting a family, to earn over $45 a week. This situation is costing New York City over $25 million a year in welfare payments alone." (*Investigation of Improper Activities in the Labor or Management Field: Hearings Before the Select Committee on Improper Activities in the Labor or Management Field*, 85th Congress, First Session, Pursuant to Senate Resolution 74, 85th Congress, Part 10, 3765, July 31, August 1, 2, 5, and 6, 1957 (testimony of John McNiff, executive secretary of the Association of Catholic Trade Unionists).)

10. Descriptions of the arrests and trial of the men behind the Riesel attack come from extensive coverage of the events by the *New York Times* and *Time*.

11. Hoffa himself was a subject of investigation by the grand jury that US attorney Williams had convened in early 1956 to look into the trucking and garment rackets. Hoffa testified before the jury for ninety minutes on June 25, 1956, and was questioned specifically about his pal Dio, including whether Hoffa owned an interest in Dio's shakedown operation, Equitable Research Associates. No, Hoffa replied under oath, he had no interest in Dio's firm. A federal prosecutor later included Hoffa's denial in a list of statements that could support charges against him for lying to the New York federal grand jury.

12. Letter, J. Edgar Hoover to Victor Riesel, May 14, 1954, Victor Riesel Papers; TAM 170; Box 11, folder 4, Tamiment Library/Robert F. Wag-

ner Labor Archives, New York University. Hoover's columns usually ignored labor issues. A guest column from June was typical. Entitled "Rumors and Fact," Hoover explained "misconceptions concerning the FBI, its functions and responsibilities."

13. Marks, "12 Who Made It Big." To the best of my knowledge, this was the first time Riesel publicly fingered Hoffa as being involved in the acid attack. His remark received no news exposure.

Chapter 2: Life Is a Jungle

1. Clark Mollenhoff, *Tentacles of Power: The Story of Jimmy Hoffa* (Cleveland, OH: World Publishing Company, 1965), 109.
2. David Nasaw, *The Patriarch: The Remarkable Life and Turbulent Times of Joseph P. Kennedy* (New York: Penguin Press, 2012), 155.
3. Charles Spalding, in recorded interview by L. J. Hackman, March 22, 1969, 70, RFK Oral History Program.
4. Mollenhoff, *Tentacles*, 126.
5. Ibid., 124.
6. Peter Collier and David Horowitz, *The Kennedys: An American Drama* (New York: Summit Books, 1984), 219.
7. Kenneth O'Donnell, in recorded interview by Sander Vanocur, 1967, provided by his daughter Helen O'Donnell.
8. Personnel file of Robert Francis Kennedy, Official Military Personnel Files, Military Personnel Archival, Archival Programs, National Archives at St. Louis, MO, and 1941–1959 Deck Logs, Logbooks, Military Records, Modern Military Branch, National Archives at College Park, College Park, MD.
9. Collier and Horowitz, *The Kennedys*, 219.
10. Drumming up publicity for the subcommittee's work was important, and Bobby showed a flair for it. After he and investigators uncovered information about a crooked millionaire hatmaker from Chicago, two FBI agents showed up and wanted everything the subcommittee had found so the Bureau could build a criminal case. Bobby held it back. He promised to provide all once the witness testified. This incensed FBI director J. Edgar Hoover. "Kennedy was completely uncooperative until he had squeezed all the publicity out of the matter he could," Hoover complained.
11. Memo, M. A. Jones to Mr. DeLoach, 09/19/59, ROBERT FRANCIS KENNEDY, Bureau File 77-51387-35.
12. "Labor Problems" serial, file 18-2-10, Committee Papers, compiled 1957-1962, Records of the Select Committee on Improper Activities in the Labor or Management Field's Case 18-2 from the 85th through 87th Congresses, Record group 46: Records from the US Senate, National Archives and Records Administration, Washington, DC.

13. "Jimmy Hoffa" serial, file 18-5-1, Committee Papers, compiled 1957–1962, Records of the Select Committee on Improper Activities in the Labor or Management Field's Case 18-5 from the 85th through 87th Congresses, Record group 46: Records from the US Senate, National Archives and Records Administration, Washington, DC.

14. Arthur M. Schlesinger, *Robert Kennedy and His Times* (New York: Ballantine Books, 1996), 142.

15. Collier and Horowitz, *The Kennedys*, 220.

16. Schlesinger, *Robert Kennedy*, 142.

17. Ibid., 80.

18. Ibid., 109.

19. Roy Cohn, recorded interview by James A. Oesterle, March 24, 1971, 2, Robert F. Kennedy Oral History Collection, John F. Kennedy Library.

20. Robert F. Kennedy, *The Enemy Within: The McClellan Committee's Crusade Against Jimmy Hoffa and Corrupt Labor Unions* (New York: Da Capo Press, 1994), 307.

21. Robert E. Thompson and Hortense Myers, *Robert F. Kennedy: The Brother Within* (New York: Dell, 1962), 112.

22. 18-page document, *Sources*, undated, file 18-244-(unlabeled), File Unit: Records of the Select Committee on Improper Activities in the Labor or Management Field's Case 18-244 from the 85th through 87th Congresses, Series: Committee Papers, 1957–1962, Record Group 46: Records of the US Senate, 1789–2011, National Archives and Records Administration, Washington, DC.

23. John Bartlow Martin, "The Struggle to Get Hoffa," part 1, "Kennedy Sets a Snare," *Saturday Evening Post*, June 27, 1959, 19.

24. United States v. Hoffa, 156 F. Supp. 495 (S.D.N.Y. 1957), decided November 6, 1957, https://casetext.com/case/united-states-v-hoffa-4.

25. Bernard D. Nossiter, "Cheasty Testifies Hoffa Sought Him as 3d Spy," *Washington Post*, June 26, 1957, 1.

26. Kennedy, *The Enemy Within*, 38.

27. "Jimmy Hoffa" serial, file 18-5-23, Committee Papers, compiled 1957–1962, Records of the Select Committee on Improper Activities in the Labor or Management Field's Case 18-5 from the 85th through 87th Congresses, Record group 46: Records from the US Senate, National Archives and Records Administration, Washington, DC.

28. Ralph C. James and Estelle James, *Hoffa and the Teamsters: A Study of Union Power* (New York: Van Nostrand Reinhold, 1965), 190.

29. "Sheriff Raided Gambling Room," *Brazil Weekly Democrat*, April 14, 1921.

30. Tom Nicholson to Ben Williamson, Reports from correspondents that were circulated to editors at the New York office of *Time* magazine, August 24, 1957, Container 141, Dispatches from *Time* Magazine

Correspondents: Second Series, 1956-1968 (MS Am 2090.1). Houghton Library, Harvard College Library, Harvard University.

31. Ibid.

32. James R. Hoffa, as told to Oscar Fraley, *Hoffa: The Real Story* (New York: Stein and Day, 1975), 29.

33. Thaddeus Russell, *Out of the Jungle: Jimmy Hoffa and the Remaking of the American Working Class* (Philadelphia: Temple Press, 2001), 14.

34. Jim Clay, *Hoffa! Ten Angels Swearing* (Beaverdam, VA: Beaverdam Books, 1965), 60.

35. Russell, *Out of the Jungle: Jimmy Hoffa and the Remaking of the American Working Class*, 29.

36. Schlesinger, *Robert Kennedy*, 140.

37. John Bartlow Martin, "The Struggle to Get Hoffa, Part One: Kennedy Sets a Snare," *Saturday Evening Post*, June 27, 1959, 19.

38. "Jimmy Hoffa" serial, file 18-5-24, Committee Papers, compiled 1957–1962, Records of the Select Committee on Improper Activities in the Labor or Management Field's Case 18-5 from the 85th through 87th Congresses, Record group 46: Records from the US Senate, National Archives and Records Administration, Washington, DC.

39. Ibid.

40. Kennedy, *The Enemy Within*, 43.

41. Ibid.

42. Teamsters official Don Vestal, summary of interviews, 1962, Don Vestal folder, Walter Sheridan Personal Papers, Box 9, John F. Kennedy Library.

43. Evan Thomas, *Robert Kennedy: His Life* (New York: Simon and Schuster, 2000), 83.

Chapter 3: Jump Off the Capitol

1. Clark Mollenhoff, *Tentacles of Power: The Story of Jimmy Hoffa* (Cleveland, OH: World Publishing Company, 1965), 154.

2. John Bartlow Martin, "The Struggle to Get Hoffa," part 1, "Kennedy Sets a Snare," *Saturday Evening Post*, June 27, 1959.

3. At the same time, Hoffa and other Teamsters officials were subpoenaed to testify at a short-lived congressional investigation run by congressman Clare Hoffman, a conservative Michigan Republican who disliked Hoffa. Hoffman was looking into complaints of shakedowns, violence, and payoffs in that city's jukebox industry.

4. Jim Hougan, *Spooks: The Haunting of America — The Private Use of Secret Agents* (New York: William Morrow, 1978), 100.

5. John Neary, "The Big Snoop: Electronic Snooping – Insidious Invasions of Privacy," *Life*, May 20, 1966, 44.

6. Bernard B. Spindel, *The Ominous Ear* (New York: Award House, 1968), 121.
7. Pierre Salinger to RFK, memo, August 27, 1957, file 18-5-239, Committee Papers, compiled 1957–1962, Records of the Select Committee on Improper Activities in the Labor or Management Field's Case 18-5 from the 85th through 87th Congresses, Record group 46: Records from the US Senate, National Archives and Records Administration, Washington, DC.
8. Robert F. Kennedy, *The Enemy Within: The McClellan Committee's Crusade Against Jimmy Hoffa and Corrupt Labor Unions* (New York: Da Capo Press, 1994), 325.
9. Walter Sheridan, recorded interview by Roberta Green, March 23, 1970, 107, John F. Kennedy Library Oral History Program.
10. Ibid.
11. Letter, Walter Sheridan to Nancy Sheridan, May 27, 1957, "Loose material" folder, Walter Sheridan Personal Papers, Box 6, John F. Kennedy Library.
12. "Labor: Dave and the Green Stuff," *Time*, April 8, 1957.
13. Ibid.
14. Ibid.
15. Ibid.
16. *Investigation of Improper Activities in the Labor or Management Field: Hearings Before the Select Committee on Improper Activities in the Labor or Management Field*, 85th Congress, First Session, Pursuant to Senate Resolution 74, 85th Congress, part 5, 1677-78, March 26–27, 1957 (Testimony of Dave Beck, president of the International Brotherhood of Teamsters, Chauffeurs, Warehousemen, and Helpers of America).

Chapter 4: Lucky Bastard

1. Jay Maeder, "Code of the Underworld Trying Johnny Dio, May–August 1957 Chapter 278," *New York Daily News*, December 26, 2000.
2. Saul Pett, "Lawyer Williams Looks at Success," *Washington Post*, October 19, 1958, E3.
3. Clark Mollenhoff, *Tentacles of Power: The Story of Jimmy Hoffa* (Cleveland, OH: World Publishing Company, 1965), 190.
4. Evan Thomas, *The Man to See: Edward Bennett Williams—Ultimate Insider; Legendary Trial Lawyer* (New York: Simon and Schuster, 1991), 109.
5. Mollenhoff, *Tentacles*, 196.
6. Unsigned memo to William P. Rogers, undated, Box 47, Criminal Division Matters, William P. Rogers Papers, 1938–62, Dwight D. Eisenhower Presidential Library.
7. Drew Pearson, "More Sidelights on Hoffa Case," *Washington Post*, August 2, 1957, D9.

8. Memo to file, Don Vestal, January 15, 1962, Don Vestal folder, Box 9, Walter Sheridan Personal Papers, John F. Kennedy Library.

9. "Jimmy Hoffa" serial, file 18-5-M, Committee Papers, compiled 1957–1962, Records of the Select Committee on Improper Activities in the Labor or Management Field's Case 18-5 from the 85th through 87th Congresses, Record group 46: Records from the US Senate, National Archives and Records Administration, Washington, DC.

10. Mollenhoff, *Tentacles*, 207.

11. Marshall Berger to Ben Williamson, Reports from correspondents that were circulated to editors at the New York office of *Time* magazine, July 20, 1957, Container 135, Dispatches from *Time* Magazine Correspondents: Second Series, 1956–1968 (MS Am 2090.1). Houghton Library, Harvard University.

12. Transcript, *United States v. Hoffa*, US District Court, District of Columbia, CR 294-57, 3016.

13. Mollenhoff, *Tentacles*, 208.

14. Ibid., 210.

15. Ibid., 211.

16. Evan Thomas, *Robert Kennedy: His Life* (New York: Simon and Schuster, 2000), 89.

17. Ibid.

18. Drew Pearson, "Pressures Cited in Washington Trial," *Washington Post*, August 1, 1957, D11.

19. Kenneth P. O'Donnell and David F. Powers, *"Johnny, We Hardly Knew Ye": Memories of John Fitzgerald Kennedy* (New York: Pocket Books, 1973), 132.

20. "Sentence First?" *Washington Post*, August 2, 1957, A12.

21. Robert F. Kennedy, *The Enemy Within: The McClellan Committee's Crusade Against Jimmy Hoffa and Corrupt Labor Unions* (New York: Da Capo Press, 1994), 312.

Chapter 5: The First Face-Off

1. "Investigations: An Inconvenient Forgettery," *Time*, Sept. 2, 1957.

2. Mary Van Rensselaer Thayer, "Kennedy Sister Joins Brothers," *Washington Post*, August 22, 1957, C9.

3. Kennedy, *The Enemy Within*, 73.

4. John Bartlow Martin, *Jimmy Hoffa's Hot* (New York: Crest Books, 1959), 49.

5. Arthur M. Schlesinger, *Robert Kennedy and His Times* (New York: Ballantine Books, 1996), 150.

6. *Investigation of Improper Activities in the Labor or Management Field: Hearings Before the Select Committee on Improper Activities in the Labor or Management Field*, 85th Congress, First Session, Pursuant to Senate

Resolution 74, 85th Congress, First Session, Part 13, August 23, 1957,
5253-54.

7. Schlesinger, *Robert Kennedy*, 157.

8. Pierre Salinger, *P.S.: A Memoir* (New York: St. Martin's Press, 1995), 61.

Chapter 6: Hoffa for President

1. John Bartlow Martin, "The Struggle to Get Hoffa, Part IV: Hoffa Takes the Stand," *Saturday Evening Post*, July 18, 1959, 30.

2. "Jimmy Hoffa" serial, file 18-5-230, Committee Papers, compiled 1957–1962, Records of the Select Committee on Improper Activities in the Labor or Management Field's Case 18-5 from the 85th through 87th Congresses, Record group 46: Records from the US Senate, National Archives and Records Administration, Washington, DC.

3. "Jimmy Hoffa" serial, file 18-5-239, Committee Papers, compiled 1957–1962, Records of the Select Committee on Improper Activities in the Labor or Management Field's Case 18-5 from the 85th through 87th Congresses, Record group 46: Records from the US Senate, National Archives and Records Administration, Washington, DC.

4. Martin, "The Struggle to Get Hoffa: Part V, Hoffa Confounds His Enemies," *Saturday Evening Post*, July 25, 1959, 30.

5. "Jimmy Hoffa" serial, file 18-5-4217, Committee Papers, compiled 1957–1962, Records of the Select Committee on Improper Activities in the Labor or Management Field's Case 18-5 from the 85th through 87th Congresses, Record group 46: Records from the US Senate, National Archives and Records Administration, Washington, DC.

6. Ibid.

7. Arthur A. Sloane, *Hoffa* (Cambridge, MA: MIT Press, 1991), 96.

8. Press release, October 7, 1957, 10E3/9/7/2-5, box 25, Committee Papers, compiled 1957–1962, Records of the Select Committee on Improper Activities in the Labor or Management Field's Case 18-5 from the 85th through 87th Congresses, Record group 46: Records from the US Senate, National Archives and Records Administration, Washington, DC.

Chapter 7: Mafia Conclave

1. Ralph Blumenthal, "For Sale, A House With Acreage, Connections Extra," *New York Times*, July 31, 2002, B1.

2. "65 Hoodlums Seized in a Raid And Run Out of Upstate Village," *New York Times*, November 15, 1957, 1.

3. Bill Bonanno, *Bound by Honor: A Mafioso's Story* (New York: St. Martin's Press, 1999), 58.

4. Richard Gid Powers, *Secrecy and Power: The Life of J. Edgar Hoover* (New York: Free Press, 1987), 332.

5. Thomas Repetto, *Bringing Down the Mob: The War Against the American Mafia* (New York: Henry Holt, 2006), 71.

6. Drew Pearson, "Washington Merry-Go-Round," *Prescott Evening Courier,* January 8, 1958, 4.

7. Jean Stein, *American Journey: The Times of Robert F. Kennedy* (New York: New American Library, 1972), 53.

8. Memo, Walter Sheridan to Robert F. Kennedy, December 10, 1957, file 18-5-2488, Committee Papers, compiled 1957–1962, Records of the Select Committee on Improper Activities in the Labor or Management Field's Case 18-5 from the 85th through 87th Congresses, Record group 46: Records from the US Senate, National Archives and Records Administration, Washington, DC.

9. Ibid.

10. Jim Hougan, *Spooks: The Haunting of America — The Private Use of Secret Agents* (New York: William Morrow, 1978), 100. Hougan's interviews with Spindel's wife and associates provide the definitive account of the wireman's extraordinary and puzzling career.

11. Arthur M. Schlesinger, *Robert Kennedy and His Times* (New York: Ballantine Books, 1996), 150.

Chapter 8: Keep the Pressure On

1. Steven Brill, *The Teamsters* (New York: Simon and Schuster, 1978), 355.

2. Ibid., 365.

3. Ibid.

4. Ethel Payne, "So This Is Washington," *Chicago Daily Defender,* May 17, 1958, 11.

5. "Labor Investigations." In *CQ Almanac 1958*, 14th ed., 11-674-11-686. Washington, DC: Congressional Quarterly, 1959. http://library.cqpress .com.offcampus.lib.washington.edu/cqalmanac/cqal58-1340149.

6. "Jimmy Hoffa" serial, file 18-5-1359, Committee Papers, compiled 1957–1962, Records of the Select Committee on Improper Activities in the Labor or Management Field's Case 18-5 from the 85th through 87th Congresses, Record group 46: Records from the US Senate, National Archives and Records Administration, Washington, DC.

7. Hugh Sidey, Reports from correspondents that were circulated to editors at the New York office of *Time* magazine, August 15, 1958, container 145, Dispatches from *Time* Magazine Correspondents: Second Serigutes, 1956-1968 (MS Am 2090.1). Houghton Library, Harvard University.

8. File 1-1-24, File Unit: Bulky Exhibit from the Select Committee on Improper Activities in the Labor or Management Field's Case 1-1 from the 85th and 86th Congresses, 1957–1960, Series: Committee Papers, 1957–1962, Record Group 46: Records of the US Senate, 1789–2011, National Archives and Records Building, Washington, DC.

9. File 1-1-28, File Unit: Bulky Exhibit from the Select Committee on Improper Activities in the Labor or Management Field's Case 1-1 from the 85th and 86th Congresses, 1957–1960, Series: Committee Papers, 1957–1962, Record Group 46: Records of the US Senate, 1789–2011, National Archives and Records Building, Washington, DC.

10. *IRS Historical Fact Book: A Chronology, 1646–1992*, Publication 1694 (12-92) Catalog Number 15037N (Washington, DC: U.S. Government Printing Office, 1993), 160.

11. Bernard D. Nossiter, "Witness Says He Was Paid By Shefferman," *Washington Post*, November 2, 1957, A1.

12. Ibid.

13. Hugh Sidey to Ben Williamson, Reports from correspondents that were circulated to editors at the New York office of *Time* magazine, August 21, 1958, container 146, Dispatches from *Time* Magazine Correspondents: Second Series, 1956-1968 (MS Am 2090.1). Houghton Library, Harvard University.

14. Ibid.

15. Ibid.

16. See Arthur M. Schlesinger, *Robert Kennedy and His Times* (New York: Ballantine Books, 1996), 159, 937, n 110, citing Robert F. Kennedy, *The Enemy Within: The McClellan Committee's Crusade Against Jimmy Hoffa and Corrupt Labor Unions* (New York: Da Capo Press, 1994), 157–8; *Investigation of Improper Activities in the Labor or Management Field: Hearings Before the Select Committee on Improper Activities in the Labor or Management Field*, 85th Congress, First Session, Pursuant to Senate Resolution 74, 85th Congress, First Session, Part 40, September 18, 1958, 15230-1; and John Bartlow Martin, *Jimmy Hoffa's Hot* (New York: Crest Books, 1959), 731–2.

17. Ibid.

18. Schlesinger, *Robert Kennedy*, 159, n108.

19. Schlesinger, *Robert Kennedy*, 159.

20. Kennedy, *Enemy Within*, 77.

Chapter 9: Promising Leads

1. Walter Sheridan, recorded interview by Roberta Greene, June 12, 1970, 126, John F. Kennedy Oral History Program.

2. Walter Sheridan, recorded interview by Roberta Greene, April 7, 1970, 124, John F. Kennedy Library Oral History Program.

3. "Legend in the Law: William G. Hundley," *The Washington Lawyer*, November 2001, http://www.dcbar.org/bar-resources/publications/washington-lawyer/articles/november-2001-legends-in-the-law.cfm.

4. William G. Hundley, recorded interview by James A. Oesterle, December 9, 1970, 6-7, Robert F. Kennedy Library Oral History Project of the John F. Kennedy Library.

5. Hugh Sidey to Harry Johnston, Reports from correspondents that were circulated to editors at the New York office of *Time* magazine, September 29, 1960, container 439, Dispatches from *Time* Magazine Correspondents: Second Series, 1956–1968 (MS Am 2090.1). Houghton Library, Harvard University.

6. "Jimmy Hoffa" serial, file 18-5-4456, Committee Papers, compiled 1957-1962, Records of the Select Committee on Improper Activities in the Labor or Management Field's Case 18-5 from the 85th through 87th Congresses, Record group 46: Records from the US Senate, National Archives and Records Administration, Washington, DC.

7. James P. Kelly, IRS affidavit, August 1, 1962, file 18-5-4456, Committee Papers, compiled 1957–1962, Records of the Select Committee on Improper Activities in the Labor or Management Field's Case 18-5 from the 85th through 87th Congresses, Record group 46: Records from the US Senate, National Archives and Records Administration, Washington, DC.

8. Ibid.

9. Bernard B. Spindel, *The Ominous Ear* (New York: Award House, 1968), 206.

10. Ibid., 218.

11. Ibid., 205.

12. Ibid.

13. *Investigation of Improper Activities in the Labor or Management Field: Hearings Before the Select Committee on Improper Activities in the Labor or Management Field*, 86th Congress, First Session, Pursuant to Senate Resolution 44, 86th Congress, 19828, July 10, 13, and 14, 1959 (testimony of Bernard B. Spindel, electronic technician).

14. Spindel, *Ominous Ear*, 210.

15. Roscoe Born and Monroe Karmin, "Anti-Hoffa Strategy," *Wall Street Journal*, October 20, 1959, 1.

16. *Detroit Times*, November 5, 1959.

Chapter 10: Primary Opponent

1. Pierre Salinger, *With Kennedy* (New York: Doubleday, 1966), 64.

2. Victor Riesel, "National Political Machine Planned By Hoffa in 1960," *The Milwaukee Sentinel*, August 8, 1959, 9.

3. George MacKinnon, unpublished manuscript, "The Making of a Judge, 1993–1994," Location 142.J.6.3B, Box 21, George E. MacKinnon papers, Minnesota Historical Society.

4. Ibid.

5. Ibid.

6. Ibid.

7. Memo, Department of Justice, Malcolm Wilkey to J. Edgar Hoover, April 12, 1960, Location 142.J.6.2F, Box 20, George E. MacKinnon papers, MHS.

8. Memo, Department of Justice, George E. MacKinnon to Malcolm Wilkey, May 8, 1960, Location 142.J.6.2F, Box 20, George E. MacKinnon papers, MHS.

9. Lou Harris, author interview, February 15, 2012.

10. David Pietrusza, *1960: LBJ vs. JFK vs. Nixon* (New York: Union Square Press, 2008), 7–9; David Halberstam, *The Powers That Be* (New York: Alfred A. Knopf, 1975), 319–320.

11. Robert M. Eisinger, *The Evolution of Presidential Polling* (Cambridge, UK: Cambridge University Press, 2003), 87–88.

12. George A. Smathers, United States Senator, 1951–1969, recorded interview by Donald A. Ritchie, August 1, 1989, Oral History Interview #1: The Road to Congress, 78, Senate Historical Office, Washington, DC.

13. Kenneth O'Donnell, interviews with NBC White House correspondent Sander Vanocur, provided to the author, courtesy of Helen O'Donnell.

14. *The Newsmakers*, WBZ Radio, Boston, January 18, 1960, Speeches and the Press series, John F. Kennedy Library.

15. Shaun A. Casey, *The Making of a Catholic President: Kennedy vs. Nixon 1960* (New York: Oxford University Press, 2009), 64–65.

16. Carl Solberg, *Hubert Humphrey: A Biography* (New York: W. W. Norton, 1984), 12.

17. Scott Reston, "Milwaukee: The Organization Men Take Over," *New York Times*, March 1, 1960, 24.

18. Associated Press, "Hoffa Suing N.B.C. and Paar for Libel," *New York Times*, May 24, 1960, 62.

19. Tex Reynolds, "Between the Lines," *Racine Journal Times*, February 8, 1960, 1.

20. "Kennedy Continues Feud with Hoffa / Valley Inn Canceled," *Oshkosh Daily Northwestern*, March 12, 1960, 13.

21. Joseph L. Rauh, recorded interview by Charles Morrissey, December 23, 1965, 38, John F. Kennedy Library Oral History Program.

22. Associated Press report, "Humphrey and Kennedy Forces Deplore Ad Citing Religious Issue," *St. Petersburg Times*, April 1, 1960, 2.

23. "Ex-state Lawyer is Linked to Teamsters and Anti-Kennedy Ad," *Milwaukee Journal*, October 2, 1960, 1.

24. Solberg, *Hubert Humphrey*, 207–8.

25. Kenneth P. O'Donnell and David F. Powers, *"Johnny, We Hardly Knew Ye": Memories of John Fitzgerald Kennedy* (New York: Pocket Books, 1973), 180.

Chapter 11: Nixon's Favor

1. Kenneth P. O'Donnell, recorded interview by Sander Vanocur, provided to the author by Helen O'Donnell.
2. Sorensen wrote draft chapters and was assigned royalties for the book.
3. Clark Clifford, *Counsel to the President: A Memoir* (New York: Random House, 1991), 306–10.
4. John Seigenthaler, recorded interview by Larry J. Hackman, July 22, 1964, 48, John F. Kennedy Library Oral History Program.
5. John Seigenthaler, author interview, August 5, 2010.
6. Ralph C. James and Estelle James, *Hoffa and the Teamsters: A Study of Union Power* (New York: Van Nostrand Reinhold, 1965), 190.
7. Arthur M. Schlesinger, *Robert Kennedy and His Times* (New York: Ballantine Books, 1996), 151.
8. Memo, C. D. DeLoach to Mr. Mohr, 4/19/60, SENATOR JOHN F. KENNEDY OF MASSACHUSETTS, 94-37374-NR.
9. Ibid.
10. Memo to file, "Don Vestal" folder, Walter Sheridan Personal Papers, Box 9, John F. Kennedy Library.
11. Victor Davis, "The Father of Scandal," *British Journalism Review* 13, no. 4 (2002).
12. Sam Kashner and Jennifer MacNair, *The Bad and the Beautiful: Hollywood in the Fifties* (New York: W. W. Norton, 2002), 37.
13. Summary of Interview, Fred Otash by Ralph F. Salerno, July 24, 1978, record number 180-10074-10198, file number 010464, Series Numbered Files, John F. Kennedy Assassination Records Collection, National Archives at College Park, College Park, MD.
14. Memo, M. A. Jones to Mr. DeLoach, 7/26/60, FRED OTASH, Bureau file 62-116606-NR.
15. Ibid.
16. One of Otash's call-girl friends did work the convention crowd, which she likely came to regret. The Los Angeles vice cops had stepped up their work during the gathering, keeping close surveillance on Hollywood hot spots such as the Ambassador Hotel's Regency Room, a widely known high-end pickup place. One night detectives spotted her there, along with "a very well known, curvaceous prostitute." The two women moved on to the Melody Room, on the Sunset Strip, where they each made a pickup—one of them an Indianapolis municipal judge who was a delegate at the convention. While vice cops watched surreptitiously, the two couples moved on to the Hollywood Roosevelt Hotel. There the two call girls booked separate rooms and began to entertain their dates—until police raided them and arrested the two women. The woman who was friends with Otash contacted the private eye, who bailed her out.

17. Marvin Miles, "Hoffa Accused of Effort to 'Crash' Convention," *Los Angeles Times*, July 9, 1960, 5.

18. Arthur M. Schlesinger, *Robert Kennedy and His Times* (New York: Ballantine Books, 1996), 204.

19. Westbrook Pegler, "Stevenson Demonstrators Financed by Jimmy Hoffa," *Human Events*, August 18, 1960, 12.

20. Ibid.

21. Norman Mailer, "Superman Comes to the Supermarket," *Esquire*, November 1960.

22. Hugh Sidey to Harry Johnston, Reports from correspondents that were circulated to editors at the New York office of *Time* magazine, September 26, 1960, container 435, Dispatches from *Time* Magazine Correspondents: Second Series, 1956–1968 (MS Am 2090.1). Houghton Library, Harvard College Library, Harvard University.

23. Ibid.

24. "Democrats: Little Brother Is Watching," *Time*, October 10, 1960.

25. Curt Gentry, *J. Edgar Hoover: The Man and the Secrets* (New York: W. W. Norton, 1991), 463.

26. Memo, M. A. Jones to Mr. DeLoach, 7/13/60, SENATOR JOHN F. KENNEDY OF MASSACHUSETTS, Bureau file 94-37374-NR.

27. Anthony Summers, *Official and Confidential: The Secret Life of J. Edgar Hoover* (New York: G. P. Putnam's Sons, 1993), 292–3.

28. John F. Kennedy debate with Richard Nixon in Chicago, September 26, 1960, Miller Center, University of Virginia, http://millercenter.org/president/speeches/detail/5728.

29. Walter Sheridan, recorded interview by Roberta Greene, April 7, 1970, 139, John F. Kennedy Library Oral History Program.

30. Louis Harris, recorded interview by Vicki Daitch, April 12 and 13, 2005, 150, John F. Kennedy Library Oral History Program.

31. "Hoffa Fails in Congress Purge Try," *Los Angeles Times*, November 10, 1960, 8.

32. *DRIVE Reporter* (newsletter of the Democrat, Republican, and Independent Voter Education Teamster political action committee), vol. 1, no. 3.

33. *DRIVE Reporter*, vol. 1, no. 2, undated but circa fall 1960.

34. "Hoffa Terms Nixon a Friend of Labor," *Los Angeles Times*, November 5, 1960, 1.

35. Marguerite Higgins, *New York Herald Tribune*, November 21, 1960.

36. Arthur M. Schlesinger Jr., *A Thousand Days: John F. Kennedy in the White House* (New York: Houghton Mifflin, 1965), 229.

37. Nicholas deB. Katzenbach, *Some of It Was Fun: Working with RFK and LBJ* (New York: W. W. Norton, 2008), 22.

38. Walter Sheridan, recorded interview by Roberta Greene, March 23, 1970, 101, John F. Kennedy Library Oral History Program.
39. Thurston Clarke, *Ask Not: The Inauguration of John F. Kennedy and the Speech That Changed America* (New York: Henry Holt, 2004), 55.
40. Jack Anderson, "Washington Merry-Go-Round," *Washington Post*, November 16, 1960.
41. Wallace Carroll, "Appointing a Relative," *New York Times*, December 17, 1960, 14.
42. "Special to The New York Times: Transcripts of Two News Conferences," *New York Times*, December 17, 1960, 14.
43. Barry Goldwater, "Appointment of Robert Kennedy Draws Fire," *Human Events*, January 13, 1961, 30.
44. Oakley Hunter, letter quoted in Drew Pearson's column, "Nixon Figured in Hoffa Delay," *Washington Post*, January 4, 1961, B17.

Chapter 12: Get Hoffa Squad

1. Transcript, Nicholas D. Katzenbach Oral History Interview I, 8, 11/12/68, by Paige E. Mulhollan, Internet Copy, LBJ Library.
2. Mortimer Caplin, recorded interview by Shelley L. Davis and Kecia L. McDonald, November 18, 19, and 25, 1991, 4 (Washington, DC: US Government Printing Office, IRS, 1991).
3. Ibid.
4. Arthur M. Schlesinger, *Robert Kennedy and His Times* (New York: Ballantine Books, 1996), 259.
5. William Surface, *Inside Internal Revenue: A Report to the Taxpayer* (New York: Coward-McCann, 1967), 123.
6. Victor Navasky, *Kennedy Justice* (New York: Scribner, 1971), 58.
7. Louis F. Oberdorfer, "Background: Oberdorfer, Lou" folder, Box 15, Victor S. Navasky Personal Papers, John F. Kennedy Library.
8. Robert F. Kennedy, *The Enemy Within: The McClellan Committee's Crusade Against Jimmy Hoffa and Corrupt Labor Unions* (New York: Da Capo Press, 1994), 173.
9. Walter Sheridan, recorded interview by Roberta Greene, April 7, 1970, 128, John F. Kennedy Library Oral History Program.
10. Navasky, *Kennedy Justice*, 405.
11. Charles Z. Smith, author interview, May 21, 2011.
12. Memo, Walter Sheridan to Herbert J. Miller Jr., April 19, 1961, "Misc. Memos: 1960–66" folder, Walter Sheridan Personal Papers, Box 12, John F. Kennedy Library.
13. Interview of Herbert J. Miller Jr., "Legends in the Law: A Conversation with Herbert J. Miller, Jr.," *Bar Report*, February/March 1998, http://educationforum.ipbhost.com/index.php?showtopic=15205.

14. Suydam was the son of the legendary *Brooklyn Eagle* journalist Henry Suydam, who advised FBI director Hoover how to use public relations to shape the Bureau's image.
15. Interview, Robert M. Morgenthau by Victor S. Navasky, "Interviews: Morgenthau, Robert M." folder, Victor S. Navasky Personal Papers, Box 22, John F. Kennedy Library.
16. Jack Turcott, "Offices Bugged, B-girls Scheme Against Delegates, Hoffa Says," New York *Daily News*, July 4, 1961.
17. Ibid.
18. Ronald Goldfarb, *Perfect Villains, Imperfect Heroes: Robert F. Kennedy's War Against Organized Crime* (New York: Random House, 1995), 193.
19. UPI, "Robt. Kennedy Stands Firm Against Hoffa," *Chicago Tribune*, July 8, 1961, Part 1, 5.
20. *National Police Gazette*, May 1961, vol. 166, no. 5.
21. Evan Thomas, *The Man to See: Edward Bennett Williams — Ultimate Insider; Legendary Trial Lawyer* (New York: Simon and Schuster, 1991), 161. The Williams-RFK conversation had to have taken place before early July 3, 1961, the start of the International Brotherhood of Teamsters national convention. When RFK dictated the memo is unclear. It was dated August 1, 1961.
22. Proceedings, International Brotherhood of Teamsters' International Convention, July 3–7, 1961, IBT0019, Series 2, Box 12, Folder 7, International Convention Records 1908–2006, Special Collections Research Center, Gelman Library, The George Washington University, Washington, DC.
23. Ibid.
24. Nancy Sheridan, author interview, April 1, 2002.
25. Memo, C. A. Evans to Mr. Belmont, 03/13/62, MISUR, Bureau file: 92-2717-487.
26. Navasky, *Kennedy Justice*, 404.
27. Interview, Edwyn Silberling by Victor S. Navasky, "Interviews: Silberling, Edwyn" folder, Victor S. Navasky Personal Papers, Box 23, John F. Kennedy Library.
28. Louis F. Oberdorfer, "Background: Oberdorfer, Lou" folder, Box 15, Victor S. Navasky Personal Papers, John F. Kennedy Library.
29. Memos, Undated, "Dept of Justice 1961–64" folder, Walter Sheridan Personal Papers, Box 12, John F. Kennedy Library.
30. Nicholas deB. Katzenbach, *Some of It Was Fun: Working with RFK and LBJ* (New York: W. W. Norton, 2008), 97.

Chapter 13: A Brazen Girl

1. Interview, Robert M. Morgenthau by Victor S. Navasky, "Interviews: Morgenthau, Robert M." folder, Victor S. Navasky Personal Papers, Box 22, John F. Kennedy Library.

2. Papers of John F. Kennedy. Presidential Papers. President's Office Files. Departments and Agencies. Justice: Levine report on FBI, January 23, 1962.

3. Arthur M. Schlesinger, *Robert Kennedy and His Times* (New York: Ballantine Books, 1996), 254.

4. Papers of John F. Kennedy. Presidential Papers. President's Office Files. Departments and Agencies. Justice: Levine report on FBI, January 23, 1962.

5. Letter, Herbert Miller Jr. to Senator Sam Ervin, March 25, 1961, Clark R. Mollenhoff papers, 1936–1990, box 72, folder 1, Wisconsin Historical Society, Madison, WI.

6. Evan Thomas, *Robert Kennedy: His Life* (New York: Simon and Schuster, 2000), 167n.

7. Interview with Judith Campbell Exner, September 20, 1975, record number 157-10002-10384, file R-1358, 29-30, series Transcript, Senate Select Committee to Study Governmental Operations with Respect to Intelligence Activities, John F. Kennedy Assassination Records Collection, National Archives at College Park, College Park, MD.

8. C. A. Evans to Mr. Belmont, 3-15-61, JUDITH E. CAMPBELL, Bureau File 92-3267-158.

9. Edwin Guthman, author interview, June 15, 2002.

10. Louis Harris, recorded interview by Vicki Daitch, April 12 and 13, 2005, 46, John F. Kennedy Library Oral History Program.

11. Andrew Biemiller, recorded interview by Sheldon Stern, May 24, 1979, 21, John F. Kennedy Library Oral History Program.

12. Ibid.

Chapter 14: Planting a Snitch

1. Arthur A. Sloane, *Hoffa* (Cambridge, MA: MIT Press, 1991), 246.

2. Victor Lasky, *Robert F. Kennedy: The Myth and the Man* (New York: Trident, 1968), 245.

3. Bill Davidson, "The Ordeal of Sam Baron," *Windsor Star*, Weekend Magazine, Vol. 15, No. 23, June 5, 1965, 2.

4. Victor Riesel, "Inside Story Told of Row in Hoffa's Office," *Los Angeles Times*, May 28, 1952, A5.

5. Associated Press, "Witness Tells Dealings with Hoffa over Strike," *Los Angeles Times*, October 30, 1962, 21.

6. Transcript, *United States vs. James R. Hoffa and Commercial Carriers*, United States District Court, Middle District of Tennessee, LAC0005, Series 7, Box 5, Folder 1, October 29, 1962 (Trial testimony: Bert Beveridge, general manager, Commercial Carriers), Special Collections Research Center, Gelman Library, The George Washington University, Washington, DC.

7. Letter, George Fitzgerald to Robert F. Kennedy, February 8, 1957. "Jimmy Hoffa" serial, file 18-5, Committee Papers, Records of the Select Committee on Improper Activities in the Labor or Management Field, National Archives, Washington, DC.

8. Transcript, Nicholas D. Katzenbach Oral History Interview I, 11/12/68, by Paige E. Mulhollan, Internet Copy, LBJ Library, 28.

9. Walter M. Miller Jr., "Bobby and Jimmy: Round Six," *The Nation*, April 7, 1962, 303.

10. Ralph C. James and Estelle James, *Hoffa and the Teamsters: A Study of Union Power* (New York: Van Nostrand Reinhold, 1965), 37.

11. Ibid.

12. *DRIVE Reporter* (newsletter of the Democrat, Republican, and Independent Voter Education Teamster political action committee), October 30, 1962, 6

13. *United States v. International Brotherhood of Teamsters* 88 Civ. 8846 (DNE) (S.D.N.Y.), 1988 (deposition, Charles O'Brien, international organizer assigned to the Teamsters' Southern Conference in Hallandale, FL).

14. Sam Baron, "I Was Near the Top of Jimmy's Drop-Dead List," *Life* magazine, July 20, 1962, 68. Kennedy had introduced Baron to the magazine editors a year earlier.

15. William A. Hatas (victim), Case 70-36555, autopsy report, Alabama Department of Toxicology and Criminal Investigation, Alabama Department of Forensic Sciences, 1051 Wire Road, Auburn, Alabama 36832.

16. Sidney Simpson affidavit, December 1, 1964, *United States v. Hoffa*, Case 15876, US Sixth Circuit Court of Appeals.

17. Walter Sheridan, *The Fall and Rise of Jimmy Hoffa* (New York: Saturday Review Press, 1972), 217.

18. Letter to Senator McClellan from Retus Riles and Frank Doughty, December 6, 1958, file 18-2-16714, Records of the Select Committee on Improper Activities in the Labor or Management Field, National Archives, Washington, DC.

19. Memo, New Orleans Area Office to Division of National Investigations, re: HOCASE, Name Check Programs, US Department of Labor, June 21, 1960, "Partin—Criminal Record" folder, Walter Sheridan Personal Papers, Box 7, John F. Kennedy Library.

20. Simpson affidavit.

21. Ibid.

22. *Osborn v. United States*, 385 U.S. 293 (1966), Decided December 12, 1966, https://supreme.justia.com/cases/federal/us/385/323/.

23. Simpson affidavit.

24. Memo, SAC, New Orleans to Director, FBI, 10/10/62, JAMES RIDDLE HOFFA, EDWARD GRADY PARTIN, MISCELLANEOUS – INFORMATION CONCERNING (Accounting and Fraud Section), Bureau File 63-7966-26.

25. Memo, Director, FBI to The Attorney General, 10/16/62, JAMES RIDDLE HOFFA, EDWARD GRADY PARTIN, MISCELLANEOUS – INFORMATION CONCERNING (Accounting and Fraud Section), Bureau File 63-7966-25.

26. Victor Navasky, *Kennedy Justice* (New York: Scribner, 1971), 419.

27. Sheridan, *Jimmy Hoffa*, 221.

28. James and James, *Hoffa and the Teamsters*, 52.

29. *DRIVE Reporter*, January 20, 1963.

30. United States Court of Appeals Sixth Circuit, 353 F.2d 789, December 29, 1965.

31. Navasky, *Kennedy Justice*, 406.

32. Memo, Director, FBI to The Attorney General, 11/15/62 JAMES RIDDLE HOFFA, EDWARD GRADY PARTIN, MISCELLANEOUS – CONCERNING (Accounting and Fraud Section), Bureau File 63-7966-NR.

33. Airtel, Director, FBI to SAC, NO, 11/19/62, JAMES RIDDLE HOFFA, EDWARD GRADY PARTIN, MISCELLANEOUS–INFORMATION CONCERNING (ACCOUNTING AND FRAUD SECTION), Bureau File 63-7966-61.

34. Navasky, *Kennedy Justice*, 420.

35. Sheridan, *Jimmy Hoffa*, 230.

36. Ibid., 251.

37. Homer Bigart, "Will the Law Ever Get Hoffa?" *Saturday Evening Post*, March 30, 1963, 68.

Chapter 15: Trouble at Home

1. Edwin O. Guthman and Jeffrey Shulman, eds., *Robert Kennedy in His Own Words: The Unpublished Recollections of the Kennedy Years* (New York: Bantam Books, 1988), 56.

2. Edwyn Silberling interview, April 15, 1991, Box 47b, 2, C. David Heymann, Robert F. Kennedy Collection, Special Collections, Stony Brook University Libraries.

3. Ibid.

4. Jay Goldberg, an aggressive, flamboyant prosecutor who used to work with Silberling in New York, had riled up locals in mobbed-up Gary with his federal grand jury. Early on, Chacharis pledged his cooperation and asked to see "the evidence" before being questioned, a request Goldberg and Silberling refused to grant. As a result, Goldberg was summoned back to Justice to meet with criminal chief Jack Miller, Chacharis, and the mayor's new lawyer, who was a member of the Democratic National Committee and who used to hold Miller's position.

5. Chacharis continued to live modestly; instead of spending the boodle on himself or his family, he funneled it into the Lake County Democratic organization to grow his power and the party's influence.

6. "Legend in the Law: William G. Hundley," *The Washington Lawyer*, November 2001.

7. Charles Shaffer, author interview, August 12, 2014

8. Walter Sheridan, recorded interview by Roberta W. Greene, June 12, 1970, 109, John F. Kennedy Library Oral History Program.

9. Ibid.

10. Ibid.

11. Ralph C. James and Estelle James, *Hoffa and the Teamsters: A Study of Union Power* (New York: Van Nostrand Reinhold, 1965), 361.

12. Memo, Langenbacher to Robert F. Kennedy, August 25, 1959, Subject: SYLVIA PARIS, Record 18-5-4010, Committee Papers, compiled 1957–1962, Records of the Select Committee on Improper Activities in the Labor or Management Field's Case 18-5 from the 85th through 87th Congresses, Record group 46: Records from the US Senate, National Archives and Records Administration, Washington, DC.

13. Subject: James R. Hoffa, Miscellaneous Electronic Surveillance References (ELSUR), box 1, vol. 3. Record Number 124-10336-10082, File Number ELSUR 92-228-1-182, 183, 185, 209, Section CR, Series DE, House Select Committee on Assassinations, National Archives at College Park, College Park, MD. These transcripts captured conversations intercepted by hidden microphones. They picked up only one side of the conversation — that of the person speaking in the bugged room.

14. Ibid.

15. Ibid., August 30, 1963, ELSUR.

16. Ibid.

17. Ibid.

18. Ramsey Clark, recorded interview by Larry J. Hackman, July 20, 1970, 41, Robert F. Kennedy Library Oral History Program.

19. Arthur M. Schlesinger, *Robert Kennedy and His Times* (New York: Ballantine Books, 1996), 608.

20. Dan E. Moldea, *The Hoffa Wars: Teamsters, Rebels, Politicians, and the Mob* (New York: Paddington Press, 1978), 161.

21. Walter Sheridan, recorded interview by Roberta W. Greene, June 12, 1970, 119, John F. Kennedy Library Oral History Program.

22. Ibid., 137.

23. William Manchester, *The Death of a President: November 20–November 25, 1963* (New York: Perennial Library, 1988), 528.

24. Steven M. Gillon, *Lee Harvey Oswald: 48 Hours to Live* (New York: Sterling, 2013), 136.

25. Walter Sheridan, recorded interview by Roberta W. Greene, June 12, 1970, 119, John F. Kennedy Library Oral History Program.

26. Walter Sheridan, *The Fall and Rise of Jimmy Hoffa* (New York: Saturday Review Press, 1972), 304.

27. Lester and Irene David, *Bobby Kennedy: The Making of a Folk Hero* (New York: Dodd, Mead, 1986), 219.

28. Charles Shaffer, author interview, August 12, 2014.

29. Ibid.
30. Memo-to-file, Melvin A. Eisenberg, February 13, 1964, File 443, Box 34, Records of J. Lee Rankin, Warren Commission papers, National Archives at College Park, College Park, MD.

Chapter 16: Get to the Jury

1. Ralph C. James and Estelle James, *Hoffa and the Teamsters: A Study of Union Power* (New York: Van Nostrand Reinhold, 1965), 49.
2. Ibid., 50.
3. John McClellan, "These Labor Abuses Must Be Curbed," *Reader's Digest*, December 1962, 98.
4. Jim Ridley, "The People vs. Jimmy Hoffa," parts 1 and 2, *Nashville Scene*, March 28 and April 4, 2002. Ridley's excellent two-part series also drew upon James D. Squires's *The Secrets of the Hopewell Box: Stolen Elections, Southern Politics, and a City's Coming of Age* (New York: Times Books, 1996).
5. *Z. T. Osborn Jr. v. the U.S.*, 385 U.S. 323, 1966, https://www.law.cornell.edu/supremecourt/text/385/323.
6. John Seigenthaler, author interview, August 5, 2010.
7. John Seigenthaler, recorded interview by Larry J. Hackman, June 5, 1970, 2, Robert Kennedy Oral History Program.
8. Walter Sheridan, recorded interview by Roberta W. Greene, May 1, 1970, 15, John F. Kennedy Library Oral History Program.
9. Walter Sheridan, *The Fall and Rise of Jimmy Hoffa* (New York: Saturday Review Press, 1972), 307.
10. John, A. Grimes, "Hoffa's Jaunty Air Fades During Tension of Courtroom Battle," *Wall Street Journal*, February 7, 1964, 1.
11. Drew Pearson and Jack Anderson, "Nixon vs. Reagan Is Real Test," *Washington Post*, May 22, 1968, B11.
12. Walter Sheridan, *Jimmy Hoffa*, 330.
13. Charles Shaffer, author interview, August 12, 2014.
14. Fred J. Cook, "The Hoffa Trial," *The Nation*, April 27, 1964, 415.
15. Walter Sheridan, *Jimmy Hoffa*, 346.
16. Al Butler, Video history, U.S. Marshal Museum, Fort Smith, AR, https://www.youtube.com/watch?v=5_NAhOO8gco.
17. John Seigenthaler, author interview, August 5, 2010.
18. US marshals later counted the coins. There were only twenty-one, worth $2.50.
19. John D. Pomfret, "Hoffa Is Guilty of Trying to Fix a Federal Jury," *New York Times*, March 5, 1964, 1.
20. "Nation: A Jolt for Jimmy," *Time*, March 13, 1964.
21. Arthur M. Schlesinger, *Robert Kennedy and His Times* (New York: Ballantine Books, 1996), 637.

22. James Reston, "Washington: Tired of Chasing People — Robert Kennedy," *New York Times*, May 6, 1964, 46.

Epilogue: In Love with Night

1. Burton Hersh, *Edward Kennedy: An Intimate Biography* (Berkeley, CA: Counterpoint, 2010), 178.
2. Edward M. Kennedy, *True Compass* (New York: Twelve/Hachette Book Group, 2009), 222.
3. Walter Sheridan, *The Fall and Rise of Jimmy Hoffa* (New York: Saturday Review Press, 1972), 382.
4. David W. Burke, recorded interview by Larry J. Hackman, December 8, 1971, 55, Robert F. Kennedy Oral History Project of the John F. Kennedy Library Oral History Program.
5. James R. Hoffa, as told to Oscar Fraley, *Hoffa: the Real Story* (New York: Stein and Day, 1975), 208.
6. Magda Crance, "Hoffa's Daughter," *Chicago Tribune*, June 9, 1991.

INDEX

INDEX

INDEX

Fifth Amendment, 4, 28, 109, 136, 139,
    142, 155, 280
    Beck and, 70–71, 96
    Hoffa and, 90, 96, 99, 104, 242
    labor unions and, 96–97, 241–43
    legislation on, 241–43
Fischbach, Hyman, 45, 46
Fitzgerald, Ella, 240
Fitzgerald, George, 95, 101, 109, 152, 248,
    271–72, 274
Fitzsimmons, Frank, 233, 339
Fonda, Henry, 240
Ford, Henry, 44–45
Forrestal, James, 29
Frey, Dorothy, 185

Gelb, Sol, 123–26
Genovese, Vito, 116
Get Hoffa squad, 6, 147, 213–33, 254, 279,
    334
    FBI and, 214, 217, 231
    indexing system of, 217
    IRS and, 215, 217–18, 222–23, 226, 232,
        233
    JFK's assassination and, 299
    jury-tampering case and, 280, 302, 306
    staffing of, 219–24
    Test Fleet case and, 247–48, 262, 266, 269
Giacalone, Anthony "Tony Jack," 284, 285,
    286, 287–88, 340
Giacalone, William "Billy Jack," 287–88
Giancana, Sam, 116, 200, 238, 239, 293
Gibbons, Harold J., 129–33, 139, 224–25,
    230, 244, 246, 302
    Hoffa and, 130–31, 132
    JFK's assassination and, 292, 296
    presidential primaries and, 160–61
Gibson, Truman, 82
Gilbert, Dan, 195–96
Glimco, Joey, 332
Goldberg, Jay, 365n4
Goldwater, Barry, 38, 87, 90, 93–95, 99,
    209–10
Graham, Phil, 91
Gray, Frank, Jr., 308
Greene, Charles, 180–81
Grimsley, Frank, 254–55, 259, 282
Guthman, Ed, 4, 33–34, 240, 291

Haggerty, James E., 230–31, 267, 309, 315,
    319, 325
Harrington, Russell, 32–33
Harris, Lou, 174, 175
    on Marilyn Monroe, 240–41
    presidential campaign and, 169–70,
        179, 181, 201, 202–3
Harrison, Robert, 190
Hastings, Al, 51

Hemingway, Ernest, 225
Hicks, George, 312, 313
Higgins, Marguerite, 206
Hoffa, Barbara (daughter), 227, 229, 250,
    308, 323, 325, 326, 340
Hoffa, James R. "Jimmy"
    1960 Democratic Convention and, 188,
        189, 194, 195, 196
    accusations against RFK by, 159, 261
    arrest of, 59–60, 61–62
    assault case against, 246–47, 251–52
    attempted assassination of, 272–73,
        274
    bribery trial of, 74–91, 124, 132, 133,
        151, 160, 311
    cash kickbacks hearings and, 108–11
    civil rights and, 131–32
    disappearance of, 339–40
    Enemy Within and, 184, 186
    espionage and, 45–46
    family of, 284–88
    garment industry and, 348n9
    image of, 43–44
    income and assets of, 136–37
    JFK and, 160, 201–2
    JFK's assassination and, 4–6, 7, 291–92,
        293, 295, 296–99, 301
    jury-tampering case against, 279–82, 297,
        299, 300, 302, 305–28, 333–35
    labor unions and, 12–22, 24, 51–53
    libel lawsuit against RFK of, 177
    Marilyn Monroe and, 239–40
    perjury charges against, 106–7, 109,
        160
    on politics, 26
    presidential primaries and, 159–62,
        172–73, 176–78, 180–81, 182
    reelection of, 227–29, 230
    RFK as attorney general and, 206, 208,
        209, 210
    RFK's death and, 339
    RFK's hatred of, 279, 328, 338
    RFK's meeting with, 42, 44, 46–48,
        54–55, 79
    RFK's personal interactions with, 61, 97,
        100, 104–5, 145
    sexual blackmail by, 189–94
    Supreme Court appeal and, 333–35
    Teamsters presidency and, 89, 106,
        111–14
    televised debates and, 200, 201
    temper of, 100, 159–60, 244, 246–47,
        258, 318, 321, 322
    threats against RFK by, 7, 254–55, 258,
        276, 293, 298
    youth of, 48–50
Hoffa, Jim (son), 227, 229, 250, 276, 303,
    308, 323, 325, 326, 333, 340

371

INDEX

ABOUT THE AUTHOR

James Neff has overseen multiple Pulitzer Prize–winning projects as investigations editor at the *Seattle Times*. The author of *The Wrong Man*, *Unfinished Murder*, and *Mobbed Up*, he lives in the Seattle area.